TROLLEY WARS
STREETCAR WORKERS ON THE LINE

Becoming Modern: New Nineteenth-Century Studies

SERIES EDITORS

Sarah Sherman
Department of English
University of New Hampshire

Janet Aikins Yount
Department of English
University of New Hampshire

Rohan McWilliam
Anglia Polytechnic University
Cambridge, England

Janet Polasky
Department of History
University of New Hampshire

This book series maps the complexity of historical change and assesses the formation of ideas, movements, and institutions crucial to our own time by publishing books that examine the emergence of modernity in North America and Europe. Set primarily but not exclusively in the nineteenth century, the series shifts attention from modernity's twentieth-century forms to its earlier moments of uncertain and often disputed construction. Seeking books of interest to scholars on both sides of the Atlantic, it thereby encourages the expansion of nineteenth-century studies and the exploration of more global patterns of development.

Jennifer Hall-Witt, *Fashionable Acts: Opera and Elite Culture in London, 1780–1880*

Duncan Faherty, *Remodeling the Nation: Domestic Architecture and the Formation of American Character, 1776–1858*

Scott Molloy, *Trolley Wars: Streetcar Workers on the Line*

William C. Dowling, *Oliver Wendell Holmes in Paris: Medicine, Theology, and* The Autocrat of the Breakfast Table

Betsy Klimasmith, *At Home in the City: Urban Domesticity in American Literature and Culture, 1850–1930*

Sarah Luria, *Capital Speculations: Writing and Building Washington, D.C.*

David L. Richards, *Poland Spring: A Tale of the Gilded Age, 1860–1900*

Angela Sorby, *Schoolroom Poets: Childhood, Performance, and the Place of American Poetry, 1865–1917*

William M. Morgan, *Philanthropists in Disguise: Gender, Humanitarianism, and Complicity in U.S. Literary Realism*

Piya Pal-Lapinski, *The Exotic Woman in Nineteenth-Century British Fiction and Culture: A Reconsideration*

Patrick H. Vincent, *The Romantic Poetess: European Culture, Politics, and Gender, 1820–1840*

Edward S. Cutler, *Recovering the New: Transatlantic Roots of Modernism*

Margaret M. Mulrooney, *Black Powder, White Lace: The du Pont Irish and Cultural Identity in Nineteenth-Century America*

For a complete list of books in this series,
see www.upne.com and www.upne.com/series/BMS.html

TROLLEY WARS

STREETCAR WORKERS ON THE LINE

SCOTT MOLLOY

UNIVERSITY OF NEW HAMPSHIRE PRESS

Durham, New Hampshire

Published by University Press of New England
Hanover and London

University of New Hampshire Press
Published by University Press of New England,
One Court Street, Lebanon, NH 03766
www.upne.com

Originally published 1996 by Smithsonian Institution Press
First University of New Hampshire Press/UPNE paperback edition 2007

ISBN-13: 978-1-58465-630-2
ISBN-10: 1-58465-630-1

Printed in the United States of America 5 4 3 2 1

Cover Caption: The cover drawing captured the usual mayhem, chaos, and
violence of an urban streetcar strike, as depicted in this confrontation in
Chicago in 1885. Photographers encountered great difficulty in capturing
these scenes because contemporary cameras and film (plates) could only
provide a blurred image of the action in these frenetic horsecar and trolley
wars. Artists, on the other hand, recreated the drama in frozen detail. The
graphic appeared on the front page of *Frank Leslie's Illustrated Newspaper,* 11
July 1885.

The Library of Congress has cataloged the original edition as follows:

Library of Congress Cataloging-in-Publication Data
Molloy, Scott.
    Trolley wars : streetcar workers on the line / Scott Molloy
      p.   cm.
    Includes bibliographical references and index.
    ISBN 1-56098-608-5
    1. Street-railroads—Rhode Island—Employees—History.
    2. Street-railroads—Rhode Island—History. I. Title.
HD8039.S82U655   1995
331.7′6138846′09745—dc20   95-8992

To my departed grandparents, Henry and Amy Molloy, who are always in my thoughts. And to my living grandmother, Virginia Handy, who has unflinchingly stood by me for a lifetime.

To my parents, David and Miriam Molloy, who never thought twice about sacrificing for their children's education. I appreciate them more every day.

To my children, Brandon, Kelsey, and Cady, the brightest jewels in the family constellation.

CONTENTS

AUTHOR'S NOTE TO PAPERBACK EDITION

In the preface to the first edition of *Trolley Wars: Streetcar Workers on the Line*, I described the difficulties in reconstructing working-class history. Unlike research libraries filled with documents of the rich and famous, laborers and their unions still have no more than a handful of notable collections of primary sources. The exchange of letters between wealthy family members, literary figures, or politicians is not duplicated in the world of ordinary people. Or if such correspondence did take place, few working families or immigrants had the prescience to hang onto it, except perhaps for wartime letters. Diaries, that staple of the well-to-do, seldom graced a plebian repository. The list of lost material for workers staggers the historical imagination. The need to survive on a daily basis left little time for industrial "hands" to build a literary trail, however meager, never mind saving the ephemeral treasure for posterity.

In the case of streetcar workers, I was fortunately able to tease out their story in large part from the extensive local newspaper coverage they received. They were good copy—interesting personalities dealing humorously with the daily vehicular and human traffic they encountered. As reporters regularly rode the trolleys, seeking gritty or funny stories about the human condition, they unwittingly compiled for posterity an occupational diary of the trolley workers, whose interaction with their passengers was an inexhaustible source of tales. If the anecdotes proved thin on a particular day, surely the next few stops would discover the Damon Runyon types for the columns of the next edition. Daily newspapers provide a chronological record of everyday life and, while they are not perfect sources by any means, they certainly assist in the reconstruction of history.

Labor unrest permeated the Gilded Age and the Progressive Era. In the 1880s, major strikes involved the Knights of Labor in many different arenas. By the 1890s, factories, construction, and mining, and the still occasional railroad strike were making headlines. Public attention centered on steelworkers at the Carnegie facilities in Homestead, Pennsylvania; textile operatives throughout New England and the East; and miners of coal and precious metal across the nation's bedrocks. These labor outbursts captured the attention of the print media and still make their way into labor textbooks as well as mainstream historical accounts. Many of these conflicts, especially, after 1905, those outside the immigrant-based Industrial Workers of the World, involved native-born, English-speaking, white males, who were not the usual suspects in the public's perception of union militancy. The introduction of rationalization, scientific management, and profit maximization broke the bonds of trust between employers and a conservative American workforce, who remained better off than most of their immigrant peers.

Trolley Wars details this change in Rhode Island among a group of law-abiding, respected motormen and conductors who fought back against the new industrial rigidity, which seemed tailor made for streetcar service, with its dependence on time and timetables. New corporate owners purchased emerging electric car systems that would attract millions of fares across the country. The new technology fulfilled its promise to provide rapid mass transit while at the same time it radically changed work and living arrangements from the more leisurely days of horse-drawn vehicles. The accompanying consolidation of the modern corporation, as witnessed particularly in the 1890s, brought about disruptive changes, not only for the cartels' employees, but for the entire service sector.

Time had run out for the small favors and courtesies that carmen and riders mutually bestowed upon each other. Horse drivers, transformed into electric motormen, no longer waited for stragglers; precise schedules ruled the routes; and detective agencies kept tabs on coin-collecting conductors. As time unsentimentally became money, the speed of the ever-larger trolley caused deadly accidents and injuries. As rails stretched to the once unreachable suburbs and rural areas beyond the horsecar's limit, fares increased to finance the construction and purchase of new vehicles and expensive electrical equipment. The modern up-tempo pace and lifestyle took their toll on the now disappearing gentility of the road that had seemed to transcend class, race (outside of the South), age, and gender. Initially, both crews and customers identified management as the culprit. The Progressive Era energized aroused citizens and forged unusual alliances between transportation workers and their passengers, fostering the illusion of a consumer crusade during the pre–World War I years. But as the years passed, relationships, habits, and cultural patterns changed so dramatically that the older, more personal way of conducting business simply disappeared from urban carriers.

Absentee and outside corporations also developed political power at all levels of government, seeking out bargain basement prices for franchises, taxes, and the right to charge for transfers to connecting lines. The business side of the labor relations chasm collared local police, the state militia, and private strikebreaking firms to keep order and maintain service. Reformers initiated electoral campaigns in voting booths as well as "guerilla progressivism" in city thoroughfares. While manufacturing walkouts shaped the contours of the period, disruptions in the trolley system had a greater impact and contemporary visibility. The localized nature of these streetcar battles accurately measured the temperature of labor relations in cities, big and small, but garnered less attention outside the immediate area, then and now. The consolidation of urban transportation would take place later, so that most conflicts involved smaller companies rather than giants like Carnegie, Rockefeller, or Pullman. Media attention for these trolley wars ricocheted from city to town as the Amalgamated Association of Street and Electric Railway Employees of America relentlessly organized transit workers across the Progressive Era landscape. Not many writers could catch their breath long enough to understand these events as something of greater significance than just a series of crippling walkouts spreading across the country.

After the original publication of *Trolley Wars*, I found, of course, more material that might have added greater detail to the book, but nothing that changed the parameters of my interpretations. I noted, for instance, how streetcar crews disseminated news and gossip among passengers, especially the conductor who patrolled a "car" collecting fares, keeping order, and sharing information, usually in the friendliest manner with patrons who were more comrades than customers. Recently I discovered a front page article in a back section of a Sunday newspaper of 1921. According to the story, horsecar crews provided up-to-the-minute details, not just about local happenings but, more important to Gilded Age riders, about the latest baseball scores!

Rhode Island's capital city hosted the Providence Grays of the fledgling National League from 1878 to 1885. Providence was one of only eight municipalities in the nation to entertain a professional baseball team at that time. The Grays, who played at Messer Park near the state's industrial epicenter of Olneyville, won two titles and were national runners-up three times. The local nine featured some of the most legendary players in those storied early years of America's national pastime. Trolley drivers actually posted the latest score and inning at the front of the horsecar. As the lethargic horses toiled on a hot summer day, the bells on the harnesses summoned fans from homes, stores, and fields to learn the breaking news about their beloved sports team. Attentive street carmen gave a running commentary of the game's highlights. More than just an exercise in nostalgia, the timely and collective distribution of entertaining information served as one more link in a chain of solidarity that joined crews, passengers, and communities. The invisible forging of this human bond, fortified in so many other ways, as noted in this book, paid great dividends when transit capital turned against transportation labor as the iron horsecar rails gave way to the steel tracks of the electric trolley and added a new hustle and bustle to human affairs.[1]

Although the exigencies of scientific management virtually outlawed the civility that characterized an earlier, slower-paced world, modern times are not totally barren of service sector kindness. In the early 1960s, when I rode a bus to and from high school, I remember a senior bus operator who used to curb the vehicle halfway down Elmwood Avenue in Providence. The driver then walked a blind passenger across this busy thoroughfare as my friends and I quietly moaned to ourselves over the loss of a few precious minutes. How the passage of time changes one's outlook! In my own transit career, I saw too many employees show up at the garage in a morose frame of mind that only worsened as the workday progressed. We made a valiant and sometimes successful effort in the union to fashion an old-time labor-community alliance despite the shackles of watches, time points, and the rush of life. We emphasized kindness and compassion to our passengers as the only right behavior in a depersonalized world seemingly out of control, slavishly following the yuppie dictate of looking out for number one. Some of us tried hard to perpetuate labor's hoary anthem that an injury to one is an injury to all.[2]

The one area I underemphasized in *Trolley Wars*, because of a lack of material, concerned the use of professional strikebreakers. Since then two provocative books have appeared that investigate the shadowy world of private detective agencies and the lucrative supplying of scabs. Robert Michael Smith's *From Blackjacks to Briefcases: A History of Commercial Strikebreaking and Unionbusting in the United States* economically and directly summarizes the use and abuse of such "services," especially in the fecund field of Progressive Era transit imbroglios. Stephen Norwood plumbs the records of the Pinkerton Agency's involvement and provides a psychological analysis as well with an emphasis on the transportation sector, in *Strikebreaking and Intimidation: Mercenaries and Masculinity in Nineteenth Century America*. Except for the occasional strike where archival information actually existed, the written record for most localities is sparse or nonexistent. I am still unaware of any specific evidence relating to the 1902 Rhode Island walkout, and I do not believe that scabs made much difference, as they did in other places, because of different political conditions and the withering local boycott.[3]

I would like to believe that, in the decade since it was first published, *Trolley Wars* has held its own. The book looks down the tracks of time to explain the development of mass transit, the subsequent speed-up in everyday life, and the outbreak of hostilities between transit operatives accustomed to a slower, more personal interaction with riders and the new investors who regarded such niceties as a slowing down of service and capacity. Although not every transit strike boasted such a pedigree, the roots of the contest usually had an earlier genesis. These often violent outbursts, while sharing customary labor-management traits, almost always highlighted some uncommon element. And that's what makes history so charismatic. The detailed timeline in *Trolley Wars* does more than just measure the thunder of the strike. The flashpoints along the Gilded Age routes illuminate societal change as well, right through the Progressive Era.

Notes

1. Patrick T. Conley and Paul Campbell, *Providence: A Pictorial History* (Norfolk, VA: The Donning Company, 1982), 100, 115; *Providence Journal*, 5 June 1921.

2. Bill Reynolds, "Scott Molloy: Man on the Move," *Providence Sunday Journal Magazine*, 10 June 1979; Maureen Croteau, "The Class of the '60s," *Providence Sunday Journal*, 28 Jan. 1979.

3. Robert Michael Smith, *From Blackjacks to Briefcases: A History of Commercial Strikebreaking and Unionbusting in the United States* (Athens, Ohio: Ohio University Press, 2003); Stephen Norwood, *Strikebreaking and Intimidation: Mercenaries and Masculinity in Nineteenth Century America* (Chapel Hill: University of North Carolina Press, 2002).

PREFACE

The task of reconstructing the lives of Rhode Island's transit workers is fraught with difficulty. Few of these men left behind diaries, letters, or reminiscences that would allow historians to understand their minds and motives. Nevertheless, trolley employees are approachable through Gilded Age newspapers. Popular journalists focused on mass transportation in the nineteenth century, particularly the crews of stagecoaches, omnibuses, horsecars, and trolleys. Daily stories about life on the road reflected the charm and adventure of primitive travel in this era. Reporters covered the colorful interaction between passengers and drivers, sometimes with unusual insight. Notices of the retirement and death of beloved crew members, who had spent legendary careers on a single route, appeared in detailed, lengthy articles, usually reserved for society's elite.

I was especially fortunate to have access to several scrapbooks of newspaper clippings that covered the careers and deaths of transit workers in the state, making my task a bit easier. The daily press of the past is essential to an understanding of this vocation and allows previously unheard workers to speak intelligently across the generations.

My interest in transportation workers goes back many years. I grew up at 350 Bucklin Street in Providence, Rhode Island, directly across from a nineteenth-century horsecar barn. In 1948, when I was two, my father took me for a ride on the last Broad Street trolley. My grandfather, an Irish immigrant, began his transit career driving a streetcar out of the nearby Elmwood Avenue garage in 1909. Two of his sons, my uncles Henry and Dick, drove buses out of the same facility. These transit genes eventually awakened in me.

My extended family displayed no affection for their working-class background when I was growing up. I was expected to attend college and did so, graduating during the turbulent 1960s. Rather than pursue a career as a junior high school teacher, I opted to apply some of my political idealism to the real world—a decision that, to my parent's chagrin, brought me back to my family's blue-collar roots.

My uncle Henry, who was business agent for the Amalgamated Transit Union, Division 618, at the Rhode Island Public Transit Authority, got me the job. Despite such connections, I was assigned to the toughest part of town for a couple of years doing night runs. On days off, I immersed myself in labor culture, keeping my college degree to myself.

I spent eleven years as a bus driver, enjoying the benefits of one of the best union jobs in the state. I made more money operating a bus than I would have as a schoolteacher. But it was the excitement of changing the world that kept me there. I attended monthly union meetings, learned *Robert's Rules of Order,* and analyzed the tricky personality conflicts that make up group politics. When I started, many of the drivers from the Great Depression and World War II era were beginning to retire. A new generation of long-haired kids, Vietnam veterans, women, and minorities came aboard. I sought to bridge the lifestyles. We bowled and played baseball together, visited the sick and injured, and tried to create a sense of solidarity.

Over the next ten years I was elected shop steward, president, and business agent. I enjoyed the rare pleasure of trying to implement new ways of doing things and sometimes even succeeded, within a labor movement that I felt had become stultified and unimaginative. We orchestrated a wildcat strike over seniority issues, increased health and safety measures, and published our own local newspaper. We joined other unions on their picket lines, sent more of our members to the 1983 Martin Luther King memorial march in Washington than any other local in the state, took public stands on American foreign policy, and were active in community activities and local elections.

During my career as a bus driver and union official, I used every opportunity to integrate a love of history with my job. I was always amazed at how little the beneficiaries of the labor movement knew about the origin and evolution of the union. I began a crusade to piece together that story. Unfortunately the division's early records were lost, so I headed for the Rhode Island Historical Society library, one of the oldest in the nation. I found some company material, but hardly an item about our union, or anyone else's for that matter. I spent months squinting at untold reels of microfilm that outlined the history of local transportation in the daily press, incidentally reaping whatever I could about the industry's work force. I devoted a week's vacation in Washington, D.C., to working at the national headquarters of the Amalgamated Transit Union, where I uncovered a wealth of information. Still, there was something missing—the human element.[1]

I had heard rumors that some of the founders of Division 618, which was established in 1913, were still alive. I tracked them down, as well as other old-timers who had joined the local in its infancy and made a career of it. These pensioners opened their homes and hearts to me and parted with old photographs, Labor Day ribbons, and other memorabilia, which became part of my vocational scrapbook and part of this inquiry's visual record. I tape-recorded many interviews with these proud motormen and conductors, all of whom have ended their journey on the tracks of time.[2]

In 1977 I published a fifty-eight-page pamphlet—complete with photographs and graphics—outlining the history of mass transit in Rhode Island and the role of traction workers and their union. That effort was more popular than academic. The union and I received quite a bit of publicity, and proud drivers and mechanics eagerly gobbled up the union-printed pamphlet. A year later, I published a more scholarly article about the landmark 1902 carmen's strike in Providence and Pawtucket in a collection of essays about Rhode Island labor history. That piece suggested further research, because many issues surrounding the violent walkout demanded closer scrutiny. At the time I was just too busy to undertake such an endeavor. But I vowed that some day I would return to that story and take a closer look.[3]

A few years earlier I had entered a part-time doctoral program in American history at Providence College. I attended full time for a semester and then accepted a job as chief-of-staff for a liberal Republican congresswoman. I was now serving labor in a legislative capacity. Meanwhile, I kept pecking away at my Ph.D. courses one at a time. I had also started teaching labor and industrial history as an adjunct professor at various schools while I was still driving a bus, and in 1986 joined the faculty at the University of Rhode Island's Labor Research Center. By then I had finished my course work and had to decide on a dissertation topic. Inevitably I chose the history of public transportation in Rhode Island and its employees.

For years I had scoured flea markets, bookstores, and antique shows, ferreting out photographs, artifacts, and stray pieces of ephemera relating to the local labor movement and especially my old union local. I had also discovered innumerable secondary and primary sources relating to that history. Most of the illustrations in this book were acquired in this desultory fashion. I became so infatuated with preserving working-class history that I advertised in out-of-state antique journals. The collection, which eventually reached ten thousand items, now resides at the Smithsonian Institution's National Museum of American History.

After recreating the story of local transit workers, especially from late nineteenth-century newspaper articles that treated horsecar and trolley service as if owned by the public, I finished my thesis and received my doctoral degree in 1991. This book has its roots in that study.[4]

One of the haunting qualities of merging a hobby and a job is the occasional confusion engendered by that marriage. There were times in an early morning mist when I drove my empty bus over a deserted, cobblestoned Point Street in Providence inlaid with old trolley tracks, wondering for a moment where I was in historical time. On suburban trips to Warwick, I passed dirt paths that once guided streetcars to the famed Rocky Point amusement park, where, during the depression, my father would ride with my grandfather holding the controls. Elderly passengers contributed to my sense of timelessness when they fumbled in their pockets, not for a bus token but a "carcheck." On my Woonsocket runs in the middle of the day—off-peak hours in the industry—the clock was turned back as dozens of older French Canadian immigrants spoke exclusively in their native tongue. Bus drivers also reflected our vocational past when they called the garage a "carbarn." Older workers often bragged how long that they had been on "the property," rather than "on the job." And when we operated the Providence to Pawtucket route we referred to it as "the pike," as in "turnpike," reaching back to the days of omnibuses and horsecars.

But if history ensnared me at times, the vagaries of modern life always brought me back to the here and now. The elderly poor might reach the end of the line and ask defensively if they could stay on board and ride back to the city to stay warm. They had no other place to go. I witnessed racial hostility on inner-city routes and carried society's outcasts home on late evening trips. But for every transit heartbreak, there were the pleasant greetings of passengers like Cam Murphy, who baked applecake for the drivers; or the aged printer who brought me a Sacco-Vanzetti defense poster written in Italian in 1921, the year he printed it as a young apprentice.

And I forever thank the union for a good life. I may be introduced as Professor Molloy to my classes and audiences, but I quickly inform them of my roots and my debts to the past. Today my greatest pleasure is to speak at union halls, which I do frequently for coffee and a donut, to remind working people of their heritage and the need to preserve it historically. And my greatest hope is that this collective act of memory will carry the notion of union solidarity imaginatively into the next challenging century.

ACKNOWLEDGMENTS

This study began as a crosstown trip and evolved over a twenty-year period into a cross-country journey, bridging vocational boundaries, spiritual frontiers, and family borders. The book has been a hobby, an obsession, and an albatross. I spent leisurely evenings scouring nineteenth-century newspaper stories, feverish summers compiling the information, and eighteen months of anxiety wondering if I could ever edit my dissertation into a manageable length. Over a twenty-year period I assembled so much material at home that I seldom had to leave the confines of my own study except to use a microfilm reader. My reference acknowledgments, therefore, are fairly limited.

My sincere thanks to the staff of the Rhode Island Historical Society, especially the director, Al Klyberg, who has opened the venerable institution to all the state's citizens; the library chairperson, Madeleine Telfeyan; and the former manuscripts curator, Cindy Bendroth. There is no greater repository of local material than the society's magnificent collection. Also of great value were the manuscripts of the John Hay Library at Brown University, whose staff was always courteous and attentive. My thanks also to Jeanne Richardson and Margaret Chevian at the Providence Public Library for assistance above and beyond the call of duty. At Providence city hall, Mayor Vincent Cianci kindly introduced me to the archives director, Carol Pace, who enthusiastically aided my research. At the University of Rhode Island, the detectives at Interlibrary Loan, Vicki Burnett and Marie Rudd, tracked down obscure tomes, statistical compilations, and elusive journal articles. They also provided my daughters with candy and treats every time we visited! At the Fortunate Finds Bookstore in Warwick, Rhode Island, the proprietor, Mildred Santilli Longo, and her late husband, Bill, supplied me with a cornucopia of memorabilia over the years, as did some of their patrons who came around for Millie's homemade soup: Joe Coduri, Tom Green, and Russ DeSimone. In Washington, D.C., the staff and officers at the Amalgamated Transit Union took great pride in assisting one of their own to compile a local history of that century-old labor organization, which has carefully guarded its significant holdings.

Because this work has been so long in the making, and because I may not live long enough to complete another one, I wanted to thank the many people in my life who have directly and indirectly helped to make it possible. I spent my undergraduate career at Rhode Island College, whose faculty was always accessible and supportive of scholarship. I remember with great affection the late Dr. Evelyn Walsh, and professors Steven Tegu, Ara Dostourian, John Taylor, Ken Lewalski, Stan Lemons, and Don Puretz. I also thank several classmates who helped: Ray Huelbig, Sheldon Mossberg, Peter Sclafani, Jim McGetrick, Ann Duffy, Arnie McConnell, John Boffa, and Dennis Cabral.

At the University of New Hampshire, where I first honed my history skills at the graduate level, I fondly recall the classes of Mark Schwarz, Don Wilcox, Charles Clark, and Al Linden. My academic and activist compatriots there were John Peterson, Paul Wilderson, Ellen Ramsey, Laura Schiebel, and Pete Haebler: still friends after all these years. I received my Ph.D. from Providence College, which also had a coterie of great professors: Paul O'Malley; Mike Metallo; the late dean of the graduate school, Fr. Cornelius Forster; the director of the Quirk Institute, Frank O'Brien, who gave me my first job in academia as an adjunct professor; and the history department secretary, my good friend, Phyllis Cardullo. My life was also changed irrevocably at PC thanks to the promethean mind of Dr. Patrick T. Conley—scholar, lawyer, and expert in state and local history. Under his guidance I crafted the dissertation that eventually became this book. I thank him for his patience and inspiration.

I owe a great debt to my colleagues at the University of Rhode Island's Labor Research Center, where I have taught since 1986: Dr. Charles T. Schmidt, director of the program, who hired me and always offered personal and professional encouragement to finish this work; also professors Matt Bodah, Carl Gersuny, Al Hoban, Elton Rayack, Nancy Potter, Clay Sink, Bob Weisbord, Larry Rothstein, Mark Grossman, Amy Tabor, Rick McIntyre, Laura Beauvais, Rick Scholl, Sue Taylor, Jim Findlay, Joel Cohen, Mort Briggs, Norm Zucker, and Leo Carroll; and my overworked secretary, Mary Pinch. Thanks also to the university's provost, Dr. Beverly Swan, and URI's most active alumnus, Jack Tempkin.

I should also note the many students who have taught me as much as I taught them, and whose careers, values, and ideals still inspire me: Helio Medina, Atiba Mbiwan, Tim Schick, Awilda Ayala Rivera, Dave Comferford, Ann Crowley, Bill Vieira, Dave Speicher, John Gilheeney, Marc Jones, Rachel Hendrickson, Tammy King Walsh, Lara Embry, Steve Kane, Gail Lepkowski, Randy Haussman, Walt Williams, Eric Barden, George Russell, Andy Welt, Marie McCarthy, Pat Brady, Dan O'Connor, Julia Londergan, George Zainyeh, Jim Cacciola, Diane Lowther, Faith Mansolillo, Chuck Marchand,

Bill McGarry, Jean Gagnier, Rob Wayss, Eric Longpre, Tim McMahon, and Azhar Aziz.

I owe a special debt of gratitude to my fellow travelers in the Rhode Island AFL-CIO, the Providence Central Labor Council, and the state labor orbit: George Nee, Chuck Schwartz, Rick Brooks, Sharon Cornu, Duane and Mary Clinker, Jack Amaral, Bill Kennedy, Theresa El Amin, Patricia Houlihan, Cathy Collette, George and Phyllis Tennian, Joyce Katzberg, Frank Montanaro, John Glynn, Luigi Nardella, Roland Rivet, John Notarangelo, Marcia Reback, Ed McElroy, Prentice Witherspoon, Mary Forgue, Al Saftel, Vilma Masciarelli, Armand Sabitoni, Tom Rotella, Karen McAninch, Jim Hart, Jack Phillips, Tracy Fitzpatrick, Morty Miller, Harvey Press, Bill Marvel, Leo Cacicio, Ron Coia, Tom Johnson, Mary Pendergast, Paul Baker, Cam Gelsimino, Micky Rooney, Anne Flood, Madeleine Lawrence, Ed Ondrasek, Edwin Sullivan, Dan Mollo, Stan Banach, Bill Turner, Larry Ward, Ken Bowling, Joe O'Connor, and Paul MacDonald.

A group of retired labor leaders and activists have also nurtured me over the last generation with their commitment to preserving labor's past: Ed Brown, the dean of labor historians in the state, whose interest in the subject preceded my birth; Larry Spitz, Rhode Island's greatest organizer and advocate for social justice; and Al Sisti, Rose Tritendi, Ann Burlak, Mike Boday, Sister Adelaide Canelas, Msgr. Edmund Brock, Arthur Coia, Frank Sgambato, Marty Byrne, Dave Kolodoff, Al McAloon, Pat O'Regan, Dick Zoorabedian, and my nonagenarian pal, Arthur Riani of the Brotherhood of Railroad Trainmen. If there's a labor heaven, Arthur will be there; he has the union's insignia already chiseled into his headstone.

I maintain close contact with many mechanics and bus drivers, active and retired, from my former job with the Rhode Island Public Transit Authority (RIPTA) and Division 618 of the Amalgamated Transit Union: Pat Macari, Manny Fernandes, Al Cardillo, Don Lopes, Tom Cute, Bill Merandi, Bob dos Reis, Ernie Gilbert, Ed Cole, Dick O'Neil, Frank Claire, Scottie McAllister, Tom Sears, Kevin Millea, Chris Mathewson, Holly Chaplin, Gordon Hunter, Jim Swanson, Jim Callary, Walter Hill, Stan Fallens, Ann Colby, Andy Santagata, Bill Bagley, Phil Maggiacomo, Bob Spencer, Mark Adamek, Bob McAllister, Don Medeiros, Burt Underwood, Russ LeTourneau, Irving Goldenberg, Phyllis Coleman, John Chadwick, George Buck, Don Fish, Jim Ruggieri, Pat Ruggieri, Jim Collins, Jerry Beaulieu, Norman Lee, Roland Daigle, Mike Solitro, Tony Rego, Ray Rogers, Ken Gray, Bill McGee, Jim Gibbons, Dave DeSimone, Ken D'Ambrosio, Joe Croce, Bill Bartolini, Tom Anderson, Bill Jencks, Tony Fonseca, Kevin Cole, Lefty Bodington, Barbara Reynolds,

Pete Ritchie, George Fagan, Jimmy Conley, Luke Gardner, George Gallagher, Bill Blair, Mike Murray, Manny Medeiros, Jerry Cobleigh, Fernando Pereira, Gus Reis, Joe Granata, and Victor Fereira.

I also remember those wonderful old-timers I interviewed in the mid 1970s, all of whom have died: Chris Daniels, Bill Thompson, Jimmy Derrick, Jim Quinn, Jim Lombardi, Manny Cunha, Alton Doe, Napoleon Rondeau, Lorenzo Sabourin, and dozens of others. I dearly miss my old friend Dick Wonson, director of scheduling at RIPTA. Dick was an avid collector of transit history, and although his interests were mainly in the technological side of the hobby, he accumulated material indiscriminately beginning in the 1940s. Dick always shared any information and material he possessed and encouraged my studies even though we often fought over scheduling problems in our contemporary labor-management relationship. Some of the scrapbooks he acquired over the years were indispensable to assembling this story. His good friend, Al Silloway, handled Dick's estate when he died and made everything available to me as well as items from his own extensive hoard of collectibles.

At the national union level, I had the great privilege of belonging to one of the most democratic unions in the country: the Amalgamated Transit Union. Jim LaSala, the union's president, and Mike Siano, one of the vice presidents, were the greatest individuals to work with, and they often cut me more slack than I deserved. Joe Jacquay, an indefatigable staff member at the Washington office, frequently helped with my requests for historical material. In the New England region, several members and officials urged me on: Jack Gallahue, Tony Romano, Ned Foley, Frank Gallagher, and John O'Leary.

In 1987 a small band of labor history buffs in the state formalized the Rhode Island Labor History Society, which had been informally organized in 1975. In this 1930s-style group, academics, workers, and activists shared their visions of a better world. Their dedication and enthusiasm has always picked me up when my spirits have flagged: Gary Kulik, Gary Gerstle, Robert Macieski, Hetty Startup, Lou McGowan, Joe Sullivan, Richard Rupp, Peter Townshend, Gail Sansbury, Mary Lee Partington, and the late Harvey O'Connor. Out-of-state activists and collectors who have helped are Jim Green, Jose Soler, Bruce Cohen, Jim Hanlan, Jane Slaughter, Marty Blatt, Lisa Lubow, Rob Weir, Ed Boyle, Ed Sullivan, Dick Oestreicher, Ken Florey, Fred Kaltenstein, John Bennett, Dave Montgomery, Stu Kauffman, Ray Boswell, John Coffee, and Ted Watts.

The Labor History Society has also been fortunate to have several benefactors who often funded projects when no one else would come forward: Bob McKenzie, who runs the all-union American Income Life Insurance Company in Rhode Island, and his philanthropic boss, Bernie Rapoport, in Texas; Marc Gursky, the feisty labor lawyer whose union lineage reaches back several generations; and the late Raul Lovett, whose counsel and generosity I sorely miss.

Thanks to my friends at the *Providence Journal*'s labor beat, who must have tired of my incessant phone calls asking them to cover one union cultural event or another: Dave Reid, Peter Perl, Ira Chinoy, Nora Toohey, John Kifney, and Carol Young; to my fellow members of the Rhode Island Committee for the Humanities: Charles Sullivan, Tom Roberts, Albert Harkness, Karen Newman, Ed Wood, and Jane Civins; and to my great friends at the Blackstone River Valley National Heritage Corridor Commission: Jim Pepper, Louise Redding, Ray Auclair, Scott Gibbs, Nancy Benoit, and Bob Billington.

Last, let me thank Steve Brier for helping me publish this work; and Doug Reynolds, Nick Salvatore, and Paul Buhle for reading innumerable drafts and never letting me off the hook until it met our expectations. A special thank-you to my editor, Mark Hirsch, who continually inspired me with confidence through this long ordeal, and to the Smithsonian's freelance copy editor, Tom Ireland. You were indeed true comrades, and I will always be indebted.

TROLLEY WARS
STREETCAR WORKERS ON THE LINE

INTRODUCTION

The history of mass transportation in the United States has long held a fascination for the public. Countless books investigate every conceivable conveyance from railroads to trolleys, from buses to subways, from canal boats to airplanes. Groups like the Boston Street Railway Association publish newsletters, issue richly illustrated histories, and organize transit buffs for trips on antique vehicles. Despite such interest, transportation workers are conspicuously absent from popular and academic narratives, as if the machines ran unattended. This book is an effort to tell their story.[1]

Trolley Wars traces the social dynamics of horsecar and electric streetcar development in Rhode Island, the most urbanized state in Gilded Age America, and follows the impact of that careening growth on the men who made the streetcars go. I argue that the development of urban mass transportation involved a battle for control of city streets and city government—a struggle that was at times waged in courts, voting booths, town councils, state legislatures, and in the streets themselves. It was a contest that drew in all kinds of urban residents. Affluent carriage owners, for instance, originally opposed any scarring of *their* roads with protruding rails that might bring unwanted travelers near their estates. Later, passenger groups, taxpayers, stockholders, and politicians in different camps fought over the question of fares, transfers, and franchises. The stakes increased considerably when locally funded horsecar service evolved into electrically powered systems financed by "foreign" capital. As outsiders took over the industry, street railways became a symbol of the wayward Gilded Age. The national streetcarmen's union, with a helping hand from riders and reform politicians, waged Progressive-era strikes that triggered violent protests and signatured the period.

Transit workers stood at center stage in these struggles. White, native-born homeowners, they were active members of their communities, belonged to local neighborhood organizations, and enjoyed remarkably cordial relations with passengers. They were social policemen and information messengers, the eyes and ears of an urban district along a route where they lived, as well. They guided and guarded their friendly patrons as new lines penetrated once isolated suburbs. The local landscape might change as urban, suburban, and rural areas overcame old geographical and social demarcations, but the smiling faces of drivers and conductors provided continuity and reassurance in an ever-changing world. Crews performed innumerable favors for an appreciative clientele, and passengers reciprocated with mutual admiration and goodwill.[2]

The decline of horsecars and the rise of electric streetcars transformed the nature of city life. Transportation was now faster, reflecting industrial America's accelerated tempo. For riders, trolleys made for quicker travel to suburban homesteads, while weekend trips to novel amusement centers perked up a population that now had a modicum of discretionary income and leisure. The convenience of electric traction also helped segregate neighborhoods by class, ethnicity, and race, and made it possible for all kinds of people to ride together democratically—and at times uncomfortably—on the same streetcar.

Nothing changed social relations or urban life more than the incorporation of the transit industry. Where small, locally owned companies once controlled horse-drawn enterprises, large corporations with no roots in the community now took charge of business, enormously expanding the system and cobwebbing urban America with trolley tracks and overhead electric wires.

But this was not all. In their quest to rationalize the industry and increase profits, corporations drew the wrath of passengers and workers alike. Although riders applauded the convenience of trolley service and the freedom to commute to work and to shop wherever they pleased, they were irked by the new dangers of electric travel and the loss of friendly amenities that had characterized local control. Faced with tightened timetables that poisoned their ability to be as courteous as before, crews found it difficult to do their jobs as safely or fraternally. "In the days before the present mad rush of life had descended upon us," a patron complained, "it was customary for the conductor to go to the assistance of an aged or lame person who was boarding or leaving the car." The sense of loss was laid squarely at the corporate door.[3]

The incorporation of the transit industry was felt most acutely by workers. For motormen, conductors, and mechanics, the out-of-town takeover promoted growing wage disparities and a deterioration of working conditions—factors that led to a sustained trade union organizing drive that was enthusiastically supported by passengers. In Rhode Island the traction company wisely grandfathered in premium salaries and seniority for horsecar veterans but instituted a lower pay scale for Irish newcomers, who fell a notch below the old-timers' vaunted status. There was a distinct generational animosity between the two sets of workers, and the hungrier newcomers eventually augmented their numbers and challenged the veterans' favored standing. As mass transit proliferated wildly, streetcar companies became at once Providence's largest employer and the flashpoint of Progressive-era protest. That conflict, at least in Providence, was not a cut-and-dry division between haughty capitalists and defenseless workers. Local management, exasperated by unreasonable and contradictory orders from an out-of-state directorate, honestly tried to please passengers and crews.

The Amalgamated Association of Street Railway Employes of America was founded in 1892, at the time of the switch from horsepower to electricity. (The name was changed to Amalgamated Association of Street and Electric Railway Employes of America in 1905.) By the turn of the century it embarked on a militant organizing program that ignited a couple of hundred strikes despite the union's sincere offers to arbitrate all disputes. These "car wars," as they were known, were notable for widespread violence and the active participation by passengers, organized labor, much of the middle class, and many small businesses on the side of motormen and conductors. The upheavals—particularly the climactic strike of 1902—also provided an opening for ethnic, reform Democrats like Mayor John Fitzgerald of Pawtucket, who championed the strikers against the hated railway as a way of undermining a corrupt local Republican machine.

This study dissects the 1902 walkout in Providence and Pawtucket, Rhode Island, as a test case for understanding a larger pattern of labor unrest and urban malaise in the country. Although these local upheavals never attained the notoriety of national strikes, their sheer number and similarity demand attention as a key to unraveling citizen frustration at the dawn of the twentieth century, a time when private trusts wrestled with the public interest.

THE PEOPLE'S CARRIAGES

In a very few years we expect to see several horse railroads through our streets. Providence is not to remain passive while the rest of the world moves, and we may depend upon it that the introduction of the horsecar is the dawn of a new era of city progress, and well worthy to be ranked with the undertakings which within a single generation have so increased our population and augmented our wealth.

Providence Evening Press, 1864

The [horse] cars are almost always well filled, many people riding short distances which before were walked.

Providence Journal, 1877

You see, the horse-car is a very democratic institution. It holds a good many people, and being open to all, it carries all kinds. You think you haven't got much aristocracy in Providence, but you've got lots of it.

Hack driver, 1883

Most public bus routes that crisscross Rhode Island today overlap track beds that once supported electric trolleys and horsecars. Before the railways, the rickety omnibus and its rough-and-tough predecessor, the stagecoach, plied these same roads on primitive turnpikes. The transportation lineage spirals even further back in time to isolated white settlers venturing into local hinterlands over frontier bridle paths.

But the transportation matrix does not stop here, either. Before the arrival of white European settlers, Native Americans had developed a system of trails through the aboriginal topography of the Narragansett Bay region. Local tribes established several narrow pathways that snaked out of the South Main Street area of Providence to outlying districts as far away as the neighboring states of Connecticut and Massachusetts. Roger Williams, the state's founder, was so impressed by the Narragansett tribe's pragmatic engineering that he called their seventeenth-century transportation web "as hard and firm as any route in England."[1]

To a degree these small paths, some six to ten feet wide, parallel the modern interstate highway system of routes I-95 and I-195 that connect the state to the rest of the world today. Some of the routes, with only minor variations, can trace a pedigree from silent Indian trails to the congested routes of lumbering Rhode Island Public Transit Authority buses four centuries later.

As inevitable as the evolution of transportation seems in retrospect, the shift from one form of travel to another created sporadic anxiety. The drive to pluralize private wayfare into mass transit engendered controversy and pitted socioeconomic groups against one another in a battle that still resonates today. When train service between Providence and Boston began in 1835, stagecoach partisans "could not conceive it possible for such a mighty enterprise as the turnpike to be abandoned without accomplishing the ruin of all who derived subsistence therefrom; and in this opinion they were supported by the prevailing sentiment of the country which regarded railroads as a curse rather than a blessing." Once the iron horse obliterated its rivals and accelerated the tempo of society with rigid timetables and schedules, owners increased fares and aggravated tempers. In 1876, the citizens of rural Georgiaville, Rhode Island, rebelled against high prices and switched to one of the few remaining stages in the state: "People are contented to ride slow and cheap," a newspaper article remarked, "rather than quick and dear." Stagecoach proprietors, however, soon sold their franchises to omnibus and horsecar interests.[2]

The horse-drawn omnibus was a transitional vehicle for mass transit. Starting in the late 1840s in Rhode Island, the "bus," as it was called, shuttled passengers along urban streets. Especially popular was the route from downtown Providence to the manufacturing village of Olneyville. A seamstress wrote, "Yesterday we had a snowstorm. The snow was falling all day, but the weather was so warm that it did not accumulate very fast, but the walking was very bad. I rode home in the Olneyville Omnibus, with eighteen other passengers." Although these slow-moving wagons were primitive interlopers in the evolution of faster travel, they did cover the distance, run regularly, and engender a "riding habit." Before the Civil War a timetable for a Providence omnibus promised an emerging middle class: "Passengers living at either end of the of the route, can leave the Arcade or bridge, five minutes before 12 M., and return at 1 P.M., giving them ample time to get their dinner and return by first trip."[3]

The railed horsecar quickly replaced the omnibus, although the tracks faithfully followed the routes of that earlier pioneer. Wealthy carriage-riding citizens initially opposed the installation of any track impediments on their streets. The convenience and comfort of the new system, however, quickly won many to the side of mass transit. In 1876 rails threaded into the emerging up-scale neighborhood of Mount Pleasant in Providence. The driver of a new horsecar stopped at a home on Atwells Avenue when signaled by a woman seemingly in distress. Her elderly husband appeared and asked the crew if they could wait a few minutes while he finished his breakfast. When the conductor informed him that the horsecars had fixed schedules, unlike the more accom-modating omnibuses, the old man seemed indignant and yearned for the good old days of personal and slower transportation. The crew trotted off at a speed of five miles per hour! By the time that electric trolleys superseded horsepower in the Gay Nineties, society had radically reset its timepiece and coped with the consequences, good and bad, of revolutionary urban and interurban travel. With the introduction of private automobiles in the early twentieth century, the carriage set regained their transportation privacy, at least temporarily.[4]

Newport, Rhode Island, exemplified the societal tension surrounding the establishment of mass transit. The city's wealthy summer colony adamantly opposed any urban transportation by rail, especially a proposed horsecar route to exclusive beach property. Although genuinely concerned about obstacles in the city's magnificent roads, status-conscious patricians wanted no working- or middle-class intruders using affordable public transportation to invade their exclusive haunts. They flexed their political and financial muscles and in 1864 forced the promoters to retreat without even scheduling an election. The incor-porators meekly surrendered to "those who ride in carriages . . . to the Beach undisturbed by this Democratic institution." Only a summer omnibus provided rudimentary public service competing with the fleet of privately owned vehicles that promenaded around town.[5]

The limited, seasonal nature of transit work in Newport put a crimp in full-time employment. Sanford Manchester, after a public-school education, worked as a hack driver in the City-by-the-Sea but left after two years for a regular position as a stagecoach driver from Providence to the Cranston village of Pawtuxet by way of Broad Street. He enlisted in the Union army during the Civil War and served three years with Gen. Ambrose Burnside. After resuming his stagecoach career, Manchester drove the first horsecar over his old route in 1865. When horsepower gave way to electricity in 1892, the veteran driver became a motorman and operated the first trolley, once again on the Provi-dence to Pawtuxet line. He died in 1901, a few weeks after ill health forced him to retire. He had spent a half century on the same route, evolving with the changing technology. Manchester's obituary mentioned that, not surprisingly, "he had a host of friends among the regular patrons." Another displaced transit worker from Newport, Crawford Titus, drove a water cart and worked in the stables of the fashionable Ocean House before seeking permanent work in Providence. Titus broke in on a profitable stagecoach route between the capital city and neighboring Pawtucket. In 1864 he operated the state's very first horsecar along the same line.[6]

The *Street Railway Journal* described Providence in the Gilded Age as a place where "everybody can see everybody else by making a few trips on a street car." Yet as Sanford Manchester knew from his career on Broad Street, local geography was constantly changing its attire. In the words of a historian of that period, "The older casual way of doing things could no longer be applied to a complex industrial society." Indeed, Rhode Island was the first urbanized, industrialized state in the nation. One observer suggested that King Midas turned it into "precious metal" after the successful, pioneering factory experiment at Slater's Mill in the 1790s. The state's emerging textile industry, distributed along a serpentine network of mill streams, specialized in woolens, cottons, and worsteds.[7]

The rise of Rhode Island's economy in antebellum America accelerated with a flood of orders during the Civil War. Suppliers outfitted the Union army and soldiers like Sanford Manchester with uniforms and blankets, while quality foundries produced a variety of weapons, engines, and hardware. Other disparate trades included a premier jewelry industry, locomotive works, rubber production, fishing, and the tourist business, catering to the elite in fashionable Newport. Through such activity Rhode Island became a rising star in America's commercial constellation during the last three decades of the nineteenth century. The points of that star, popularly known as the five industrial wonders of the world, included five of the nation's premier manufacturing establishments. These businesses had a multiplying effect on the rest of the state's economy. Spin-offs transformed Rhode Island into a beehive of machine shops, foundries, and block-long brick mills.[8]

The nerve center of this commercial activity was the city-state of Providence. Despite its diminutive size, the demographer's scales counted more people in the capital city in 1900—175,000—than had lived in the entire state just forty years earlier. As the twentieth largest city in the United States by the turn of the century, Providence was one of the nation's ten industrial leaders, with a number-one ranking in the production of worsteds, number two in woolens, and number five in cottons. Politically, however, it remained a wealthy Gulliver shackled by dozens of Lilliputian rural towns that controlled political machinery through a corrupt Republican Party.[9]

Rhode Island's bold entrepreneurial vision in the commercial arena was not matched by a progressive outlook in the political sphere during this period.

The explosion of manufacturing and banking activity found no counterpart in a democratic system of proportional representation and free suffrage. Left in the wake of the state's dramatic and rapid economic transformation was an antique and discriminatory political structure. Most industrial and foreign-born workers in Rhode Island did not have the right to vote because of property qualifications, a situation that would have implications for mass transit. The advancing industrial state became less Jeffersonian with the realities of an increasing immigrant population. Modernization and commercialization helped democratize daily and popular life, including transportation services, but did little to assault the aristocratic ramparts of Rhode Island's political economy.[10]

Within this societal framework manufacturing became intertwined with transportation. Historian Maury Klein admits frustration when trying to disentangle one from the other: "The chain of connections seems hopelessly circular, tempting one to take two aspirin and turn in relief to a novel or magazine. Yet the chain is not so much circular as it is a spiral in which the factors reinforce one another and gain momentum as they move through time." Providence began experimenting with horsecar service in a secure industrial infrastructure and expanding population base that had already nurtured a railroad and shipping fleet.[11]

When Rhode Island dispatched troops to the bloody battlefields of the Civil War, native sons assembled in Providence. They arrived by stage, train, and omnibus or simply walked. The soldiers who returned could ride new horsecars home to some parts of the city with one of their compatriots, Sanford Manchester or Crawford Titus, at the controls. Another returning veteran, Daniel F. Longstreet, had enlisted in the Fourth Rhode Island Infantry as a drummer boy at age fifteen. When he mustered out in 1865, he noted with great interest the installation of tracks in his neighborhood. He became a conductor. His career progressed to clerk, superintendent, and eventually founder and president of the American Street Railway Association.[12]

The general assembly had passed legislation in March 1861 to incorporate Rhode Island's first three lines. These initial steps signaled a jockeying for potentially lucrative routes rather than a rush to immediate construction. Almost three years passed before a fare was collected. Horsecar advocates were "men of capital interests in the section of the city or suburban district which the particular road was designed to benefit." These real estate boosters believed that faster transportation would entice potential homebuilders to their suburban holdings. The early vagaries of the Great Rebellion dampened speculation until the war turned in the North's favor. Returning veterans, ready to use their bonuses for down payments, gave a shot in the arm to horsecar development. A writer for the *Providence Journal* described the local economy near the end of the conflict: "Money was abundant, prices were advancing, fortunes were being made in a day, and the tidal wave of land speculation which reached its flood in '73 had just begun to flow . . . but it gave us our horse car lines."[13]

Promoters had to raise significant amounts of capital, which certainly surpassed any sums required for stage and omnibus development but fell short of railroad investment. The incorporators of the state's first horsecar enterprise, the Providence, Pawtucket and Central Falls Railroad, pledged $100,000. A more serious obstacle than raising money and the experimental nature of the local system was a peculiar right granted to Rhode Island cities by the general assembly. According to the statute, town councils had to schedule a municipal election to determine whether or not a steam railroad and, by implication, a horse railway, could lay tracks "upon and over or along any of the public highways." Voters had recently rejected a mile-long freight track through the downtown area between a wharf and storage depot.[14]

There was more to this exercise in extreme democracy than urban aesthetics and street safety. Because the state constitution disenfranchised more than half the residents of Providence by requiring naturalized citizens to own real estate in order to vote, the affluent and conservative enjoyed a disproportionate political influence. With such a truncated electorate, transportation questions had important social implications that did not always meet the eye. Pioneering horsecar lines in other cities had employed raised rails, or a "gutter track," which protruded above the street surface and easily damaged carriage and wagon wheels. Rhode Island's private vehicle owners bristled at street impediments seemingly designed to incur accidents, disrupt independent travel, and open exclusive thoroughfares to lower-class penetration.[15]

As Civil War profits expanded a local moneyed class, an out-of-state observer remarked, "The number of private carriages one sees in the business streets of Providence is suggestive of . . . one of the wealthiest cities in the union." A veteran hack driver concurred: "The keeping of a carryall and hired man is so common now as to occasion no remark." He guessed that some two hundred families could afford the $2,500 for a team, vehicle, and coachman. The *Providence Morning Star,* however, estimated the number of family carriages to be "up among the thousands." Several thriving businesses catered to the private coach trade by offering a wide variety of contemporary styles: landaus, coupés, and phaetons. Furthermore, the well-off paid no fees to register their vehicles. As long as a small group of qualified voters could veto route selections, horsecar promoters had to placate these influential carriage owners.[16]

The Providence city council scheduled a vote, coinciding with the 1863 spring general election, to determine if the Providence, Pawtucket and Central Falls Railroad could lay tracks. Holding such referenda was time-consuming and expensive, so two possible routes were presented. Even though the proposed lines overlapped considerably, a second choice might prevent another tally in case one route proved objectionable. The council also felt obliged to point out on the ballot that the railway in question was horsepowered and not steam-driven. The promoters diplomatically agreed to install rails that would not interfere with local street traffic. Hiram Thomas, president of the horsecar company and editor of the *Providence Evening Press*, explained in his newspaper column that "the substitution of what is known as the Philadelphia flat rail, for the obnoxious patterns first used, has wrought an important change in the practical operation of street railroads, and won to their warm advocacy many who violently opposed them. It is this improved rail which will be laid down here." Other street vehicles actually rode on top of these updated flat rails for a smoother ride, and the remaining omnibuses were outfitted with a flanged front wheel for this purpose. Managers of the railroad and the city council further allayed the concerns of the public, or at least that part of the citizenry that could vote, by displaying models of the improved track at all ward rooms on election day. A letter to the *Providence Journal* predicted the plebiscite would turn on one issue only: "The kind of rail used in street railroads determines the question whether they are a universal public convenience or an unmitigated nuisance."[17]

Local newspapers editorialized in favor of either route, and several gushed over the potential benefits to Rhode Island. Hiram Thomas anticipated suburban commuting and proclaimed that the horse railroad would "open up for building purposes a large track fitted for the residence of classes who are more than willing to reside at some distance beyond the thickly settled portion of the city, if they can go to and from their place of business without too much loss of time and at a light expense." Another newspaper praised the route along the old Pawtucket turnpike, which traveled "through a beautiful region of unoccupied lands, which have recently been platted as house lots and are now in the market." In another editorial, Thomas added a dose of boosterism: "In a very few years we expect to see several horse railroads through our streets. Providence is not to remain passive while the rest of the world moves, and we may depend upon it that the introduction of the horse car is the dawn of a new era of city progress, and well worthy to be ranked with the undertakings which within a single generation have so increased our population and augmented our wealth." The *Providence Journal* gave its endorsement, too: "Horse railroads have been constructed in most of the large cities; and with great success, everywhere promoting the public convenience, increasing business, and raising the value of property."[18]

With such widespread enthusiasm for the new horsecar system and an acceptable rail pattern, both routes won approval in all city wards by a large majority. In his annual address, Mayor Thomas Doyle declared that management's choice of flat rails overcame "the principal objections which have been urged against them." With the city's carriage set temporarily assured of minimum inconvenience and uninterrupted use of the streets, the state's pioneering horsecar line collected its first fares on May 26, 1864.[19]

The tracks from Providence to Pawtucket followed the route of Indian couriers, stagecoaches, and omnibuses. Thirty-minute service and ten-cent fares, two cents less than the omnibus, delighted the public. The *Pawtucket Gazette* reported, "All with whom we have conversed on the subject are much pleased with riding in the cars where the track is straight and unbroken by turnouts." The four-and-a-half-mile trip took forty-five minutes. An omnibus transferred passengers from downtown Pawtucket to the neighboring village of Central Falls on a regular schedule. Drivers and conductors were "so busy that time for rest or refreshments could not be found," especially on Sundays, when most citizens enjoyed a day off.[20]

Class pretensions in Providence were not as pronounced as those in Newport, but people recognized the possibility of antagonism through the introduction of mass transit. A gray-bearded hack driver analyzed the situation for a local reporter. "You see, the horse-car is a very democratic institution. It holds a good many people, and being open to all, it carries all kinds. You think you haven't got much aristocracy in Providence," he concluded, "but you've got lots of it." The larger question of social and physical mobility for all classes and ethnic groups would became an unstated but burning issue later in the century, when electric trolleys opened up all areas of the state to rapid transit.[21]

Other entrepreneurs quickly joined the ranks of horsecar enthusiasts. The general assembly incorporated four more "animal" railways. "The success and popularity of the Pawtucket line," according to the *Providence Journal*, "opened the eyes of enterprising men in all parts of the city. During the spring of '64 there was horse-car talk on every side." Furthermore, without the social worries of the beach crowd in Newport, local editors endorsed the new horsecar routes: "They furnish a cheap, safe and agreeable mode of communication between the city and the suburbs and between different points within the city." The *Providence Daily Post* remarked on the momentous changes: "To those of us who remember when there was no omnibus in Providence, the idea of a thorough system of street railways is something startling."[22]

A horsecar passes above Pawtucket Falls in the 1880s. The mills along the Blackstone River, already ancient by the end of the nineteenth century, were among the first factories built at the beginning of the industrial revolution in the United States.

During the 1860s horsecar promoters hurried to invest in America's new urban transportation market, clogging streets with horsecars and courts with legal challenges. Boston, in 1860, hosted twenty competing lines. By 1886 there were 525 horse railways in the United States scattered among 300 municipalities. The voters of Providence, exercising their right to authorize or reject proposed routes, sanctioned three more during the presidential election of 1864. Seven separate concerns now held legitimate city charters, although the Pawtucket route was the only operational one. Proprietors began to wonder among themselves whether the congested streets of the capital city could accommodate so many competing lines.[23]

The *Providence Journal*, in its self-appointed role as civic guardian, suggested a merger. William and Amasa Sprague, scions of the state's most important textile empire and possessors of a valuable charter, orchestrated the unification of the city's horsecars. The general assembly passed legislation to create the horse-powered Union Railroad Company in January 1865. The new board of directors included representatives from most of the former independent lines, with the exception of the innovative Pawtucket enterprise, which remained unattached. Shareholders chose Amasa Sprague as president and his brother, William Sprague, the state's junior United States senator, as a director. The company issued consolidated stock worth $515,000 and limited the issue to $700,000.[24]

The Spragues' initiative and bankroll accelerated the spread of rails, or "iron claws," as they were commonly called in newspapers of the time. The Union Railroad's first horsecar jogged into service between Market Square in downtown Providence and the industrial village of Olneyville on Washington's Birthday, 1865. The driver, John Benchley, was a veteran of omnibus and sleigh service, and he ended a fifty-year transit career on the electric trolleys. A ten-minute headway was established to this important textile center. The *Providence Journal*, reflecting the views of the commercial establishment, predicted "a decided appreciation of property in that section." During the summer the Spragues opened five more lines, corresponding to the original route plans of the merged railways. Although the Union Railroad did not expand further for another decade, patronage grew steadily along the twenty miles of existing "threads of silver." In August 1865, for example, conductors tallied more than one-quarter million fares, including nine thousand passengers on one pleasant Saturday. Patronage spiraled to four hundred thousand in July 1869, and in 1872 the traction enterprise recorded over one-half million fares in eight different months. "The cars are almost always well filled," stated a newspaper account chronicling the growth of mass transit in Providence, "many people riding short distances which before were walked."[25]

Although the fledgling enterprise blunted any potential opposition when it agreed to employ flat rails, winter weather introduced a new controversy among old antagonists over control of local streets. Storms often interrupted travel in that era, and the Spragues used a "mammoth roller" pulled by oxen to compress snow. Frequently the Union Railroad employed small passenger sleighs but could not afford an entire substitute fleet. With the riding habit on the increase, patrons wanted more service, especially during inclement conditions. However, the summer carriage set, turned winter sleigh riders, pressured the city to limit plowing and prohibit chemical melting. As the popularity of horsecars swelled the ranks of mass transit advocates, town authorities informally allowed the clearing of snow by the Union Railroad.[26]

Cursing barriers and bare spots caused by illegal plowing, sleigh owners lobbied the mayor to enforce the law. During one blizzard the railway etched a clearing on the tracks, producing huge snowbanks that impeded sleigh travel.

The street commissioner ordered laborers to break down the ramparts, pushing snow back onto the rails. City workers and company crews dueled furiously to undo each other's toil, shoveling snow on and off the tracks to the delight of an assembled crowd. A group of children joined the fray and almost buried a stalled car. The police chief had to restore order between competing interests.[27]

Horsecar patrons potentially represented a much larger constituency than carriage and sleigh owners. Their growing numbers meant political influence despite voting restrictions. The 2,400 commercial freight carriers in the city who, unlike owners of private vehicles, paid to register their wagons, drays, and hacks also learned the benefits of plowed streets: "It is in the horse-car track that the milkman, the butcher, the baker and the merchandise truck find a roadway." Only 15 of the city's 185 miles of streets were paved in 1870. Always eager to mediate civil disputes, the *Providence Journal* suggested, "There is ample room for sleighs in near a hundred miles of unobstructed streets within the city limits, to say nothing of the whole boundless continent beyond, where the speed and mettle of noble steeds can be tested unchecked by municipal regulations." The same opinion piece further chided owners of private vehicles: "The number of people who depend upon the cars to carry them daily between their homes and places of business is very large—much greater than can be accommodated by any other means of conveyance—and many of them have fixed their place of residence in reliance upon the cars."[28]

A letter to the *Providence Morning Herald* the following month added more socioeconomic spice to the debate. The author criticized the selfishness of "some of the men who can afford to ride in their own carriages" for their opposition to plowing. He rhetorically asked who was really complaining about cleared roads: "not the poor man, certainly, for the street car is his carriage; not the invalid, for the horse car carries him to and from his work and store; not the laboring man, forced upon the suburbs by high rents; not the resident of Olneyville, East Providence or South Providence, who visit our lecture rooms, halls and associations by the aid and conveyance of the cars." But the *Morning Star* praised the work of the Union Railroad: "It is only on the occasion of a storm or some serious impediment to locomotion, that the blessings of a horse railroad are fully appreciated." (Patrons were a diverse group, as the writer of the letter to the *Morning Herald* pointed out, and they built a following for mass transportation.) The Providence city council amended the snow-plowing ordinance but mandated the removal of embankments. Such a legal compromise hinted at a growing acceptance of mass transit in the community in spite of the political power of the carriage set.[29]

When the Union Railroad proposed double-tracking portions of fashionable neighborhood streets to handle more riders, local estate owners hired a lawyer to halt construction. A parallel set of rails eliminated the need for turn-outs, small track spurs that allowed an outbound horsecar to pull over while an inbound car could proceed. Although another line increased capital costs, it also expedited trips and strengthened the riding habit through greater speed and convenience. Although several retired politicians testified against ex-panded service near their genteel estates, other witnesses, including a local minister, took the side of ordinary commuters, complaining about "the present delays and inconveniences suffered by the public under the single track sys-tem." In another blow to minority control of the streets, the city council author-ized double-tracking.[30]

At the same hearing, counsel for the Union Railroad reminded wealthy opponents, "Nothing had advanced the price of real estate so much as horse railroads." Even during the first year of operation, the influence of mass transit was reflected in "for-sale" advertisements. Real estate agents trumpeted the proximity of homes and undeveloped land to horsecar routes. One auctioneer highlighted a piece of property as "easily accessible from the centre of the city, being on the line of the Union Railroad (now nearly completed)." Transit ser-vice, even before the inauguration of a route, increased property value. If estab-lished homeowners were unmoved by this argument, as businessmen they had to be inspired by the horsecar's larger impact.[31]

Despite the obvious benefits of urban service, city and state officials eyed the new carrier warily. The general assembly, in granting charters, enacted for-mal regulations protecting private travel. Voters had to approve routes, and carriers had to give two weeks' notice before construction so owners of adjacent property could sue for possible damages. The legislature also ordered horsecar enterprises to issue annual reports. The state railroad commissioner, who for-merly regulated steam trains only, now had jurisdiction over the animal railway. Another section of the regulations mandated fines or imprisonment for horsecar or carriage drivers who obstructed one another on the streets, because the animosity between private and public interests lingered.[32]

Transit entrepreneurs had to dodge another barrier once past the regula-tory dictates of the state. Some municipalities subjected railways to stricter local ordinances than before. Providence, for example, stipulated road upkeep: the companies were required to "keep and maintain in good order and condition, by paving, repaving and repairing, whenever necessary, at their own cost and expense, the streets that may be occupied by their rails, so that said streets may be safe and convenient to travellers with their teams, carts and carriages, at all seasons of the year; and on streets and parts of streets not paved, said company shall pave between the rails, and two-and-a-half feet outside of each rail." If carriers evaded repairs for more than ten days, the city could terminate the franchise. Town fathers also held an option to subcontract necessary restoration and bill the railway. Under extreme conditions, the town could even tear up the tracks. Mayor Doyle created a railroad committee to oversee burgeoning transit activity and issue regulatory ordinances, and the city council levied annual road taxes.[33]

This flurry of regulatory action reflected a growing concern about Rhode Island's new era of transportation. The city council and, to a lesser degree, the legislature willfully imposed these stringent and exacting rules. They cautiously guarded government prerogatives regardless of any expected benefits from expanded transportation service. Over a generation of experience with the wily and volatile forerunner of American big business, the railroad, had hardened honest public servants in making contractual arrangements. The municipal rot that infected Gilded Age America partially originated in the machinations of railroad barons who corrupted public bodies in search of unrestrained freedom of action. Initially, state officials did not allow railroad malfeasance to degenerate to levels that prevailed elsewhere. Local vigilance withered, however, as railroad, horsecar, and electric trolley service became more lucrative.

For their part, the state's newspapers usually backed a free-enterprise vision of railway expansion. Provisions in horsecar charters, according to one daily, onerously placed the company "at the mercy of the City Council, which may even, after the cars have run one year, order the rails taken up at the company's expense." The *Daily Post* asked if mass transit could operate under such conditions: "From seeming to be almost unanimous for railroads, we have come to be looked upon as having so great an antipathy to them as to place them almost completely beyond our reach." The editorial also wondered if "the railroads are to be taxed too heavily to allow their business to be a very profitable one," citing provisions for road paving in particular. Hiram Thomas, both editor and transit entrepreneur, attacked obstructionists: "They fight against it, but they will find it as fruitless as the attempt of Dame Partington to mop the Atlantic out of her dwelling when its huge waves were rolling in through the door." On the other hand, a rival newspaper chastised Thomas for demanding "one privilege after another." A member of the new railroad committee complained that the horsecar charter was "a better proposition than a corporation ought to have, to monopolize the important streets through which the road is desired to pass."[34]

Despite the sincere vigilance and caution of most politicians, the Union Railroad and its electric successors would undermine taxation and regulatory control. Like the steam railroads, these profitable transportation enterprises perfected a degenerative system of political favoritism and municipal graft to protect their empire. As early as 1864 the *Manufacturers and Farmers Journal* accused Hiram Thomas and his Pawtucket line of trying to subvert local prerogatives: "They prominently appeared at two different sessions of the General Assembly in an effort to have the right of voting upon street railroad propositions taken from the citizens of this city altogether." The cumbersome yet democratic privilege to choose routes was soon overturned, although the right to vote was still limited. In this instance, corporate high-handedness probably served the interests of a majority of the disenfranchised over those of the voting elite.[35]

Although the influence of mass transit on urban growth, property values, and suburbanization would mushroom in the electric trolley era, the horsecar provided a slow-motion preview of things to come. "The days of Providence, as a village, have passed," a *Journal* editorial noted. "The horse railroads, perhaps, decided that. The new hospital helped. The introduction of water settled it beyond peradventure." Looking ahead, the same article pondered a local metropolis with more public parks, schools, and libraries; hotels, theaters, and a new public market. The reverie reached its denouement, as was customary in the local press, with Providence overtaking Boston as the region's premier town: "Thus, while building up a noble city, and increasing our home market, we shall gain the energy by which to secure a large portion, perhaps second to no city, of the interior trade of New England and the commerce following therefrom."[36]

In his 1864 annual address, Mayor Doyle discussed horsecars in some detail. He tried to balance the city's need for revenue against the danger of discouraging industry and transportation with regressive taxes: "Care should be exercised not to make the restrictions so burdensome as practically to prevent the building of the roads. It will be time enough to impose a heavy tax when it shall be found that their earnings will warrant it." In return, he demanded a unified system of tracks rather than a competing web of rails crisscrossing one another. Doyle threatened to withhold a franchise into the city's commercial center at Market Square until rails on both sides of the Providence River were completed; "otherwise our citizens in passing from one point of the city to the other will be subjected to a change of cars, additional fare and other inconveniences."[37]

The pioneering era of mass transit in the 1860s and 1870s featured a shifting alliance of proponents and opponents of horsecar service. The carriage set originally objected to tracks that might interfere with private travel and routes that might bring unwanted passengers by their own front doors. Eventually the elite embraced mass transit, and some even abandoned expensive carriage travel for the inexpensive and reliable horsecar, even if it meant rubbing elbows with workers and immigrants. As the Union Railroad prospered, former foes purchased the company's valuable stock. Middle-class passengers regularly patronized service, and most working-class customers rode on special occasions or Sunday outings. As horsecars girdled the city, the *Providence Journal* commented, "Business establishments and places of trade are gradually driving back the population from the centre of the city and the constantly improving facilities for reaching the outskirts in every direction are contributing much to the same result." Another elite, the Union Railroad's charismatic work force, would play a major role in this process and significantly change the equation of street control.[38]

AN EXCEPTIONALLY INTELLIGENT
CLASS OF MEN

What a car conductor don't know about every regular patron of the line isn't worth knowing.

Providence Morning Star, 1886

Few complaints are made to the company against the men for incivility, and as the public well knows on all of the routes in the city, the conductors and drivers are as a rule very gentlemanly in their treatment of passengers. . . . They are an exceptionally intelligent class of men.

Providence Journal, 1892

The passengers were very friendly with the drivers and conductors, and many times if the regular riders were late for their cars, they would whistle for us to stop, and we would wait for them to come out. In all the thirty-eight years I have worked for the company, I have found that if the conductor was gentlemanly and courteous to the public, that the public would be equally so to them. The regular riders always had a friendly greeting for the drivers and conductor when they entered the car, this we appreciated, and it made the day's work pleasanter for both.

Retired horsecar conductor, 1926

Benjamin R. Jepson began a fifty-five-year career with the Union Railroad in 1871 at age fourteen. He started as a "hill boy" on Eddy Street, attaching extra mounts to passing horsecars about to ascend one of Providence's many inclines. Once at the top of the hill, he would lead the horses back to the bottom and await the next vehicle. He also spent several years as a hostler and night watchman for the railway before graduating to full-time horsecar service, "the goal of all youngsters in the business then." As a rookie driver he spent "4 years, 10 months, and 19 days" on one route before finally accumulating enough seniority to operate the Eddy Street run, where he had started his career. He lived directly on the line and passed by his home twenty times a day. When electric streetcars were introduced he easily made the switch to motorman on the same route, pulling out the first trolley at 5:06 A.M. daily. He was active in local fraternal groups like the Ancient Order of United Workmen and the Odd Fellows. He later served as sergeant-at-arms for the street carmen's union and was a revered warden for the Providence Central Labor Council. When he retired in 1927 Jepson had spent decades on the same route, changing to an easier line only for the last few years of his career. The day after he was pensioned he inadvertently showed up for work, unable to break the habit of a lifetime.[1]

Clarence "Pop" Spear started his railway service as a seventeen-year-old hill boy, the same year Ben Jepson broke in. After completing his informal apprenticeship program, he drove the first Mount Pleasant horsecar. He operated the initial electric trolley on the same route a generation later. After serving that community for thirty-three years he switched to the Elmwood Avenue line until his death on the job at age sixty-seven, a veteran of fifty years of duty. Spear was a union activist and a great prankster, beloved by colleagues and passengers who anointed him with the nickname "Pop" for his decades of service. In 1911 he originated an annual reunion of horse-era veterans that featured a small parade with a restored horsecar filled with old-timers. Providence residents cheered the spectacle and the memory of a simpler and bygone era. Pensioners wore different-colored badges signifying years of service, and the top of each badge contained an embossed photograph of Pop Spear on a horsecar.[2]

When he retired in 1910 at age seventy, William Leonard Vinton was allegedly the oldest working street railway employee in New England. He started his transit career in 1864 on a local farm, driving a four-horse team. He received fifteen dollars a month and board. Although he eventually doubled his salary there, he decided to become a horsecar driver at the Union Railroad five years later. "I used to come in now and then to get loads of manure," he said, explaining how he changed jobs, "and they knew what I could do when it came to handling horses. I got in ahead of nearly 200 other applicants anyway." Because of his experience and maturity, Vinton trained for only an afternoon before being assigned his own car on the South Providence route, where he toiled almost continuously for the next forty-two years. He switched from driver to the higher-paying job of conductor early in his career and worked during the 1902 strike, unmolested by protestors. He was active in a fraternal order and lived only a few blocks from the carbarn. Upon retiring, Vinton authored a short poem that was published in the local newspapers. It could have served as a collective epitaph for several generations of transit employees:

> Today I leave the cars on which
> I've been so very long.

Motorman Clarence "Pop" Spear was a legendary figure on the Providence transit system for fifty years. Here he operates the first electric streetcar on Providence's Mount Pleasant route in December 1893. The conductor on the left, David Allardice, was another union activist.

And so that now I've been "retired"
I'll sing my little song.

So many years I've been "right there"
On 'bus, horsecars and electrics, too,
That I know the question will be asked
"What will he ever do?"[3]

These three streetcar workers, like thousands of their colleagues in Rhode Island and elsewhere, operated the new vehicles that undergirded industrialization, urbanization, and suburbanization during the Gilded Age. As opposition to new modes of travel withered, railroads became the country's commercial arteries, and public transportation evolved into the nation's capillaries, moving workers, customers, and residents to jobs, stores, and homes. In various vehicles, primitive and sophisticated, mass transit helped design and develop urbanization and its dialectic, suburbanization, and increased the value of real estate in both sectors. Public transportation, especially when it became rapid, changed America forever by accelerating the division of neighborhoods

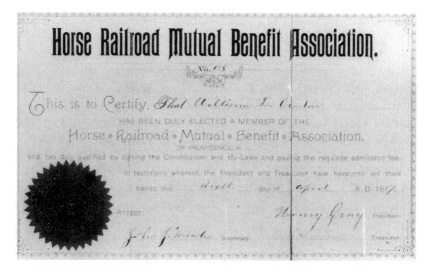

The Horse Railroad Mutual Benefit Association provided health and burial insurance to transit workers in the Gilded Age. It served as an incubator for the street carmen's union. William Vinton drove farm horses and a horsecar, and became a trolley conductor before he retired at the age of seventy.

by class, ethnicity, and race. Horse railways and electric streetcars quickened life's tempo, simultaneously creating leisure time and new popular forms of amusement.

Although these transit-driven changes were accomplished gradually, traction workers and their patrons witnessed the daily dismantling of a preindustrial world order from a horsecar bench. While drivers and conductors unwittingly facilitated this societal alteration as part of their job, they also reflected old ways. The labor historian Herbert Gutman wrote that the period's workers "lived through an era of extreme social change and social disorder, but carried with them meaningful and deeply felt traditions and values rooted in the immediate and even more distant past." Crews who traveled the same lines for decades provided continuity and reliability to several generations of the same families, who rode in their stagecoaches, omnibuses, horsecars, and trolleys. Yet increasingly rigid timetables presaged the forthcoming world of modern scientific management. Drivers and conductors were usually married family men, white, and native-stock Protestants who belonged to several fraternal organizations and lived within walking distance of local carbarns. Many of them had served in the Civil War, and most of them had agricultural experience and values, exemplified by long workdays and dependence on horsepower. The horsecar, a hybrid between farm life and industrialization, represented the future, but at a manageable pace. The horse, at least until it was replaced by electric motors a generation later, pulled a manufactured body that was a combination train and stagecoach. In control of these vehicles were familiar faces who carried friendly greetings. They distributed community information gleaned from thousands of daily trips a year on the same line. Urban transit workers were sentinels of a preindustrial world who guided their customers into a new industrial frame of mind.[4]

The affluent veneer of the times camouflaged the proletarian ribs of a hardworking society. Behind the props and sets that the affluent built at Bristol, Newport, and Providence's East Side, a massive work force toiled innumerable hours to create the wealth at the top. The Gilded Age, the Gay Nineties, and other conventional views of life in nineteenth-century America hid the arduous reality of working-class life.

Employees of the Union Railroad shared a demanding lifestyle with their neighborhood peers. Yet status and salary nudged them ahead of others on the working-class circuit. These "Knights of the Road," as they were often referred to in the press, were urban aristocrats in a nation of laborers, farmers, and mill hands, especially in a medium-size city. The urban historian Samuel Hays described the preindustrial American world "as a face-to-face community in which human relationships were established in personal contact over limited areas." That characterization rang true in many places long after the introduction of large-scale corporate enterprise and no more so than on horsecars and trolleys.[5]

For some native-born American workers the initial transition to industrialism meant deskilling, as artisans involuntarily slipped into the ranks of factory labor. At the same time, this vocational demotion opened up a slew of new semiskilled jobs for American farmers and immigrant peasants, although they often relinquished whatever tentative hold they had on yeoman sovereignty in exchange for these salaried positions. When independent stage operators and omnibus drivers lost their autonomous jobs to larger corporate transit services, they surrendered a degree of self-reliance as well. As they boarded horsecars or electric streetcars to make a living, they too became wage earners, but the nature of the work left them a notch of freedom with minimal supervision. They enjoyed, in the words of an English historian, "mobility of the workplace." Their accommodating demeanor and envied employment earned the carmen a vaunted and admired position in society's pecking order. If they felt justifiable pride in their line of work, it did not go to their heads. They might seat a gentleman at the suburban end of the line but soon be reminded of the period's financial vagaries when they passed through the poorer part of town at the beginning of the route.[6]

Transit workers first carved a niche in American folklore during the heyday of the stagecoach, when drivers checked the nation's pulse along their scattered routes. Wayfarers respected their knowledge of "horseflesh" and current news. According to a local article, operators were greatly admired. "The driver also acted in the capacity of an express carrier of all kinds of small parcels, had charge of the mails in transit, and was the trusted bearer of many important messages and missives, which he delivered with the air of a man who was of some consequence in the world." One of the last stage operators in Rhode Island started his career during the administration of Andrew Jackson. He was still driving in the 1890s, "in determined spite of and with a kind of contempt for those modern conveyances the steam car and steamboat." Like many other drivers who toiled endless hours, he was an owner-operator who hung on after prudent businessmen would have abandoned the enterprise. An interurban electric railway eventually replaced his coach.[7]

Transit employees in Gilded Age America, like their blue-collar counterparts in other lines of work, could be sure of one thing: long hours. And unlike the agricultural background that many of them came from, there was no seasonal slack. John Benchley, who operated the first Union Railroad horsecar, remembered: "We worked from early morning until late at night without any regard to time." Later in his career he ran a "matinee" route from noon to midnight, with only short breaks at the end of each trip. Another horsecar veteran claimed that "working days were measured by the rise and set of the sun rather than any prescribed hours of labor."[8]

Although a day's labor had been whittled to twelve hours by the 1870s, there was a wrinkle. In mass transit, riding patterns generally determine trip frequency and service. Carriers need more employees and cars for rush-hour traffic than off-peak periods. Drivers and conductors often worked split shifts with several breaks ranging from thirty minutes to a few hours. A schedule could stretch to sixteen hours with no compensation for intervening time. On busy holidays, a crew might toil for eighteen hours without relief. Before occupational specialization hardened, drivers and conductors sometimes swapped positions to break the monotony of such a routine.[9]

Transit workers accepted these demanding schedules, but elongated shifts took a toll. "It wasn't anything unusual for a horse car driver when he got at the end of the line, to sit down for a snooze," an old-timer confessed, "and sometimes it was necessary to send out to see why he wasn't showing up, only to find his snooze had developed into a protracted sleep." Late-evening drivers often tied the reins to the front of the car on the final trip to the carbarn and joined the conductor inside the horsecar for a nap. Through habit the horses usually stopped at the barn, but one night a team kept going. The embarrassed crew slept through the extracurricular ride before pulling in several hours late. Despite grueling schedules and occasional sleepiness, drivers and conductors seldom missed work or appeared late. Ben Jepson logged fifty-five years for the Union Railroad with only one "miss" when "his faithful alarm clock went back on him." [10]

"Those were the good old days," joked one old-timer about the horsecar's first decade, "when a fellow WORKED from 4:30 in the morning until 5:30 in the afternoon, THIRTEEN hours a day, seven days a week, 365 days a year." There were no scheduled days off in that period. No paid vacations. Employees could be excused by arranging for a "spare man" to relieve them for a few hours or a few days. Transit crews were such an integral part of everyday urban life that any absence was quickly noticed by riders. Vacations, however brief, were reported by the newspapers. One account cited a conductor who visited friends in Massachusetts; another announced that several employees went fishing; a third trumpeted the news that a crew member took an unusual two-week break. [11]

Like Pop Spear and Ben Jepson, aspiring drivers and conductors usually served an apprenticeship as hill boys before being broken in under the supervision of an "old hand," who indoctrinated the rookies in the culture of street railroading. They willingly worked the "list," or "slate," temporarily replacing full-time workers. John Wall, who drove from 1886 to 1924, remembered: "While running 'spare' we were supposed to run from any car house in the system regardless of where we lived. Each evening we were assigned a car for the next day, and if it was an early one, we often had to walk from our homes, sometimes many miles in order to get there and start on time. When we were not assigned a car, we had to report at the office before ten in the morning and remain until noon time before being excused." The Union Railroad did not compensate spare men for "report" time. This reserve force often cajoled full-time operators into taking a break in order to get in a few trips and earn something. Once these employees secured full-time positions, they usually moved close to the carbarn to avoid long, early-morning treks to work. [12]

Transit crews labored as hard as other workers but earned a better salary for most of the nineteenth century. They received two dollars a day at the inception of the Union Railroad. By the 1870s conductors enjoyed a daily stipend of $2.50, drivers $2.25, better than what their counterparts earned in New York City, Saint Louis, and other metropolitan areas. Extra remuneration for the conductor reflected an attitude that a rewarded fare collector would be less likely to steal. Although drivers seemed to acquiesce in this arrangement, one publicly complained that he deserved equal compensation for operating at the "worst end of the car." Most employees, however, considered horsecar work a source of "good pay." Furthermore, transit workers valued steady, year-long employment over seasonal or part-time work. Skilled tradesmen might earn more, but construction jobs were often irregular. Because of the seven-day workweek, drivers and conductors were assured of an extra day's earnings. Also, they were paid weekly, unlike workers in other industries, who were paid once or twice a month. Transit salaries remained constant until 1894, when out-of-state owners reduced wages for all new employees to two dollars, the same stipend as thirty years before.[13]

The Spragues and their successors, at least until the electrification of the lines, purposefully used good wages to attract and retain the best personnel. When a potential competitor threatened the Union Railroad's monopoly, management sounded a warning: "Instead of the gentlemanly young men that as a rule now look after the safety and comfort of yourselves and families as they ride over the streets of the city, you will find a band of underpaid and overworked hirelings whose only recommendation is that they will work cheaper." A few days later at the same public hearing, the superintendent of the Union Railroad argued that higher wages brought "a better class of men." Such admissions by the era's captains of industry were not standard fare, especially in the field of mass transportation. The *Street Railway Journal*, for example, editorialized, "The employer has no more responsibility for the comfort of men of whom he buys services than of him of whom he buys hay."[14]

Employees, on the other hand, openly complimented liberal policies at the Union Railroad. The state's industrial commissioner printed a series of anonymous interviews about local job conditions. A horsecar driver, although voicing a number of concerns, ended by saying, "We are working for the best railroad company in this country." When a driver wrote an unsigned letter to the *Providence Morning Star* complaining about conditions, a colleague quickly replied, "There is not a man who works for the Union Railroad Co., outside of this would-be kicker, who has any fault to find but what he has always been used as a gentleman by the management of this company." Veterans who retired after the turn of the century endorsed labor relations as "one big happy family." On a punishing holiday like the Fourth of July, when carmen toiled fourteen to sixteen straight hours, the owners diplomatically paid a fifty-cent bonus and distributed free lemonade at all carbarns (a dose of ginger was added to the beverage to prevent stomach cramps). Through thick and thin, transit employees pledged allegiance to the Union Railroad and practiced loyalty until the syndicate came and abandoned small courtesies and personal favors to them. Their identification with management paralleled that of the railroad brotherhoods.[15]

To ensure a quality pool of applicants beyond the draw of good wages, the Union Railroad employed a stringent reference policy. One employee remembered being told to have "a good reputation, be fairly well educated and be recommended by two prominent men." An article in the *Providence Journal* commented, "There are always plenty of applications for places on the cars, but the men who hold the places do not often resign." Fourteen years later a similar analysis in the same newspaper reported a similar phenomenon: "A large number of horsecar conductors and drivers cling to the brakes and punches for many years." More than a third of the work force had a dozen years' seniority; this was "a very contented class of men." Local university students even sought summer employment to augment tuition payments. Work-force stability remained a hallmark of horsecar operations in Rhode Island until the vicissitudes of electrification disrupted employee permanence.[16]

Job qualifications were very different for the two main classifications in transit service. "The conductor," according to the railway's first rule book, "is expected to see everybody within the car who may want to get out, and everybody without who may want to get in, each on the first indication of their wish." In this endeavor the conductor controlled the car's bells, which signaled the driver to stop and go. He had to be alert constantly and was forbidden to sit down while on duty. The Union Railroad suspended six for this infraction in one year. The company also required daily housekeeping chores: the conductor was required to "keep his car clean and in good order, and dust the seats and clean the windows and lamps every morning before starting." He was also accountable for any neglectful damage to the horsecar. A local newspaper described the job as combining "the strength of Solomon, the patience of Job, the meekness of Moses, and so on."[17]

Once patrons were safely aboard, the conductor diplomatically performed his most serious duty: collecting fees and tickets. "He must take every fare, but must never twice ask the same person to pay. If he takes counterfeit money it is his loss; if he gives too much change, he alone must bear it." At the end of each trip he had to count and separate cash fares and a great variety of tickets. The Union Railroad supplied each conductor with a hand-held register, and, according to the *Providence Journal*, there was "great indignation among the conductors when the bell punch appeared." Fare collectors felt the machine impugned their integrity, although management said it had instituted the new policy to protect conductors' reputation by forcing them to tally each payment in front of the customer and eliminate any suspicion of fraud.[18]

Mark Twain popularized the conductors' protest:

> Conductor, when you receive a fare,
> Punch in the presence of the passenjare!
> A blue trip slip for an eight-cent fare,
> A buff trip slip for a six cent fare,
> A pink trip slip for a three cent fare,
> Punch in the presence of the passenjare!
>
> *Chorus*
> Punch, brothers! punch with care!
> Punch in the presence of the passenjare![19]

Several conductors actually resigned in a huff. Although the Union Railroad admitted it had no evidence of organized pilfering, other metropolitan railway companies had uncovered stealing. Passengers also objected to the bell punch as a "badge of disgrace" for their beloved crews. As a newspaper reporter stated, "In a city the size of Providence, each prominent conductor is better known by the masses than the Mayor of the town." One patron wistfully recalled, "Then there was no coin collector such as now makes the relationship between the passenger and street company an impersonal thing." This public annoyance with the railway hinted of an emerging alliance between riders and transit crews. Passengers even encouraged conductors to pocket fares in protest. Although liberal wages gave pause to any larcenous thoughts, packed vehicles facilitated stealing, and some did not resist the temptation. Unlike transit companies in other cities, the Union Railroad employed no "spotters" or detectives during the horsecar era, a testimony to employee honesty.[20]

While tempers would cool over the register issue, overcrowded horsecars irritated passengers more than any other contemporary mass-transit problem and taxed the skill of driver and conductor alike. A reporter described a Pawtucket car with 135 passengers crammed into a vehicle with twenty-four seats: "They were hanging on by the eyelids, toes, and all sorts of ways," the journalist bemusedly wrote. "Some dropped off soon after starting, in fact, they were dropping off all the way, and those who dropped footed it home." Another reporter exclaimed, "It has been said that a horse car cannot be filled so full but what it will hold one more." In one instance, youthful riders climbed atop an overloaded vehicle for a seat on the roof. Another time, a sideboard broke from the weight of twenty patrons. Drivers had to gauge stopping distances differently with such heavy loads, and conductors toiled feverishly to collect fares. Transit companies preferred the profit of "standing freight" to the double expenditure of running two cars in close proximity to provide seats for all passengers. When the Union Railroad was forced by overwhelming patronage to increase service to the state's textile center, the *Providence Journal* marveled: "A car every five minutes to Olneyville! It was but a few years since an omnibus once in thirty minutes was thought to be ample accommodation."[21]

Drivers and conductors faced various problems on the road. A driver had to have "considerable physical strength" and be "a man in whom a phrenologist would find 'form' large." A patron remembered that drivers were "as solid as the Rock of Gibraltar." They had to be ambidextrous enough "to drive three or four horses with one hand and work the brake with the other without even the slightest confusion between the two." The driver's greatest enemy, however, was not his team but the weather. The Union Railroad did not equip the fleet with vestibules, sheltered compartments at the front of cars. Open-faced vehicles exposed drivers to winter's teeth, although some preferred the unprotected freedom of motion. John Wall described his gear: "In cold weather we usually wore an overcoat down to our feet, under this one or two sweaters, and a short coat, a pair of felt top boots, over these a pair of overshoes, a scotch cap well down over our ears (nothing visible except our noses), and one or two pair of mittens, with the temperature down below zero, the rain and sleet beating in on us with no protection whatever." Contemporary opinion attributed the crew's good health and longevity to these conditions. Providence haberdashers advertised "Heavy Felt Ulsters" expressly for drivers. The jackets cost $5.50, more than two day's earnings.[22]

One newspaper explained why such uniforms were needed on a rail jaunt along the old Pawtucket Turnpike: "No colder place than across the 'flats' this side of the horse-car barn can be found anywhere but in Greenland." A driver turned meteorologist described a frigid winter as "the result of trying to blow the north pole down this way so as to save going in search of it." The local press expressed great sympathy for carmen in such conditions, the *Providence Journal* commenting that "blinding sheets of snow . . . rendered the occupation of the drivers anything but agreeable." Passengers too felt the sting of cold-weather transit. At times riders had to push derailed cars through snow embankments and back onto the tracks. "Lumps of snow and ice get under the flanges of the wheels," a passenger moaned, "and the cars bound from the track like a bolting politician." Once "a load of shivering freight" borrowed

Pawtucket motorman Joseph C. Fiske (right foreground) poses in front of his snow-encrusted trolley in 1895. Streetcars lacked a protective vestibule in front until after the turn of the century. Fiske, a union activist fired during the 1902 strike, later spent almost fifty years as a railroad engineer.

shovels from local residents to liberate a stalled horsecar. During a blizzard vehicles operated off the tracks, "just bumping along as best they could," a retiree recollected. "People didn't mind rough riding in those days, the extra bumping kept them from freezing to death in the cars, so they really liked it."[23]

Once rails were cleared, drivers faced another dangerous situation. Water quickly froze on brakes and metal tracks, turning some downhill routes into toboggan runs. Operators unhitched teams and walked the animals while the conductor guided the vehicle to the bottom. "Each car gained momentum," marveled a witness, "as it speeded down the decline and whirled around the curve at Fountain Street with the velocity of an express train." When one horsecar began gliding before the team was detached, the driver somehow managed to free the horses safely while the car was in motion. Fearing a crash, several patrons unnecessarily jumped from the sliding machine. John Wall reminisced about the rough treatment: "This would shake up the passengers some-what," he explained, "but they always laughed and were very good natured about it. (Nowadays I presume they would sue the company for injured nerves.)" The unavoidable danger, shared excitement, and give-and-take assis-tance between riders and crew helped cement this unusual service alliance.[24]

Another consequence of bad weather nettled horsecar employees: "storm tables." Whenever there was a significant accumulation of snow, the Union Railroad cut back the number of trips and added as many as six horses to the driver's charge. One winter, hostlers hitched extra teams thirty-six days in a row. To make up for the cost of this seasonal problem, the Union Railroad paid crews only by the trip, regardless of time spent on the road. "When your Car is not run, on account of the weather or other reasons, you will report for extra work," the company ruled, "and payment in such cases will be made either by the trip or by the proportion of the day's work at the prescribed rates." One contemporary union estimated, "The employees have to sacrifice from 25 to 50 per cent of their pay and undergo exposure to the weather such as no other class of people, with the exception of the police." One driver explained, "In storm time we only have six trips a day, which we get paid $1.50 for, and drive four horses." The *Morning Star*, sympathetic to the plight of workers, editor-ialized, "It would not make a large inroad on the company's plethoric sur-plus, should the hardworking help be paid double rates for trips run on 'storm time,' thus bringing their pay up to the rate made on other days." Even the management-oriented *Providence Journal* admitted that lost wages were "quite considerable in the winter." The employees circulated a petition asking for full wages for storm time, but to no avail. The company's largesse was unilateral and not subject to negotiation with workers. Crews acquiesced as long as over-all treatment was fair and considerate.[25]

Pleasant weather, on the other hand, also brought problems. Intoxicated patrons, especially on evening horsecars nicknamed "bartender's carriages," harassed other passengers and challenged crews. In response to public com-plaints, the state railroad commissioner ordered the posting of this notice on all horsecars: "No disorderly, or otherwise obnoxious person, whether under the influence of liquor or not, will be allowed to ride upon this car." Drivers now legitimately passed by potential troublemakers, who often waited for a return trip to retaliate. William Vinton, because of his size and wrestling skills, had few problems removing any agitators. One conductor who ejected a ruffian at an amusement park confronted dozens of "toughs" on his next run. He bran-dished a revolver to scare them away. On other occasions a vandal broke four horsecar windows before being subdued; a delinquent threw a knife at a conductor; and "one dirty fellow, who deserved a beating," attacked a conductor with a cane. Passengers often came to the aid of the crew in such circumstances because adventure on the streets of Gilded Age America had a certain attraction. A newspaper account noted that "queer incidents in the [street] railroaders' career are as numerous as mosquitoes on a hot summer's night in a swampy wood."[26]

Accidents, although infrequent, were another source of headaches. Despite stringent city ordinances that limited horsecar speed to five miles per hour in the city and seven miles per hour outside the business district, mishaps did occur with the slow-moving vehicles. The quickened tempo of urban life took its toll on crew members, riders, and pedestrians: "I can't hold the reins in one hand, keep my other hand on the brake, keep my eyes on the horses, ring up fares, answer questions of patrons, watch for passengers on side streets and do other things that a driver has to do according to the rules governing our duties," an operator complained, "and at the same time keep a sharp watch on children who steal rides to see that they are not injured." When management used one horse team to pull two horsecars but employed only one conductor for the tandem vehicles, employees protested that the practice was dangerous and inconvenient to waiting passengers. Conductors refused to patrol the second car, and the Union Railroad backed down when a newspaper reported public complaints: "A company doing the large amount of business which the railway is doing, should have enough men to attend to it properly."[27]

Compared to the proliferation of collisions in the upcoming trolley era, local drivers established an enviable safety standard. Ben Jepson, for example, had only one real accident during a fifty-five-year career because he adhered to the principle that "drivers of teams and automobiles and pedestrians are all deaf, dumb, and blind." There were only a handful of yearly injuries and a rare death during horsecar service. In 1886 the Union Railroad carried 82,000 passengers on Memorial Day and a whopping 97,000 on July 5, almost a third of the state's population. The *Morning Star* complimented the carrier for its impeccable record: "The carrying of the vast number without a single mishap speaks volumes for the excellent service of the company." The newspaper, which often criticized the Union Railroad for other reasons, praised the conscientious crews: "In no other city are conductors and drivers more careful for the safety of their passengers, and when persons are injured it is almost invariably by their own carelessness." When incidents occurred, regular patrons put their crews in a good light by filling out favorable accident reports, which the company required.[28]

Drivers and conductors were as solicitous of their horses as of their passengers' safety. The Union Railroad maintained a stable of magnificent animals in carbarns along each route. The flagship Olneyville facility, for example, housed almost four hundred. The purchase, training, and care of these animals was a major capital investment, one that transit companies protected diligently. The American Street Railway Association's official journal was filled with suggestions on how to prolong a horse's usefulness, and the organization created a standing committee on the health of animals. In Rhode Island an elite foreman was expected "to know every horse in his care as a mother knows her child. He must know the tastes, temper, endurance, gait and general characteristics of each horse. He ought to be something of a doctor and nurse as well." Hostlers nicknamed each of their sixteen charges and fed them carefully prepared meals. Veterinary attention probably surpassed any medical service the employees received. Horses worked only three hours a day, covering about fifteen miles, and were retired after three years of service. The Union Railroad sold them at a popular annual auction, where local citizens got a bargain and the company recouped some of its investment.[29]

From its inception, the transit carrier admonished its crews to pamper these teams. "You must use your horses with care and treat them kindly," the first rule book stated. "You will not . . . use a whip except when absolutely necessary, and any abuse of your horses will subject you to immediate discharge." Drivers had to slow horses with reins, not the car brake, and inspect shoes and harnesses daily. In the face of such unequal care, the Rhode Island Knights of Labor made a pitch to local crews: "One is apt to think that the employes are not as valuable as are the horses employed." William D. Mahon, founder of the national streetcarmen's union a few years later, similarly complained, "It is a fact that in the early days the horse received much better treatment than the car man who drove him. Men could easily be replaced even at the miserable wages paid," he mused, "but a horse cost money."[30]

These salvos fell on deaf ears. Reflecting their own agricultural upbringing and previous experience with horsepower, local carmen obediently and cheerfully respected their teams. They depended on the horses' performance as much as management or patrons did. A forty-five-year veteran remembered fondly, "I had those creatures so well trained that they understood and minded every word I spoke to them, for I never used reins." Drivers often became so possessive of certain horses that they came to work regularly to prevent another colleague from using their "hitches." As one old-timer remarked at the end of a thirty-eight-year career, "The drivers were as careful of their horses, as if they owned them," despite frequent challenges to the drivers' patience. When an Olneyville car stopped due to an excited animal, the *Morning Star* observed,

"During the delay there was no abuse of the balky horse, and not an oath or angry word was heard from either one of the horse car men." In rare instances of mistreatment, public reaction cut deep. "George Johnson, driver of Elmwood car No. 35, was complained of yesterday for cruelly beating one of the horses attached to his car," according to the *Manufacturers and Farmers Journal.* "It is understood that the animal is balky, and that Tuesday as well as yesterday much excitement was caused by the driver's treatment of it." Passengers were furious. These infrequent incidents caused great embarrassment to all Union Railroad employees, who employed peer pressure to prevent such behavior. The horses' royal treatment, at least in the Gilded Age, when horsepower mattered, did not trouble crews or lead to unionization locally.[31]

The real union in those pioneering horsecar days was the one between patrons and carmen. Despite a company prohibition against "unnecessary conversation with passengers," drivers and conductors, like professional salesmen, cultivated a fawning clientele. Conductors especially were skilled conversationalists who bantered and joked with customers, employing their personalities as a vocational skill. When one veteran concluded a forty-one-year calling, a newspaper article lamented a vanishing way of life in industrialized Rhode Island, recalling a time "when patrons on the few lines that radiated out from Market square felt a personal interest in the men who drove the horses and collected the fares, and when each conductor had his own particular following." Another seasoned driver spent a lifetime in transportation, operating a stagecoach, horsecar, fire engine, and finally a Union Railroad trolley. Before he moved to Rhode Island, "persons from all over the eastern portion of Massachusetts went out for the sole purpose of riding with him" on the stagecoach. William Vinton recounted three decades of toil as a conductor: "I knew intimately all the regular passengers. . . . I never had to ask the people who travelled with me where to stop, for I knew their streets as an elevator boy knows the floors for the regular occupants of a business building. Even now when I have a car full of 'regulars' I don't call the streets, but if there are any strangers on board I do." That first generation of transit passengers must have felt like intruders on the avenues of the carriage set, but drivers and conductors negotiated the geographical and social terrain for their dependent riders, especially those passing through an upper-class community for the first time.[32]

The obituary of another venerable transit worker mentioned that "he ran cars almost entirely on the so-called Elmwood avenue lines, and thus became well known and liked by the hundreds of the company's patrons between the Elmwood barn, Butler avenue on the East Side, and along Smith street, as his schedule sometimes directed him." Another enterprising conductor, a stickler for mathematical figures like many of his coworkers, kept a personal record of his passengers for eighteen years. He rang up 2,181,487 fares and collected almost $110,000 in cash and over $1,000,000 in tickets, while traveling over 340,000 miles. Although the company was eventually bought out, changed its name to the Rhode Island Company, and became the United Electric Railways after bankruptcy, the personnel remained constant.[33]

During these busy careers, drivers and conductors performed innumerable courtesies for passengers above and beyond the call of duty. Daily intercourse mandated respect and gentility unexperienced in most other walks of life. John Wall encapsulated that philosophy when he talked about his life as a horsecar conductor: "The passengers were very friendly with the drivers and conductors, and many times if the regular riders were late for their cars, they would whistle for us to stop, and we would wait for them to come out. In all the thirty-eight years I have worked for the company, I have found that if the conductor was gentlemanly and courteous to the public, that the public would be equally so to them. The regular riders always had a friendly greeting for the drivers and conductor when they entered the car, this we appreciated, and it made the day's work pleasanter for both." An experienced patriarch of stagecoach, omnibus, horsecar, and trolley service practiced civility as a driver. He learned "to always turn out when he met another vehicle and give the other vehicle the right of way and he would never have any trouble." As the pace of Gilded Age society accelerated, some old indulgences perished. When Pop Spear's horsecar replaced the Mount Pleasant omnibus, a steady rider yelled from his front door to ask if the new crew could wait a few minutes for him to finish breakfast. They apologetically told him that the faster tempo of horsecar service prevented such courtesy any longer.[34]

Employees did other favors that reinforced their camaraderie with passengers. Crews frequently turned in lost pocketbooks and wallets, sometimes containing significant amounts of money. Conductors sold individual tickets for five cents, instead of in blocks of twenty as required by the company, thus saving the customer a cent. The Union Railroad disciplined fare collectors for not charging double when shoppers carried large packages or workers dragged a tool box on board. At times conductors allowed mothers to suspend baby carriages from a handle on the back platform or winked at itinerant peddlers, who often used horsecars as private hacks to drag their wares across town for a single fare. As a favor to patrons and local businesses, crews frequently delivered parcels and newspapers "all along the line." One Olneyville shopkeeper hesitated to criticize the Union Railroad's service at a city council hearing so as not to offend the many carmen that patronized his store. The council itself even refused to hire a candidate for constable because he allegedly insulted a conductor.[35]

Transit workers, many of whom lived in the same neighborhoods as their passengers, served as reliable information bureaus to the general public: "If these employees keep their ears open they certainly can obtain a great deal of information useful or otherwise. The conductor's appealed to for his opinion on all sorts of subjects." The *Morning Star* commented, "What a car conductor don't know about every regular patron of the line isn't worth knowing." Such knowledge and intimacy only enhanced the crews' respectable standing in the community.[36]

These kindnesses and familiarity, sometimes contrary to company policy, ingratiated riders to the carmen. "Few complaints are made to the company against the men for incivility," noted the *Providence Journal*, "and as the public well knows on all of the routes in the city, the conductors and drivers are as a rule very gentlemanly in their treatment of passengers. . . . They are an exceptionally intelligent class of men." The *Morning Star* complimented the operation, too: "The cleanliness of the vehicles, the good character of the horses, the intelligence, gentlemanly deportment and accommodating spirit of conductors and drivers, all make traveling from one part of the city to another and to the suburbs as pleasant as a vacation excursion." Crews had another reason to protect their reputations and polish their images: accusations and criticism led to surveillance by company supervisors and detective agencies in other cities. Horsecar crews in Rhode Island escaped that fate until the system's electric expansion.[37]

More often than not, passengers registered appreciation, not complaints. Drivers and conductors received a variety of Christmas presents. A veteran fondly recalled, "Just about this time of year, the old horse car drivers were particularly accommodating, for more than one turkey or chicken found its way to their homes, the gifts of patrons along their way." Broadway residents in Providence brought hot meals to crews on winter holidays, and a Prairie Avenue rider contributed coffee and doughnuts on a cold day in February. Ben Jepson remembered a blizzard that stranded the crew overnight: "Some of the neighbors dug out to us and were more than good in bringing out sandwiches and things, and a bakery wagon that was plowing through stopped and left us a load of cookies. One woman brought out a big tureen of hot soup." In warmer weather a greenhouse proprietor in Cranston supplied local carmen with Easter flowers. Riders occasionally chipped in to help an injured employee or pay for vandalism, which ordinarily was charged to the crew. When employees formed a mutual benefit association, thousands of patrons attended fund-raising concerts and fairs. Carmen seldom left railway service for other work, and the newspapers usually noted passengers' regret in such instances.[38]

Not all transit workers were angels, of course. Some "knocked down" fares for themselves. A passenger confessed, "I had a friend who put himself through college by working as a conductor in an open car in the summer vacation— and put himself through comfortably." Some crew members occasionally argued with customers. Rookie drivers and conductors could try the patience of patrons and coworkers alike. "A good many people when they want to stop a horse car sing out 'hay' to the conductor," observed the *Morning Star:* "'Grass' would be more appropriate to yell at the green conductor who persistently keeps his back turned on running, screaming passengers." The city of Pawtucket employed small "bobtail" horsecars with a driver who doubled as a conductor. According to an irate patron of this line, it took "a public gymnastic performance" to attract the driver's attention. Such rudeness was uncommon. Transit workers seemed to police their own ranks to prevent public criticism and ridicule. The superintendent of operations said, "The men are honest, capable and faithful. . . . there is not so good a set of men upon the horse-cars in any other city in the country." Dismissals were rare. The one bad habit that no one could seem to prevent, however, was flirtation. "It is wonderful how many beautiful girls do succumb to the wiles of the horse car conductors," observed the *Morning Star.* "They are the source of much trouble to many a doting parent."[39]

Conductors and drivers promoted a sense of brotherhood within their own ranks, waving fraternal acknowledgment to one another as their routes continually crisscrossed downtown. As a group they were outdoorsmen, uncomfortable in the confines of a manufacturing plant. "The man who has had his car seldom goes back to work in the shop." One youngster, fresh from pastoral Maine, became an industrial apprentice in Olneyville: "Bill made a try at it but, after his life in the open, being shut up in a mill did not appeal to him and he proceeded to get a job as conductor on the horse cars." Farm work and horse experience developed an urban wanderlust, a need to keep moving, if only along a familiar, repetitive route. A Progressive-era study of Providence's labor force concluded that railway employees "come from the rural districts or from the mills and factories, and others from clerical positions to get the benefit of work in the open air."[40]

Horse carmen socialized whenever their limited leisure time permitted. They chatted, philosophized, and argued during many split shifts at the various carbarns. They went on sleighing parties, practiced polo and baseball, and played practical jokes. Pop Spear, the venerable horsecar driver, bet the crew of two cars in front of him that he could reach the carbarn first. The others quickly accepted, figuring there was no way he could pass them on a single track. Once they were out of sight, Spear drove his horsecar off the rails and down a trackless side street to the carbarn. When his rivals arrived they found him smugly smoking his pipe. Male bonding was further enhanced between drivers and conductors, who often formed lifelong partnerships on the same line. Employees also presented gifts to grooms and retirees, serenaded coworkers on special occasions, and made collections for and visited the sick and injured. Conductors and drivers wore black mourning ribbons on the job and served as pallbearers when a colleague died. Every carbarn would send a delegation to the funeral, and many devoted passengers would attend as well. This camaraderie rivaled that of other uniformed services in military, police, and fire companies.[41]

The vast majority of Rhode Island railway employees during the horsecar period were born in the United States of English descent. Few non-English names graced a Union Railroad roster until after the system was completely electrified and working conditions deteriorated. Then transit employment no longer had an exclusive appeal to native Yankees. Irish Americans, in particular, replaced old-stock employees. In 1895, 639 of the 786 Rhode Islanders who worked for the Union Railroad were native born; 81 came from Ireland, although some second- and third-generation Irish were employed but not listed by ethnicity. An academic study of Providence just before World War I concluded, "The street-car employees are mostly Americans." In larger cities the work force included more immigrants.[42]

Drivers and conductors discussed establishing a Gilded Age fraternal order like the local police lodge, and they incorporated the Horse Railroad Mutual Benefit Association in 1884. One hundred seventy of the approximately 250 drivers and conductors joined and paid weekly dues. Like similar institutions in that era, it served as a primitive health care and burial insurance plan. Later that fall, the association provided a nurse and a dollar-a-day compensation to its first beneficiary. After the driver's death the group made a per-capita assessment of two dollars for the widow. If a member's wife died, the organization contributed 100 dollars for funeral expenses. The group, assisted by a women's auxiliary, held a week-long public fair to raise money. Local businesses donated cash and merchandise. Patrons, in a hotly contested election that rivaled any political contest and included more voters, chose a favorite driver and conductor. Winners received an expensive new uniform. Later the group hosted a series of popular annual concerts. Within a few years almost all employees had joined this dynamic organization, which they would later use as a springboard to unionization.[43]

The same year horsecar employees organized the association, other local workers, affiliated with the Knights of Labor, formed the Rhode Island Central Labor Union to unify the state's disparate labor force. More than half were foreign born in the 1880s, primarily Irish, British, and French Canadian. Many were unskilled and uneducated but found ready employment in the teeming, but cyclical, textile industry, which commanded the lion's share of local manufacturing capital. In that era, more women worked outside the home in Rhode Island than in any other state and made up 10 percent of the Knights' local membership. Similarly, the number of Catholics was high: by the turn of the century, Rhode Island was the first state with a Roman Catholic majority. Child labor was also endemic. At its height, the Knights claimed a dues-paying membership of over 13,000 of the 71,000 workers in manufacturing and mechanical pursuits.[44]

The Knights' new Central Labor Union introduced legislation to limit factory work to ten hours a day. Sponsors of the bill exempted street railway employees, knowing that the Union Railroad and its workers would probably object to any loss of pay. There is no evidence that drivers and conductors protested the exclusion or made any overtures to the new labor body. During that period the Knights of Labor began a brief but meteoric rise to prominence in working-class wards across the country. They were especially active and successful in organizing approximately fifty assemblies of horsecar workers in militant, big-city operations across the nation. The Rhode Island Knights solicited local drivers and conductors in its weekly newspaper, *The People*, but apparently made few inroads among these conservative and contented employees. Many of the carmen were taxpayers who owned enough property to vote under the state's restrictive franchise. With a large contingent of Civil War veterans in their ranks, they leaned toward the Republican Party. On the other hand, Irish Catholics dominated the state Democratic Party and the Knights of Labor. Although horsecar employees did not wave the bloody shirt at Irish workers, many of whom had served in the war on the same side, there was a distinct socioeconomic chasm, going back to the 1842 Dorr War, when both sides squared off in a local power struggle. Furthermore, Yankee drivers and conductors may have feared a loss of status in the Knight's vocationally mixed assemblies of skilled and unskilled workers, although the order did its best to stay nonpartisan in local politics. This cautious attitude toward industrial organization dovetailed with the railroad brotherhoods' antagonism to general unionism among train workers, as practiced by Eugene Debs's American Railway Union.[45]

Carmen at the Union Railroad had grievances, to be sure, but they

FRANK LESLIE'S
ILLUSTRATED
NEWSPAPER

No. 1,555.—Vol. LX.] NEW YORK—FOR THE WEEK ENDING JULY 11, 1885. [PRICE, 10 CENTS.

The Knights of Labor led a violent horsecar strike in Chicago in 1885. Superior wages and excellent working conditions in Rhode Island prevented such uprisings. Frank Leslie's Illustrated Newspaper, *July 11, 1885.*

viewed them in a larger context. For the most part, they were satisfied with their lot in life. Many of them had labored on farms where the length of the workday challenged even a horsecar schedule. They willingly accepted the doting care horses received, even if it was at their own expense. In return crews never experienced the economic insecurity that so many trades and textile operatives, organized by the Rhode Island Knights, underwent during the financial upheavals of the late nineteenth century. Steady pay, a company-imposed system of seniority that protected older workers with choice runs, and a sense of belonging and importance reinforced daily by appreciative passengers and coworkers provided a contentment few other workers could match. There was never a layoff until the Great Depression of the 1930s. Under ordinary conditions these carmen were conservative. But when the Union Railroad disrespected precedent, pride, or citizenship, traction employees reacted with uncharacteristic fury, supported by a phalanx of passengers, a unity that transcended generation and social class. When "foreign capitalists" bought the Union Railroad and transgressed the customary workplace culture by paring wages, upsetting work conditions, and depersonalizing labor-management relations, employees then made a belated turn to trade unionism, drawing upon their organizing experience with the beneficial association.

THINGS WERE REDUCED TO A SYSTEM

You may readily discover how important it is to secure faithful and efficient service from conductors and from that you will be able to estimate the amount you can afford to pay to make the position so desirable, and the means of detection so ready and complete, as to stop both the inducement and the opportunity for peculation.

Union Railroad Superintendent Daniel Longstreet, 1877

The Union Railroad Company has ever been alive to the interests of the people, and its managers have done not a little towards building up the city and bringing into demand the hitherto unsalable land in the suburban districts.

Providence Morning Star, 1883

The red ball hangs aloft my love, the moon is shining bright, we'll skate a couple of hours, love, at Roger Williams Park tonight. That is if I can raise the price of four horsecar tickets, and one ice cream with two spoons.

Providence Morning Star, 1886

In an era when railway managers barked orders like military officers and expected their employees to respond accordingly, drivers and conductors at the Union Railroad discovered an unusual ally in the firm's front office. As a child, Daniel F. Longstreet did agricultural chores at 3:00 A.M. before going to public school each morning. In 1862 he enlisted in the Fourth Rhode Island Infantry at age fifteen. Although still a teenager he was promoted to head a large field hospital before mustering out at the end of the Civil War. When Longstreet returned to Providence he was surprised at seeing horsecar tracks "into the section of the city where my home was." He began to think of a transportation career: "I had become accustomed to long hours and exposure. It seemed to me that the life of a conductor would be an agreeable one, and I made the necessary application." He started work in 1865 on his nineteenth birthday. Laboring sixteen hours a day, he earned the standard two-dollar salary, "ample for all my necessities."[1]

Longstreet recounted later in his career how dismayed he was at "the utter lack of system and accountability in the conduct of the business." His military nature bristled at imprecise rules, haphazard schedules, and questionable collection procedures. "I had just passed three years under circumstances which demanded the strictest sort of discipline . . . and these things were very annoying to me." He took it upon himself to compile his own timetable, established a system of passing other cars on single tracks, and issued zone checks to ensure full payments on his two-fare suburban run. He was so frustrated by the disorganization and seeming lack of advancement that he was prepared to leave the transit field. In less than a year, however, he was promoted to clerk and given free rein to institute personnel policy while the superintendent was preoccupied with rail construction.[2]

More than anything else, the unregulated collection of fares nettled Longstreet, "not only for financial but for moral reasons. There was no system for accounting for money received," he complained. "It was the custom to keep tally with pennies, and at the end of the day to turn in as many fares as you could find tallies. It was said that some of the boys would spend the tallies (by mistake) for beer, sandwiches or cigars, and in that way unconsciously reduce their living expenses. Whether this was true or not, they certainly had the credit of being dishonest." In his new position as clerk, he diligently recorded daily receipts for all lines, toiling late into the evening. He compared income from different conductors on the same route, trying to uncover dishonesty. He introduced the bell punch, creating an uproar among his colleagues and inspiring Mark Twain to compose his "passenjare" jingle. Longstreet's sole interest seemed to be ensuring a verifiable collection system "which would enable the conductor to maintain his honesty before the public."[3]

One would not expect such invasive innovation to endear the young Civil War veteran to either coworkers or patrons. However, he made sound trade-offs to ensure a top-flight work force. He unilaterally reduced the workday to twelve hours with no loss of pay, issued natty uniforms, and increased wages. By contrast, the president of the largest Boston street railway asked, if one "can get efficient conductors and drivers for say thirty-five cents a trip, why should he pay fifty cents?" Later in his career Longstreet endorsed a ten-hour railway workday if scheduling flexibility could be maintained. Drivers and conductors began to affectionately refer to him by his initials, "D. F." Nor was he one-sided in his administration of justice in a class-conscious, Gilded Age America. The Sprague brothers, owners of the Union Railroad, also had a lifelong interest in horse racing and were the local proprietors of one of the country's premier tracks. Longstreet became secretary-treasurer of that corporation and uncovered unexpected fraud among wealthy racers when a party misrepresented an animal to enter it in an inappropriate class. He then notified other establishments around the country to keep the perpetrators from the sport altogether. The same rational mind that organized local transit operations then established a national trotting association with standardized rules and regulations. "Things were reduced to a system," he wrote years later about his various endeavors during this period.[4]

Longstreet proved as solicitous of patrons as he was of employees, reasoning that a first-rate operation drew a concomitant clientele and work force. In 1873 the Union Railroad continued to fulfill its side of the bargain by equipping the popular Elmwood line with a half dozen sparkling new horsecars. These state-of-the-art vehicles featured safety brakes, upholstered seats "with the best hair," superior ventilation, and lamps etched with route names. "They are of the most elegant and convenient style and finish," complimented the local press, while the industry's national organ paid homage by describing Rhode Island cars as "scrupulously clean and attractive." William Sprague, president of the Union Railroad, promoted his enterprising clerk to secretary-treasurer in 1870 and superintendent two years later.[5]

Longstreet and the Sprague brothers planned to upgrade the rest of the fleet, but the panic of 1873 toppled the family's textile company. Their network of financial interests was so intertwined with the Rhode Island economy that the empire's demise strained the state for years to come. The Spragues forfeited the Union Railroad in 1876 in a controversial bankruptcy takeover. The Spragues also lost the family homestead in Cranston to real estate interests, who, ironically, subdivided the land into a horsecar suburb. The Union Railroad, however, continued to prosper, and its stock reached $180 a share by 1881.[6]

Longstreet retained his position under the new owners but faced a recessionary "scalping knife." The board of directors proposed cutting wages to two dollars and eliminating the rented bell punches. "It seemed to me," he lamented, "to be undoing in a minute what we had been years in accomplishing." Longstreet pleaded with them: "You may readily discover how important it is to us to secure faithful and efficient service from conductors," he argued, "and from that you will also be able to estimate the amount you can afford to pay to make the position so desirable, and the means of detection so ready and complete, as to stop both the inducement and the opportunity for peculation." He went on to defend his philosophy of recruiting the best horsecar crews and favorably compared the price of premium labor to the annual cost of one stolen fare per trip: $17,100. "The great obstacle I had to contend with always," he complained, "was that other roads did not pay as much wages, or did not keep up their roadbed and equipment as we did. My argument was that we got the equivalent in a better service which was bringing to us a relatively better business." The board followed his advice.[7]

As long as the Union Railroad "included" passengers and workers in its daily considerations, there was a sense of sharing and commonweal that kept muckrakers, labor unions, and disgruntled individuals at bay. The company controlled street operations, but in a benevolent fashion. Before the age of corporate takeovers, expansive railway policies dovetailed with public desiderata. The horsecar system, as primitive as it was, provided ordinary citizens with legitimate access to the carriage set's city streets and made most thoroughfares thoroughly public.

Longstreet, as a go-between in this process, was a real-life Horatio Alger whose pluck-and-luck demeanor symbolized the age and made him a winner with employees and riders. Although he patrolled a horsecar for only a brief period as a conductor, he was one of the boys. During a career that was a perpetual experiment to improve service, he personally invented variations of safety devices, snow plows, brakes, wheels, roller bearings, and other features. The *Street Railway Journal* carried a photograph of his improved track, called "the Longstreet Rail." Under his direction the Union Railroad earned extra revenue by marketing advertisements in horsecars, renting surplus sleighs and omnibuses, and selling horse manure for fertilizer, taking in $7,000 on that alone in one year. He also made the company self-sufficient in other ways, authorizing the construction of horsecar bodies and the establishment of a paint shop. The Union Railroad also employed its own talented blacksmiths and horseshoers. The company constructed a popular model depot with public urinals and water closets in downtown Providence. And later in the century, during slack winter months, Union Railroad mechanics and carpenters built rides at two local amusement parks.[8]

Despite tough economic times, Longstreet convinced the board to expand service in the 1870s. Approximately sixteen major routes or extensions snaked into new areas of Rhode Island under his direction in the next ten years. Track length increased from thirty-five to fifty-five miles. Industrialization, population, and mass transit nourished each other, making Rhode Island the most urbanized state in the nation. Despite being a novelty in 1865, the Union Railroad exerted a centrifugal pull on residents, stretching the narrow boundaries of the inner city outward to new commuter suburbs. The animal railway became so popular that steam railroads offered a left-handed compliment by promising affluent commuters a comfortable respite on the train: "You need not ride for half an hour in a crowded horse car."[9]

Although street and steam railroads used tracks as a common denominator, their similarity during horsecar times was limited. As America's first Big Business, so to speak, the railroad industry led the way in rationalizing and systematizing service and tackling a wide array of everyday problems that would bedevil other enterprises in the coming decades as the nature of commerce changed. At the time Longstreet made his preliminary experiments, he anticipated the future direction of urban mass transportation. During his pathbreaking career, horsecar schedules and traffic volume were still footnotes to the iron horse's complex grid of passenger and freight travel. But Longstreet's work at the Union Railroad set the stage for what was to come in the industry.

This urban–mass transportation revolution, according to urban historian John Stilgoe, became an escape route to lower rents and a rural ideal as downtown business districts transformed themselves into high-rent administrative, commercial, and financial centers. Wealthy homeowners led the exodus, followed by the middle class, skilled tradesmen, and some immigrants and laborers, who clustered in less desirable neighborhoods. Specialization shattered old, integrated business centers, where rich and poor once lived and worked in close proximity to one another. The *Street Railway Journal* reported a "desire to separate the residence from the shop."[10]

As rents for housing skyrocketed around the old downtown business district and former homes were renovated or torn down for commercial development, workers had no choice but to find cheaper living quarters, even if that meant including the cost of daily fares in a family budget. "Providence more than most cities is a manufacturing place. Its different enterprises require a large number of skilled workmen," observed the *Providence Journal*. "It will soon be indispensable, then, that within striking distance there shall be enough tenements to be had at reasonable rates, to retain this class of workmen, if our city is to maintain its present prosperity." Some claimed that laborers were already "forced upon the suburbs by high rents." A letter to the editor a generation after horsecar service commenced said the same: "Now the class of people who ride on these various cars, for the major part, are those who labor for a living, and in most cases for small wages. It is the laboring portion of the people who support this interest."[11]

Rhode Islanders from all walks of life responded by boarding horsecars to "remote regions" of the city in search of open land. German immigrants founded the Providence Cooperative Building Lot Association to procure homes at affordable prices. Land values accelerated in suburbs as well as in the inner city, but supply and demand met in amicable adjustment in the "outlands." Buyers could tolerate some land speculation because prices were cheap to begin with, and their lots soon appreciated favorably. As the economy rebounded in the 1880s, even those of moderate means could build, and new, inexpensive construction material encouraged the out-migration. Incentives, gimmicks, and free horsecar tickets to prospective buyers lured customers for a look at the suburbs. With such widespread popularity, Longstreet orchestrated transit expansion and the hiring of additional crews, often relatives of current employees.[12]

One of the most interesting and representative transit developments occurred in the neighborhood of Elmwood, just southwest of downtown Providence in Cranston, Rhode Island. Once accessible only by "long, hot and dusty rides" on an omnibus, Elmwood quickly became the darling of Providence, a "smiling suburban village." The coming of the Union Railroad enhanced earlier development in the community and transformed it into a horsecar suburb. Lower Elmwood, closest to downtown, became a mecca for middle-class shopkeepers, grocers, and working-class producers, who populated local side streets. Unskilled Irish workers inhabited the adjacent West Elmwood section, serving as factory hands, gardeners, and general laborers.[13]

Elmwood Avenue, the main artery, soon hosted a ribbon of genteel estates comfortably beyond the plebeian neighborhoods. As early as 1867 a realtor described a home there in a transit framework: "This property is situated on one of the great avenues leading from the city, directly on the line of the Elmwood Horse Railroad, the cars of which pass and repass half hourly through the day." Merchants, financiers, builders, and professionals moved to the aristocratic settlement. This affluent invasion led to an annexation drive. Providence offered an array of city services unmatched by the still bucolic town of Cranston. "We do not wonder that the citizens of Elmwood and South Providence, so thickly settled and whose vacant lots are being so rapidly occupied," editorialized the *Providence Journal*, "should feel the need of those advantages which a City Government can alone afford." Newcomers wanted police and fire protection, city water, street services, and school facilities. In 1868 Cranston relinquished the area to Providence.[14]

Elmwood continued to expand due to the availability of mass transportation. The Union Railroad built a modern carbarn on Bucklin Street at the end of the line, near present-day Columbus Square. Although patronage was minimal there, the company wisely foresaw rapid land development in the area. Realtors soon trumpeted it as "the most rapidly growing section of the city . . . near the termination of the Elmwood Horse Cars."[15]

A sizable colony of drivers and conductors, most of them married, clustered around the new facilities, minimizing their own trek to work for early-morning pullouts. Steady employment and good wages enabled a remarkable 71 percent of the 281 carmen listed in the Providence city directory to own their own homes in 1891, the last full year of exclusive horsecar service. The street railway industry officially encouraged the hiring of middle-aged family men—"old residents of the city"—who were "more amenable to discipline." Employees Benjamin West, Frederick Lockwood, and Arthur Barney purchased houses directly on Bucklin Street, within a few blocks of the Union Railroad office. Young, unmarried transit workers often boarded with older colleagues, turning fraternal bonds into family ties. Horsecar drivers Joseph Feeley and William McKeon, for example, rented from fellow driver Benjamin West at 208 Bucklin Street. Frank B. Cottle, a driver who owned a home at 38 Redwing Street, around the corner from the company stables, sublet to his brother James, also a driver.[16]

Four blocks from the carbarn, Potters Avenue bisected Bucklin Street and was home to nine Union Railroad workers: four conductors; three drivers; a clerk; and a hill boy, who attached extra horses to cars. Only the hill boy boarded; the others were homeowners. The nine lived fairly close to one another at the following Potters Avenue numbers: 15, 154, 301, 367, 369, 456, 468, 477, and 522. This housing pattern was repeated around the company's other carbarns. Although living close to work was not unusual in that period, the carmen became part of the very suburbanization they fostered on the job, leapfrogging to commuting's outer limits. On and off the job, fraternity in the neighborhood reinforced workplace and community interaction.[17]

Passing by their own houses, inbound and outbound, a dozen times a day, horsecar crews kept an eye on the community. At lunchtime, near the end of the line, a driver or conductor worked both positions while his partner stopped at home for a quick lunch. Like local post offices, neighborhood carbarns became a gathering place for gossip and fraternity. Children especially liked to come look at the horses, particularly if a colt was being broken in for street service. Conductors, who seemed to know everyone along a route, might solicit colleagues and friends for a local cause or charity at the company stables. One enterprising crew member, later a union activist, sold 1,356 tickets for the annual meeting of the community's literary association, seventeen times as many as the runner-up.[18]

Services proliferated along the line as the population expanded. The Elmwood Store, a suburban emporium, offered a variety of goods "at prices so low that money can be saved by purchasing, even though the purchaser should have to include horse car fares." The Providence Riding School for Ladies and Gentlemen offered lessons at tony prices. A brochure advised customers to board horsecars and included a schedule. The Eagle Nursery featured 300,000 fruit and ornamental trees and was "easy of access by the Elmwood horsecars that pass it every quarter of the hour."[19]

Business and urban transit sustained each other in a commercial symbiosis. The Union Railroad's Elmwood route was one of the most patronized lines in the system, second only to booming Olneyville. The development of Roger Williams Park, a mile south of Columbus Square, and the Bucklin Street carbarn further enhanced the area. The company extended its Elmwood tracks there and introduced the bloomer horsecar, a vehicle without sides. "The change from the hot, close-atmosphere box cars, to the delightfully cool and airy open ones, was too great to be thought lightly of, and the cry was for more," according to a newspaper. Bloomers brought the feel of a private summer carriage to the average citizen for a six-cent fare. Rides became an amusement as much as a way to reach a particular destination as small bits of Gilded Age discretionary time evolved into mass leisure.[20]

After lengthening the route, the Union Railroad built a $15,000 gothic "Waiting House" on Crystal Lake. The What Cheer Cottage, as it was called, contained a celebrated soda fountain of Mexican onyx, which had been exhibited at the Centennial Exhibition in Philadelphia. The carrier also constructed a passenger depot, "gladly welcomed by thousands of people who like to visit the park but who do not like to fight for seats and standing room in crowded horse cars." This "architectural gem" featured "exquisite wood carving in bold relief, bountifully adorned with cathedral glass in high colors." Sunday cars ran on a remarkable five-minute headway to the new facilities. The *Providence Morning Star* commended Longstreet's first-class handiwork and solicitous regard for passengers: "The Union Railroad Company has ever been alive to the interests of the people, and its managers have done not a little towards building up the city and bringing into demand the hitherto unsalable land in the suburban districts." A year later an omnibus left the new park depot for the Auburn Post Office two miles away, moving public transportation even further south into rural outposts off Elmwood Avenue. The omnibus would stake out a new route for the coming of the electric streetcar a decade later.[21]

In 1887 Daniel Longstreet and another Union Railroad director started the Park Land Company to capitalize on Elmwood's popularity. The *Providence Journal* commented on one of his sales: "There will be inaugurated on Saturday at Auburndale a grand auction sale of land such as never before been seen in this State." The plats lay adjacent to Roger Williams Park on Elmwood Avenue. Agents distributed hundreds of free horsecar tickets to prospective bidders, provided clam chowder at the What Cheer Cottage, and featured a balloon ascension. The 292 lots sold for top dollar, about fifteen cents a square foot. The area was advertised as having the advantages of "city and country combined," and the *Journal* summarized its attractiveness: "Its pleasant location, readily accessible by steam or horse railroad, the possession of facilities in the introduction of Pawtuxet water, gas and sewerage, the establishment of street grades and curbing, its proximity to Roger Williams Park which insures the best of sanitary conditions and attractive surroundings, and the easy terms upon which a site for a cozy home can be secured, form a combination of inviting conditions which cannot but convince those seeking an investment that the economy and comfort offer most satisfactory inducements."[22]

By the late 1880s horsecar and carriage traffic so choked Elmwood Avenue that residents lobbied for a widened thoroughfare. A local citizen's committee hosted a meeting of 850 presided over by a successful downtown retailer who owned a Queen Anne mansion there. A band played while civil engineers showed stereoscopic slides of proposed improvements. Car tracks would be moved to one side of the expanded street, freeing up the rest of the avenue for carriages and other vehicles. Residences would lose part of their front yards. Planners predicted property values would spiral dramatically. The city council eventually authorized improvements, although some of the private carriage set complained to no avail that "the line of horse cars is taken out of the street and put into the door yards of most of us," a reminder of the initial rail battles of the 1860s and the now-changing demographics of the transit industry. Designing was brilliant and just in time for electric streetcars.[23]

Elmwood's experience with real estate and mass transportation was unusual only because of the park's development. Horsecar service ignited real estate speculation and building booms locally and nationally. Festivities usually marked the inauguration of modern transit facilities; a community's coming of age. The Branch Avenue line connected the manufacturing village of Wanskuck, stronghold of the Knights of Labor, with downtown Providence. On opening day in 1883 some two thousand children, "talking all languages," greeted the first vehicles. Working-class residents decorated their homes, exploded fireworks, and sponsored a celebration ball and parade. Emerging middle-class communities like Mount Pleasant hosted upbeat commemorations, while private-carriage wards like Elmwood gave catered receptions with polished entertainment. Frugal carriage owners could now hire weekend drivers and commute to the office during the week. Even middle-class clerks occasionally rode a horsecar home for lunch. And workers and their families enjoyed holiday excursions on the line.[24]

The horsecar served as a conveyor belt between city and suburb wherever

A crowded Providence horsecar on the way to a football game in the 1880s.

it traveled that first generation. Urban dwellers could ride into the country or move to more spacious and less expensive homes. Some rural residents packed up and headed to town for industrial employment and a taste of urban life. "There is more business in the city than ever before," the *Providence Journal* reported, "and the people in rural Rhode Island are from time to time giving up work on the farm and getting down nearer to the centre of trade." Paradoxically, the influx of commuters to horsecar suburbs began a deterioration of the very paradise they hoped to enjoy. As the animal railway and lot development penetrated even the wilds of Cat Swamp on the East Side, one writer lamented civilization's march: "The wild forest and swamp land, known to us and our fathers, is fast becoming unrecognizable, as the trees are removed, the waters drained, and new streets formed." Utility services proliferated as the horsecar carried in its train gas lighting, sewers, city water, and other improvements in the infrastructure.[25]

Part of Longstreet's plan to reduce things to a system in the process of horsecar expansion caused bitter resentment. The Union Railroad introduced a commonplace scheme in the railway industry to secure funding from neighborhood landowners, builders, and businessmen to pay for new routes. The northern Providence suburb of Mount Pleasant, for example, petitioned the railway to construct a line. The company refused unless community leaders contributed $25,000. "After much persuasion and diligent canvassing," a local developer raised the sum but insisted on service at least every half hour in return. The Union Railroad demanded similar terms for service to Providence's East Side and the industrial village of Thornton. Whether Longstreet initiated this funding strategy or was simply carrying out the orders of the board is unknown. However, he defended subsidies, citing a $40,000 land-acquisition bill on the East Side alone. He later carped that some businesses defaulted on their pledges. Longstreet also complained that the last six lines of the Union Railroad built in the 1880s were profitless despite 800,000 miles of annual service. Original city routes, he claimed, subverted convenient but unprofitable new service. Despite these entanglements, requests for new lines continued unabated.[26]

Although the Union Railroad enjoyed a monopoly of horsecar service, there were no laws preventing competitors from carving out an independent route. Prospects for remuneration in such a venture were questionable. Several groups in neglected areas threatened to arrange for transportation with alternate carriers. At times these business interests went so far as to incorporate a new line, trying to pressure the Union Railroad into acting first. With a virtual stranglehold on service, the railway could trump rivals and provide horsecars—for a price. On a few occasions speculators tried to anticipate the company's future direction by securing rights to a route and selling the franchise at a profit later. In general the legislature and city councils stipulated that lines had to be completed within a short time to prevent such ventures.

Property owners on Providence's College Hill posed the greatest threat to the Union Railroad's control of the streets when they pushed for service in the 1880s. College Hill, or Quality Hill, as it was mockingly called, rose impressively over the old commercial district and harbor. Wealthy colonists settled in nooks and crannies overlooking the growing city. Brown University sat atop the slope. Famous Benefit Street, with its eighteenth-century mansions, hugged the midsection of the hill. A 15-percent grade prevented horsecar service, and although the Union Railroad built routes around College Hill to the east and west, residents complained they "had to go downtown by way of Warren," a nonsensically long journey.[27]

The installation of a cable tramway, the only one ever constructed in New England, engendered a number of competing interests, reviving memories of battles over street rails in the 1860s. East Siders split into opposing camps, for and against the novel system. Carriage owners argued with speculators, and advocates of public transportation locked horns with those who demanded exclusive neighborhood privacy. While the debate on Quality Hill raged, tramway incorporators, including many prominent Rhode Island businessmen, did yeoman battle with the well-heeled Union Railroad. The legislature and Providence city council hosted a series of thirty-eight hotly debated public hearings, and the *Street Railway Journal* reported a "cable war."[28]

Preliminary charter discussions in the Rhode Island senate drew witnesses and spectators. When several women testified the venture would disturb East Side tranquility, "A Believer in Public Accommodations" answered in a letter to the editor: "The ladies over east and on the banks of the river, who live in humble houses, and have no horses, carriages or drivers, and who for themselves and little families would enjoy the convenience and comfort of horsecars, were not present." Samuel J. Nightingale, a prominent real estate broker whose family attempted to incorporate a horse railroad in the area, sold several local estates purely on tramway potential.[29]

Advocates for the system circulated petitions along the proposed route. Newspapers dissected the results, gauging sentiment among private estates and renters, and even computing attitudes among owners by the amount of property they owned fronting the street. By any measure, residents overwhelmingly endorsed the tramway. The general assembly granted a charter. The Providence city council, under the auspices of the railroad committee, scheduled another round of volatile hearings. Prominent community residents and investors testified. Wealthy backers, who stood to gain from the new road, championed adequate transportation. Others took the Union Railroad to task in an assault that grew with each succeeding year. One politician assailed the carrier's bottom line: "They have enriched themselves out of the city and its citizens." A real estate agent cited beggarly square-foot values on top of College Hill and needled Daniel Longstreet, who stood to make a small fortune in his own speculative deals near Roger Williams Park: "At Auburndale our friend here gets 15 cents."[30]

Longstreet, accustomed to grandstanding criticism from a partisan city council, reeled from the elite's hostility. At the next hearing he attacked tramway advocates as spoiled: "It is but natural that they should look after their own interests and provide themselves with an expensive cable railway as they would with an expensive carriage of any kind," he said, echoing the rail controversies of a generation earlier. Longstreet then tackled the specter of competition: "If you grant this petition," he pleaded before the railroad committee and city council, "others will be emboldened by their success to ask you for like privileges." He predicted chaotic railway service. Competitors, he charged, would use catchpenny workers, lame and blind horses, and faulty rails. "Then and not til then," he said, "would the falsity of the communistic idea that it is possible to get something out of nothing be fully realized." In the columns of the national transit press he characteristically attacked competitors as foolhardy dreamers: "It is a wild scheme, with no possibility of its ever becoming a commercial success." And on it went. These kind of utility battles would intensify during the next few decades and afflict towns and cities across the United States, paralleling, but in a more public fashion than, the conflict over steam-railroad mergers and franchises.[31]

The council finally voted to grant a tramway charter. The cable road would stretch over College Hill and continue to Olneyville over the Union Railroad's tracks, cutting into its most profitable franchise. Longstreet had desperately tried to forestall this option by allowing the cable interests to use his company's rails, but only into downtown Providence from the foot of College Hill. Commercial groups in Olneyville encouraged competition, hoping to lower fares. "The business men of Olneyville want three-cent fares so that their customers will not ride past their stores to the city; the real estate owners want three-cent fares to induce the workers in Olneyville factories to take residence." One storekeeper, however, attacked the rival line: "He [the storekeeper] has no fear that the track would be injurious to his trade, but a large number of employees of the Union Company trade with him, and they were all so well treated by their employers that they are eager to have all opposition blocked." The carrier's largest carbarn was in Olneyville, and its employees populated the entire area.[32]

On December 11, 1889, the Providence Cable Tramway Company conquered the once insurmountable hill. Thousands of residents and onlookers lined the streets to cheer, some for enhanced financial opportunities, others for improved transit service. The company tested the cable and provided free rides for several weeks, a stellar public relations performance. Sets of cars meant to hold 36 somehow accommodated 130 without the usual complaints. With the operation a reality, the Union Railroad approached the Cable Tramway Company and tendered a bountiful offer to buy the road for $130 a share. Tramway entrepreneurs, including some of the most powerful citizens in the state, had bested the Union Railroad and made a profit to boot. While the senior carrier suffered a public relations defeat and paid top dollar for the enterprise, it maintained a virtual monopoly on railway service. The upcoming electrification of mass transit and the added capital expense of that power would discourage even the most well-heeled investors in the future. For the public, the end of competition meant an end to external pressure, which had forced the Union Railroad to maintain service, improvements, and expansion.[33]

From a bottom-line perspective, railway management showed shrewd

New England's only cable car system ran on Providence's College Hill beginning in 1889. The owners challenged the Union Railroad's traction monopoly in Rhode Island.

acumen. Once the Spragues had developed a basic horsecar network, their successors studiously sought community subsidies for future construction projects. Patronage on new, unremunerative lines buttressed ridership on older routes, but there was no easy way to measure this feeder phenomenon then. The Union Railroad was willing to take a chance only if businessmen and land speculators in unserviced regions took a gamble too. Almost every route built after 1876 involved a subsidy to the company for neighborhood horsecars. The Union Railroad was not monolithic, however, in its approach. Management scrutinized each community. In Pawtucket, it formed a holding company, allowing others to chance a loss if the enterprise failed. The carrier did not modernize the East Providence system until a competitor threatened the monopoly and local taxes underwrote an expensive bridge to connect the two cities. On the East Side of Providence, the railway procrastinated for years before tramway entrepreneurs forced the issue by building a successful road.

Carrier intransigence was not confined to route expansion. The Union Railroad fought tax assessments and road maintenance provisions with even greater vehemence. The president of the Providence city council assessed the situation precisely: "The Union Railroad Company is a monopoly of capitalists, who care not so much about exemption from present payment as exemption in the future, ten or twenty years hence." Squabbles over taxes began with the inception of service. Town fathers passed an ordinance charging the Union Railroad 1.5 percent of gross receipts. Later, the city of Providence had to seek a state supreme court ruling forcing the carrier to make back payments. Daniel Longstreet argued that such a measure was a disincentive to expand: "When the city shows a deposition to sit on us arbitrarily, the less miles of track we lay the better."[34]

Management retreated to the friendly confines of the general assembly, petitioning for a charter amendment to curtail city control of the enterprise. The railway also issued a public memorial explaining its decision to seek redress at the legislature: "As each year the city council is changed, . . . [and] the action of one city council cannot bind its successor, it would seem that the whole business and investment of the railroad company is subject to every impulse of popular feelings or prejudice, and liable to injury or destruction." Although the assembly eventually let the charter amendment die in committee, political pressure forced Providence to settle for a smaller, $8,000 annual tax tribute instead of the more lucrative percentage rate. The memory of that political maneuver would resurrect similar efforts in the upcoming electric era, when the Union Railroad found the legislature even more hospitable to its demands in the face of mounting public pressure to control streets through increased taxation.[35]

These lofty financial battles over route subsidies, tax payments, and franchises never unilaterally aroused public indignation. The average rider was more concerned with the liberating effects of mass transportation and whether or not there were enough seats on a horsecar. When the Union Railroad appealed to the state legislature, it opened a Pandora's box by discussing the cost of rides. The horse railroad charged a basic fare of six cents, and ten cents on longer suburban runs. Nationally, an ordinary fare was five cents, and the carrier did issue books of twenty tickets for one dollar. But the *Providence Journal* complained that the company refused to offer tickets on board horsecars, preferring to sell them "at inconvenient places, where few passengers would call." The *Morning Star*, generally supportive of the Union Railroad in other matters, scolded that "the six cent fare is a [Civil] war rate, and it seems as though it was time to return to a peace basis." Conductors already sold single five-cent tickets as an unsanctioned courtesy to working-class patrons.[36]

In 1881 the Union Railroad carried over eight million riders. Despite the inconvenience of obtaining tickets, 53 percent of patrons used them. Most blue-collar families paid the six-cent fare for occasional rides rather than invest the sizable sum of a dollar for a discount package. People in wealthier neighborhoods bought tickets more frequently than those in lower-class enclaves: riders on the Broad, Elmwood, and Broadway routes bought tickets more often than those in less affluent areas like Cranston, Mount Pleasant, and Pawtucket. Longstreet disingenuously informed the legislature, "We have for years wished to sell packages of 5 tickets for 25 cents in the cars." The company estimated that a more liberal policy, however, would boost ticket usage to 88 percent of all riders and cut into the railway's one-cent-per-passenger profit. Despite several depression years, the Union Railroad averaged a steady 7.95-percent investment return. That profit, while not lavish by industrial standards in Rhode Island, was not insignificant, either.[37]

Closely related to fare structure was a policy that incensed the average passenger more than any other issue: transfer tickets. "Give us cheaper fares, or transfer tickets, is the cry of the laboring man," editorialized the *Morning Star* as it outlined the expensive burden of switching horsecars downtown for an additional fare and repeating the process on the way home. "The adoption of transfer tickets in this city would allow many of the patrons of the Union Railroad Company to eat jelly cake who are now compelled to go it on plain, old-fashioned, Rhode Island johnny cake."[38]

The coupling of the system's original routes with others provided crosstown rides for one fare. The Olneyville cars, for example, traversed Broadway to downtown Providence and then trekked to the East Side for six cents. When the Smith's Hill line opened, the Union Railroad attached it to the Elmwood Avenue route. These tandem circuits usually combined a longer route with a shorter one for a single fare. Later, new lines terminated in the city, and connections to other areas required another payment. The *Morning Star* printed a cute description of the budget predicament: "The red ball hangs aloft, love, the moon is shining bright; we'll skate a couple of hours, love, at Roger Williams Park tonight. That is, if I can raise the price of four horse car tickets, and one ice cream with two spoons." The Union Railroad finally swallowed the ticket pill and sold the more affordable books of five on the horsecars. A Cranston Street conductor reported a typical response soon after: only one cash fare from forty-one passengers. The transfer controversy, on the other hand, festered for another generation and helped turn passengers against the company in the electric era.[39]

Despite the success of the Union Railroad during its first quarter century of service, the system's growing complexity and increasing capital requirements forced management to economize. At times public relations took a back seat to the corporation's bottom line despite the compromising efforts of Longstreet. Passengers, grown accustomed to the convenience and comfort of urban mass transportation, grumbled about carrier shortcomings. Drivers and conductors, while pleased at the expansion of horsecar service and job security, were shocked when the Union Railroad stopped partially subsidizing the mutual benefit association as part of its cost-containment measures.

On top of this, management's most visible, articulate, and effective spokesman, Daniel Longstreet, went to work for the West End Street Railway in Boston in 1888. At a farewell party for the general manager and several other successful Providence entrepreneurs who were also relocating to Boston, the local elite lamented the departure of so many talented businessmen to the city's arch rival. Toasts to Longstreet's honor by the governor and other political kingpins, as well as the presentation of a silver salver, paled before his most cherished memento. Coworkers at the carbarn where he started his career presented him with an embossed photograph of the stables and several horsecars. Almost 100 colleagues had their names inscribed on the framed emblem.[40]

Before leaving Providence, Longstreet used his organizational talent to spearhead the formation of the American Street Railway Association, the industry's national organization. His quest for knowledge and order led him to visit other transit properties around the nation, seeking out information and new techniques. He marshaled his wide network of acquaintances to build a foundation of managerial solidarity among a group of independent and often jealous railway operators. The association met for the first time in Boston in 1882, a decade before the establishment of the national streetcar union, and spoke the language of solidarity before takeovers would shake the industry. One railway president pleaded with his peers: "Above everything else, let the members of this Association foster a brotherly regard for each other, so that, when we meet in strange cities, we shall be as brothers. There shall be no North, South, East or West with us," he concluded passionately. Longstreet, who served as president of the group in 1893, confessed that he only wanted to establish on a national level what he had started in Rhode Island: "a liberal policy with employees and the public." Although the Railway Association never followed those precepts closely, the organization honored him as its "father."[41]

In his inaugural address as president, during the Panic of 1893, Longstreet reminded his listeners, "The faithful employe and the roadbed and equipment should be the last to suffer." His local legacy of progressive personnel and customer relations would soon be buried by the political machinations of electric streetcar service, although his immediate successor at the Union Railroad brought similar diplomatic skills, seniority that had begun in 1866, and sensitivity to his colleagues. New company policies forced horsecar crews to question the carrier's noblesse oblige and brought passengers and transit workers closer together in common cause against the Union Railroad's corporate owners in an attempt to influence the operation of the enterprise.[42]

THE SUGAR RAILROAD

Those who know how I feel in regard to the use of boodle in elections know how it enrages me to have these quasi-public corporations furnish a corruption fund to prevent the free expression of the will of the people.

Hiram Howard, state representative, 1891

You see we have the public sympathy and support on our side. The people are with us. Most of us were born and brought up in this city and have worked for the company a long time. Everybody knows us, and I think we are a pretty popular lot of railroad men.

Anonymous conductor, 1893

Now that it [the Union Railroad] has become the property of a syndicate of foreign capitalists, whose sole object is to squeeze out all the money they can out of it, it is not surprising to find the help growing restless and discontented especially when they see a dispossession on the part of the controlling powers to reduce wages by employing new men.

Pawtucket Evening Post, 1894

For almost thirty years the Union Railroad had been a permanent fixture on the Rhode Island landscape. This premier horsecar system gave Providence a claim on modernity and progress, while familiar faces and friendly greetings from drivers and conductors gave urban life an aura of familiarity and manageability. Although ownership had changed hands in the 1870s, day-to-day management officials were as well known and liked as the crews. Like the Spragues, the new proprietors were local capitalists, as were most of the stockholders. When new routes penetrated the suburbs, the expansion was slow and calculated, seldom disrupting the gentle cadence of everyday life, which was still poised between the preindustrial, antebellum world and the industrial vortex that was surely taking over.

Between the advent of horsecar service in 1864 and its termination in 1894, the vehicles changed little in Rhode Island or elsewhere. They were made more comfortable, stylish, and safe during that span thanks to managers like Daniel F. Longstreet, but their overall appearance across three decades was indistinguishable. And the horse? Owners had to pay more, and hostlers learned how to choose and train them better, but the beasts evolved no more than the cars they pulled. Then came the revolutionary force of electricity, which overturned the technological status quo with greater energy than most political upheavals exerted on government. Electrification created an enhanced world of applied science as well as a novel realm of social science. David Nye, historian of electricity, wrote, "Electric traction has been studied primarily as a form of transportation, without recognizing that it also became a vehicle of political ideologies, or seeing that it altered the city's image, and together with spectacular lighting was involved in turning the urban landscape into a spectacle. A machine's social reality," he emphasized, "is constructed, and emerges not only through its use as a functional device, but also through its being experienced as part of many human situations which collectively define its meaning." [1]

The trolley created a new mobility and speed in everyday life. Urban, suburban, and rural geography were telescoped into one another. Housing patterns, real estate speculation, consumerism, and entertainment all felt the occult impact of a vehicle that Oliver Wendell Holmes described as a "broomstick train," with its ungainly pole to the overhead wires, and William Dean Howells as "fabled monsters." Terence Powderly, grand master workman of the Knights of Labor, presciently assessed the significance of this force for workers during a speech in 1879. He predicted that rapid urban transit would liberate wage earners from the evils of tenement life: "A day will shortly dawn during which no horses or mules will be seen drawing our steel cars, they will be propelled by an invisible force that shall revolutionize the streetcar transportation in all our cities and towns. Men will be enabled to have their homes away out in the country and by the aid of electricity go to and from their work in less time than they now use in walking a few city blocks. Then instead of being subjected to the temptation of the saloon, which he must pass, the workingman may take the electric car at the door of the workshop or mine and ride it miles away to the door of his home. The extra two hours that enemies of the eight hour day begrudged him," Powderly triumphantly concluded, "will be devoted to the cultivation of a garden plot." [2]

Powderly's benign characterization differed little from the descriptions of electric traction promoters. The editors of the partisan *Electrical World* phrased it in language that was always painful to Providence boosters, living in the shadow of Boston's New England supremacy: "The time is not far distant when the existence of a horse railway in a community will be a matter of reproach and regarded as indicating a backward state of civilization." In a short decade of fitful but successful experiments, inventors proved beyond a doubt that they could speed urban travel dramatically. Their trials and research caught the eyes of entrepreneurs and speculators ready to take title to the nation's newest investment opportunity. Perhaps they could not recreate the national trusts that dominated other sectors of the economy, but on a local and regional level, the prospects seemed staggering.[3]

Horsecar companies were profitable, but the desultory nature of animal locomotion and the attendant cost of purchasing and caring for animals limited profits. "Discussions at early meetings of the American Street Railway Association on the causes of cholic, or debates over whether chloride of lime or sulphate of iron was the better disinfectant for manure pits, gave way," according to the organization's historian, "to complex interpretations of dynanimeter readings, presentations on designs for electric transmission materials, and other subjects that could be understood only by highly trained technical experts." Although the initial capital costs of electrification would be expensive, intense competition between General Electric and Westinghouse drove down the cost of motors from $4,500 to $750 in just six years. Operating expenses declined to as little as 40 percent of horsecar service, and patronage skyrocketed. The United States Department of Commerce and Labor conservatively estimated that national operating costs plummeted more than 10 percent between 1890 and 1900. Benjamin Jackson, an influential Union Railroad director, admitted that the owners expected a 25-percent cost savings. The increase in capital investment was enormous: from $150 million invested in horsecars in 1882, to $2 billion in electric traction a generation later. Similar action marked the interest in other utilities, such as natural gas, telephones, and residential electric power. Burton J. Hendrick, a careful researcher of street railway financiers for *McClure's Magazine*, noted after the turn of the century, "Every city has had its traction speculators; nearly every one can point to its traction millionaires. As usual, however, the richest opportunities have fallen to the lot of a few energetic men." Their methods paralleled those of other captains of industry and usually meant the loss of local utility control, which is what happened in Rhode Island, too.[4]

When he left Providence, Daniel Longstreet bequeathed another valuable legacy to the Union Railroad: a belief in a faster energy mode than horsepower. Always looking to the future, in 1892 Longstreet and the Spragues authorized some of the earliest experiments in the United States utilizing naphtha engines on horsecars. "I got it into my head that 'horses had got to go,'" said Longstreet. Although unable to overcome engineering problems, the Union Railroad successfully introduced a charter amendment to the general assembly establishing "the right to use any motive power over any of the tracks." Surprisingly, Longstreet admitted: "It is well known that I opposed all electric schemes. It was not because I knew less, but because I knew more about the practical requirements than those who were promoting the schemes." A decade later the company engaged the Rhode Island Locomotive Works to test electric motors on horsecar bodies. Ironically, an independent horsecar operation in the rural northern town of Woonsocket, Rhode Island, initiated trolley service in 1887, the first of its kind in New England. Although the line only lasted a few months due to technical problems and some community opposition, it prompted the *Providence Journal* to assess transit prospects: "The contest of the future, then, is not between electricity and the horse, but between electric cars and electricians." If Woonsocket had maintained regular service for a year or so it might have made claim to being America's first electric streetcar operation. Richmond, Virginia, claimed that distinction about the same time with uninterrupted service.[5]

Another independent Rhode Island entry into the electric power sweepstakes challenged the Union Railroad in 1889. Newport, Rhode Island, never even fielded a horsecar operation because of fierce opposition by summer colonists who wanted no street rail system or tracks interfering with carriages and exclusive beach retreats. Transit incorporators shepherded legislation through the general assembly but camouflaged their real intentions by chartering the Newport Horse Railroad Company and then building an electric system. Wealthy carpetbaggers declared class war and threatened to buy up stock and disband the operation if they could only identify stockholders. William Astor and August Belmont, who later introduced subways to New York City, led the opposition. After a ruling by the state supreme court, however, the trolley began service.[6]

The Union Railroad, although a pioneer in searching for alternate methods to horsepower, hesitated to embrace the emerging but primitive and expensive electric technology of the late 1880s. The promise of engine propulsion opened a bewildering array of inventive opportunities in the United States. The initial decade of electric service pitted different methods and applications against one another in a lucrative race to establish an accepted operational standard. In the spring of 1889 the Union Railroad petitioned the Providence city council to experiment with storage batteries on several city routes. If successful, battery-powered streetcars eliminated the need for poles, overhead wires, and other appurtenances on constricted streets laid out in the colonial era. Wireless energy also tempered public anxiety about accidental fires and electrocutions. Just before trial runs began, a New York court enjoined all battery use until several patent disputes were settled.[7]

The Union Railroad quickly changed plans and took city officials to Boston to examine an overhead electric system developed by the West End Street Railway, Daniel Longstreet's new employer. When the carrier decided to embrace this technology, with its unsightly grid of aerial wires, management braced for an onslaught of hostility. The Union Railroad hired the popular, veteran city clerk of Providence, Henry V. A. Joslin, to blunt criticism. Joslin, a Brown University graduate, possessed "a cyclopedic knowledge of local affairs." (His colleagues toasted him as irreplaceable and reduced the salary of his successor.) At the same time, the governor appointed a new railroad commissioner, Edward L. Freeman, a key Republican legislator and insider, who could be counted on "to do the right thing" for the Union Railroad. Furthermore, the company engaged city solicitor and former railway critic, Col. Nicholas Van Slyck. Management cunningly enlisted outspoken adversaries and turned them into company partisans. These appointments, while perfectly legal, added to the carrier's stable of influential politicos and helped demoralize opposition in the electric era.[8]

The city's railroad committee opened hearings on electric propulsion in the summer of 1890. They dragged on for a year. Affluent neighborhoods sent in petitions against the ungainly electric apparatus, while downtown merchants and the Providence Board of Trade endorsed it, expecting a legion of new customers. The telephone company, on the other hand, vigorously fought the system, fearing electrical interference with conversations. Opposing sides mobilized voter support, presented conflicting expert testimony, and predicted dire consequences if the other side prevailed. William Roelker, the carrier's counsel and a key Republican legislator, concluded arguments with seasoned reasoning. He credited horsecar travel for increased population and property values but warned that the region required even faster transit to compete in the world of the future. Furthermore, he said, the electric streetcar would eliminate horses, dust, and manure from local streets. As to individual protests against electrical rigging: "They always want them put near some other fellow's house." Nor, he honestly observed, could the rural ideal be prolonged in a twentieth-century metropolis: "People cannot live in a large modern city and have the quiet and retirement of the country."[9]

While waiting for a railroad committee decision, the Union Railroad announced a general cash fare reduction from six to five cents. Several of the longer suburban routes that ordinarily cost a dime were also cut to a nickel. Riders were ecstatic, especially on the heavily patronized Pawtuxet and Pawtucket lines. Some twenty workers who commuted daily to factories in Providence each gave five antique pennies to their conductor as a playful celebration of reduced prices. The railroad committee expeditiously and unanimously endorsed the Union Railroad's petition to electrify. The full city council voted to deny the request, citing potential hazards, but in reality stalling for financial concessions from the carrier. The company's annual report for 1890 underscored its wealth: another handsome 8-percent dividend for the tenth year in a row and a fleet of 1,515 horses and 301 horsecars.[10]

The Union Railroad amended its petition to limit electrification to two experimental routes only: Pawtucket and Pawtuxet, the recipients of the company's recent largesse in reducing fares. Corporate magnanimity had been used simply to buy community support and blunt antagonism. The railroad committee approved the amended petition, and a few days later the full council began deliberations again. Discussion centered not so much on electrification, which was a foregone conclusion by that time, but on the amount of compensation the Union Railroad would pay for lucrative electric franchises. The new city clerk, D. F. Hayden, corresponded with counterparts in American and European cities to determine tax rates and formulas. The full council finally gave its blessing but warned, "Providence is very much behind her sister cities in securing an adequate return for the use of the public streets." The council would wait to see how the trolley performed before acting. The battle for the streets had permanently entered the domain of high finance.[11]

By the end of the year the Union Railroad was testing electric streetcars along Broad Street into Pawtuxet, a five-mile journey. The inaugural public trip ran on January 20, 1892. Riders and curiosity seekers squeezed into trolleys all day and evening. There was universal approval of the speed and comfort of the new conveyances except when plodding horsecars got in the way along parts of the route. The railroad commissioner, although a company partisan, reflected local sentiment when he reported, "Citizens who formerly opposed the establishment of electric lines have changed their views and in many cases have been among the most ardent supporters of a system of traction which they have come to recognize as the most beneficial to their property interests and the most conducive to their personal comfort and convenience." The Union Railroad anxiously prepared to extend electric service but demanded franchise concessions from the capital city, which eagerly anticipated new tax revenue from a modernized and enriched carrier. Another controversy began in the framework of Rhode Island's increasingly corrupt political arrangements.[12]

Since the Dorr War in 1842, the Republican-run "*Journal* Ring" had controlled state politics by disenfranchising a majority of voters and maintaining a legislative cabal that denied proportional representation to Irish-Democratic urban strongholds like Providence, Pawtucket, and Newport. The ring was led by a triumvirate: Henry Bowen Anthony, United States senator and *Providence Journal* editor; Ambrose Burnside, Civil War general and Anthony's colleague in the Senate; and Charles "Boss" Brayton, who orchestrated the day-to-day legerdemain from the Rhode Island statehouse for the corrupt GOP despite several damning U.S. congressional investigations of his activities. Anthony died in 1884, and Burnside a few years later. Their deaths ironically strengthened the ring: Brayton carried the incubus to a new generation of schemers, who modernized graft from more sophisticated profit ventures. Brayton optimistically loosened voting restrictions so that propertyless immigrants could vote in mayoral and state-office races only; power was retained in the general assembly and the city councils, especially the restricted office of alderman, whom only the affluent could elect. Ring coffers were replenished through influence peddling by emerging utility monopolies. Nelson W. Aldrich, who replaced Burnside in the Senate, performed diplomatic service in Washington, where he became "general manager of the United States" due to his legislative wizardry and influence. He joined forces with Marsden J. Perry, who built a local energy empire and became known as the state's utility king.[13]

Transit management sought sanctuary in the friendly chambers of the general assembly. Union Railroad partisans on the city council initiated a bill in the legislature to allow moderate taxation of corporations and utilities in exchange for twenty-five-year monopoly franchises. The resolution empowered city councils to assess a 3-percent gross receipts tax. The bill passed into law in May 1891, and the city council hailed it as a great victory. City coffers would take in $50,000 a year, a much greater sum than the flat tax of $8,000. The Union Railroad enthusiastically accepted the greater tax burden in exchange for an ironclad monopoly to replace the uncertainty of the present arrangement.[14]

The passage of the act raised a storm of protest. In a stinging editorial, the *Providence Journal* warned of inherent dangers in assigning exclusive privileges to gas, electric, railway, and telephone monopolies. "There is no such thing possible as turning the city over to the corporations bound hand and foot and powerless to help itself for a quarter of a century." The Advance Club, a group of reform industrialists, condemned it. The Rhode Island Business Men's Association asked, "What can we say for the representatives of our city who for personal position or gain are interested for these corporations and who are recreant to their trusts?" The association called for municipal control of utilities, predating union demands by a decade. The city's elite aldermen, beholden to the Union Railroad for campaign funds, debated the act but also declined to overturn it. In July 1891 Democratic representative Lucius F. C. Garvin, a radical physician, reformer, and advocate of a single tax on land, introduced a bill to limit franchises to seven years. It failed, but a public hearing on the issue featured speakers who chastised the city council as spineless.[15]

Hiram Howard, jewelry and silverware manufacturer, Advance Club president, and Democratic state representative from Providence, sent a revealing personal letter to Adin B. Capron, Smithfield grain dealer, Republican speaker of the state house of representatives, and future U.S. congressman. The two officials, although from different parties, had been lieutenants in the Civil War together and shared a warm camaraderie. Capron had apparently written to Howard first, advocating a "spirit of friendship" with state utility interests in an attempt to blunt Howard's criticism of corporate power. Howard, the reformer, refused any overtures and lectured his friend privately: "Those who know how I feel in regard to the use of boodle in elections know how it enrages me to have these quasi-public corporations furnish a corruption fund to prevent the free expression of the will of the people." He labeled the 1891 franchise legislation, "An Act to permit the Union R. R. Co., the Narragansett Electric Light Co., the Providence Gas Co., and the Providence Telephone Co. to loot the tax-payers and citizens of Providence." He further attacked the exclusive nature of the contract: "One provision of the Act shuts out all competition and makes the corporation the masters of the servants of the people." Howard concluded by citing a recent visit to the Toronto Railway Company, whose franchise included a formula four times more remunerative for the city than the Providence tax plan.[16]

Newly elected mayor William K. Potter called for repeal of the franchise law just as trolley service began in Providence. At the same time, an emboldened Union Railroad prepared a stunning charter amendment to further its interests. The company influenced the legislature to pass a ten-section act stripping Providence of the right to unilaterally close routes, a prerogative that went back to the 1860s. In exchange, the amendment reduced the franchise to a twenty-year period and sweetened the capital city treasury with a 3-percent gross tax for five years, followed by a negotiated increase of up to 5 percent. Significantly, the bill prohibited any railway competition for existing services. The Union Railroad justified its demands by documenting $2 million in costs to electrify the system and the need to borrow more capital for further modernization. The company produced letters from several local and national banks refusing to bankroll utilities shackled by onerous city ordinances. A communication from the New York firm of Drexel & Morgan contained a certain irony in corrupt Rhode Island by declaring that lenders hesitated to fund municipal ventures, "the existence of which depends largely upon the judgment or caprice of politicians." In an article entitled "A Valueless Franchise," the *Street Railway Journal* reported that "banks would have nothing to do" with the Union Railroad.[17]

Even smug politicos recoiled at Union Railroad boldness. Alderman, and future mayor, Edwin D. McGuinness said the measure should be labeled "an act to legalize highway robbery"; another politician predicted there would be no transfers for twenty years. The *Providence Journal* reported that the issue was a lively topic of popular debate. At a state senate hearing, the Union Railroad reiterated the need to raise capital, especially with petitions for electric service expansion coming from so many communities. The city negotiated a few points and added some minor protections in the final bill. At the same time, Narragansett Electric Company obtained a similar franchise from the general assembly. The gas and telephone monopolies made separate contracts directly with the city.[18]

The whirlwind activities that engulfed Rhode Island utilities in the last decade of the nineteenth century funneled into a political tornado in February 1893 when the real reasons for the jockeying became clear. The *Providence Journal* announced that a New York syndicate had been quietly buying up Union Railroad stock since January. Prices spiraled from $205 to $250 a share. Majority owners, like president Jesse Metcalf, had already sold out. Representatives of the syndicate distributed a circular offering $250, and close to a third of the twenty thousand outstanding shares had already passed over. Prior to this no more than a handful of stock was ever offered publicly. Shareholders consisted of seventeen corporations and 284 individuals, most of whom lived in and around Providence. "No other transaction of recent years has created such intense interest among all classes," the newspaper reported, "and the outcome is eagerly awaited."[19]

Excitement mounted as the public waited to see if the syndicate could gain control. The *Journal* assigned fifteen reporters to interview stockholders. Several "looked upon the whole thing as an outrage against their personal loyalty toward Providence." Others cherished individual shares as heirlooms passed down through two generations. Some expected even higher prices. Three bankers "did not like to see the control pass out of the city, but they were not in the company for motives of patriotism, but for money." Several Union Railroad directors, ignorant of behind-the-scenes machinations to market the enterprise, refused to trade. "I prefer that it should have passed into local hands," sniffed a director. "It isn't pleasant after we've spent time and laid awake nights in devising means by which money might be saved for the corporation to have it pass into the hands of outsiders." Within a few weeks, purchasers owned fifteen thousand shares and total control. Narragansett Electric stock edged up nine dollars as well in anticipation of profits from supplying electricity to the burgeoning railway. The syndicate was finally identified as the New England Street Railway Company, chartered in New Jersey by eastern capitalists. Marsden J. Perry had been the local point man with a Union Railroad director.[20]

Providence Journal editors sarcastically expected a "beneficent despotism, because long experience has taught absolute rulers that it pays to deal liberally with their humble subjects." The same syndicate bought the Pawtucket Street Railway at $100 a share, even though the operation had never paid a dividend. The lure of profitable electric service was that strong. The president of the Pawtucket road allegedly sold at $96 a share when private sales brought $125 a bit later, further implying the work of a few behind-the-scenes operators. Takeover plans had been carefully crafted for several years. One Providence city councilman predicted months before either sale, "You will find in one year or two that this road has been sold to the Philadelphia syndicate, and that the present stockholders have enriched themselves enormously by the sale." William Roelker, one of the raiders, lied outright: "In regard to . . . a Philadelphia syndicate, . . . there was not a shadow of truth in the statement."[21]

With 95 percent of Union Railroad stock purchased, the corporation named three new directors: Nelson W. Aldrich, Marsden J. Perry, and William Roelker. Aldrich was elected president. He said the company would invest $3 million in electric modernization. A holding firm, the United Traction and Electric Company, was organized in New Jersey to run the Union Railroad. Soon after, the *New York Times* published a long exposé that detailed political lobbying and a traction payoff between Nelson Aldrich and the nation's Sugar Trust. Aldrich, according to the article, masterminded an increase in duties for imported sugar in 1890. The United States House of Representatives had sent legislation to the Senate calling for a forty-cent tariff on every 100 pounds of foreign sugar. Aldrich, as virtual chairman of the Senate Finance Committee, worked assiduously to inflate the sugar tax to sixty cents. These protective duties brought windfall profits to the American Sugar Refining Company of New York. The *Times* estimated that Aldrich's maneuvers in the Senate produced additional earnings of $35 million by discouraging imports of refined sugar.[22]

When Aldrich planned to enter the potentially lucrative, yet untested, electric railway field in Providence, he required funds to finance the changeover from horsepower. In the words of the *Times*, "A large amount of money was needed to carry out all the plans which Mr. Aldrich had. He did not have it, and appealed to such capitalists as were his friends for assistance. The Sugar

Trust was one of those corporations which was asked to help Mr. Aldrich to a good thing, and it responded with $1,500,000 of cash." John E. Searles, treasurer of the American Sugar Refining Company, immediately became a director of the United Traction and Electric Company. Aldrich vehemently denied any wrongdoing. In Providence, copies of the *Times* sold out, and second-hand copies fetched fifty cents.[23]

Some in Rhode Island were not taken by surprise at the news. During a Democratic rally before the takeover, a speaker from New York lambasted Senator Aldrich: "We in New York call election money 'sugar.' Senator Aldrich is said to have brought sugar here and to have got it from the Sugar Trust." The *Times* also called the Union Railroad the "Sugar Railroad." The *Providence Evening Times*, mouthpiece for local Democrats and a good bromide to the Republican press, howled in indignation at the senator's role: "His conduct in the Union Railroad franchise matter furnishes evidence enough to connect him with one of the most odious monopolies ever fastened by a degraded legislature upon a suffering state." Lincoln Steffens, in his famous 1905 essay, "Rhode Island: A State for Sale," described the situation: "Aldrich joined Perry; he became a partner in his scheme; he delivered Brayton and Brayton's System; and, besides the actual government of his state, Senator Aldrich brought, to back the scheme, capital from out of the state."[24]

Although many Union Railroad stockholders expressed concern about an out-of-town takeover, within a few weeks most swallowed civic pride and sold at a handsome profit. Another interested group was not so fortunate. Drivers and conductors had enjoyed steady employment and premium wages since the inception of railway service in Providence. Daniel Longstreet's liberal salary policy attracted an honest and dedicated class of worker. In return, horsecar employees shunned unionism, especially overtures from the Rhode Island Knights of Labor, who had successfully organized such workers elsewhere. Local drivers and conductors also enjoyed rudimentary social benefits from a popular mutual benefit association.

Still, veteran transit workers, who had spent a lifetime in street railway service, often on the same route, reacted nervously to the syndicate. In 1893 their counterparts in Worcester and Boston, Massachusetts, initiated a drive to form a regional union. According to the *Providence Journal*, "The consolidation of the various street railway lines is given as the cause of this move for self-protection by the employees." The *Pawtucket Evening Post* was more direct in its indictment: "Now that it [the Union Railroad] has become the property of a syndicate of foreign capitalists, whose sole object is to squeeze out all the money they can out of it, it is not surprising to find the help growing restless and discontented especially when they see a dispossession on the part of the controlling powers to reduce wages by employing new men." Providence carmen met in March as part of that effort. About 150 Union Railroad workers attended a three-hour meeting hosted by the Rhode Island Central Labor Union. Rank-and-file sentiment appeared to be against formation of a union at that time; employees felt they could still trust management and protect their interests without radical action, a reflection of three decades of amicable labor-management relations and a feeling that employees shared in the company's street control.[25]

Longstreet's successor, Albert T. Potter, minimized a union drive. "I have too great confidence in the men to fear anything like a concerted movement against the company," he declared. "I have been with the road myself since 1866; some of the employees have been with us since the Union Railroad first came into existence in 1865, and many of them could decorate their sleeves with four five-year stripes if such was the custom among horse car men. Up to within a year or so ago this road had paid its men higher wages for twenty years than any other like concern in the country." He believed that seniority and salary would ensure worker loyalty. The *Street Railway Journal* recognized the qualities of officials like Potter: "A superintendent who knows his business can establish and maintain relations with his men such that strikes may become difficult or impossible."[26]

A few weeks after the union meeting, employees tested company resolve by asking for a ten-hour day. Although the workday was still about twelve hours, split schedules stretched some shifts from fifteen to eighteen hours. As a petition to reduce hours circulated between carbarns, a rumor began that wages would be cut by 20 percent. Signatures suddenly became scarce, and startled employees decided to forego the request. One driver remarked, "I guess the fellows who strike in at 6:30 in the morning and get through about 11:30 at night, will have to keep it up a while longer." Wages remained steady, out-of-work hostlers trained as motormen, and union talk subsided.[27]

A year later rumors circulated again that the United Traction and Electric Company would cut salaries. Former city clerk Henry Joslin, now secretary of the Union Railroad, denied plans for a reduction but said he was unsure of syndicate plans. State representative William Roelker unequivocally promised there would be no salary cuts but admitted that directors had discussed the issue. That confession sounded a defensive alarm. Independent-minded carmen, veterans of stagecoach, omnibus, and horsecar service, finally organized a labor union. The *Providence News* reported, "The board of officers consists of some of the oldest, most reliable and conservative men on the cars."[28]

Disgruntled employees gathered to discuss forming a local division of the Amalgamated Association of Street Railway Employes of America, realizing that they could no longer stand alone against an impersonal syndicate with headquarters in another state. Although the parent organization was less than two years old, urban railway workers had banded together in primitive unions in New York City as far back as 1861. The Knights of Labor had unionized thousands of drivers and conductors around the country during the 1880s. When the Knights' empire crumbled later that decade, the fledgling American Federation of Labor began advocating the organization of electric railway employees. Samuel Gompers, founder of the A. F. of L., advocated strong, independent national unions representing skilled and craft workers, unlike the Knights, who mixed workers from different industries into the same local assemblies. A later history of the national carmen's union would criticize the commingled structure of the Knights: "A carpenter, shoemaker, and a baker, who knew nothing of the conditions of railroad work, would settle the grievances of street railway employes."[29]

The federation sanctioned Gompers's plea for a national organization to represent trolley employees. He issued a call for a convention in Indianapolis in 1892. Fifty delegates responded from twenty cities, representing independent locals, Knights of Labor assemblies, and several railway unions directly affiliated to the federation. They voted to "rescue our occupation from the low level to which it has fallen" and endorsed training programs, higher wages, shorter hours, sick benefits, and industrial arbitration.[30]

Organizers from the Amalgamated appeared at the first Providence meeting. The Rhode Island Central Labor Union called it the biggest gathering of workers since the heyday of the Knights and enthusiastically welcomed the popular carmen into the ranks of the local union movement, however tentative the crews were about joining the bandwagon. Providence newspapers headlined the meeting. The *Providence Journal* remarked ruefully, "Under the local management the men were assured of satisfactory treatment, and there was never the least dissatisfaction among the employees." The syndicate had changed all that, and a feeling of unrest permeated the work force. Drivers, motormen, and conductors hoped the union would protect them from wage reductions and suspected importation of cheap out-of-state replacement workers. The *Journal* further commented, "The New York capitalists desire the road to make larger returns . . . by reductions in salaries and the cutting down of running expenses."[31]

Zachary Taylor, president of the local, had already been suspended along with several other activists. Union Railroad general manager Albert Potter declared, "Not a single man has been threatened, and not a single man has been laid off." He later backpedaled, admitted the suspensions, and agreed to allow them to return to work, but already there was talk of a strike. One conductor told a reporter: "You see we have the public sympathy and support on our side. The people are with us. Most of us were born and brought up in this city and have worked for the company a long time. Everybody knows us, and I think we are a pretty popular lot of railroad men."[32]

The conductor and his coworkers realized that public animosity toward the railway syndicate remained red hot. Any action by employees was sure to act as a lightning rod and direct local frustration against the carrier and its unpopular leadership. The company assured horsecar veterans there would be no salary reduction, although a new scale would be instituted for newcomers: two dollars a day, the same salary the Union Railroad started with in 1865. Potter was surprised at the vinegar reaction to the plan by insecure old-timers. The next union meeting brought in more recruits, most employees now doubting any good-faith promises from the syndicate. Members set a one-dollar initiation fee and twenty-five-cent monthly dues. Two more union meetings were held, and membership reached about five hundred, almost the entire work force.[33]

The union proposed a city ordinance to require licensing of motormen, making it difficult to hire strikebreakers in case of a walkout. At least half the employees were registered voters, an unusually high percentage in a state that limited the franchise to as few as possible, and their popularity at least got them a hearing. Streetcar workers also formulated plans to enlist the support of other A. F. of L. unions for a possible boycott, again realizing the need for a coalition against an out-of-state corporation. Providence carmen officially affiliated with the Amalgamated as Division 39, with eligibility for strike pay of five dollars a week. However, the union's constitution forbade a walkout unless the company refused arbitration. The membership had to authorize a strike by a two-thirds vote and seek approval from the parent body. Talk also centered on a ten-hour day and a daily wage of $2.15. A union delegation prepared to visit General Manager Potter to discuss grievances. Potter refused, and in August union president Zachary Taylor resigned. A new slate took office.[34]

The Providence city council committee on ordinances debated whether to invoke a twenty-dollar-an-hour fine for unlicensed operators in case of a strike. Future Providence mayor Edwin McGuinness represented carmen and argued that railway employees should be licensed like hackmen. The city, he pleaded, should determine competency, not the Union Railroad. At the next hearing, Potter falsely warned the council that municipal licensing would make

Providence liable for accidental damages caused by motormen. He then gave a shocking and unwarranted description of horsecar veterans. The *Providence Journal* reported, "He explained that during the horse-car period of the street railway business it became the rule to find places on the cars for all those who had failed in other businesses; as a consequence it became a sort of dumping ground for all those who had grown old and worn out." Not even the Union Railroad's bitterest enemies had ever portrayed employees in such uncomplimentary terms. His unkind and inaccurate portrayal underlined concern about a syndicate that could turn an old friend and coworker like Potter into a hired gun. In fact it had been rumored that he was going to be dismissed as part of a general housecleaning. Potter, with his own job on the line, outlined a new selective hiring process that would reject four of every five applicants and put the old-timers on notice that they were expendable. The American Street Railway Association commented, "New blood and new capital entered the field, but many of the old customs and old employes remained."[35]

The licensing ordinance died in committee, but no labor union had been so cordially received in city chambers before. As a counter to union initiatives, the Union Railroad instituted the company-dominated Street Car Mutual Benefit Association to compete with the more independent Horse Railroad Mutual Benefit Association formed a decade earlier and run by the employees themselves. The concept of management-oriented health and welfare gained credence nationally as a shield against the Knights of Labor, who offered group benefits to their members. The Amalgamated, which inherited the Knights' mantle in the street railway industry, provided some minimal coverage to its constituents as well and needled the owners' ulterior motives in endorsing mutual benefit associations: "There has never been one of them yet that has been a success to the company, and more than one of them have turned out by thoroughly organizing into a trades union." But disciplinarians in the industry came to see the value in controlling even the limited recreation time of workers. "The policy of keeping the employees around the car house during their spare hours," according to the editors of the *Street Railway Journal*, "is undoubtedly correct." One company official proclaimed, "Yes, we know all about them and where they are in the habit of spending their leisure time. Everything we hear about the men when on duty or off goes upon our record." The Buffalo railway system opened a two-floor club and gymnasium that featured billiards, showers, and a library that was available to family members in the evening. A few intrepid owners even suggested profit sharing as a way to keep the unions at bay. The Amalgamated poked fun at these fanciful schemes: "What does a man working 14 or 15 hours a day want with a club room or library?"[36]

The new mutual benefit association at the Union Railroad came under strict company control and provided insurance like its predecessor. A carman from each barn joined the board of directors, paralleling the structure of the union's executive board. Dues were eight dollars a year with an initiation fee of five dollars. By 1900 the death benefit was only one hundred dollars, an amount that was "to be made larger when the membership . . . increased sufficiently to warrant doing so." Similarly, despite a five-dollar-a-week sick benefit, only four hundred dollars had been distributed, indicating that few motormen or conductors joined. In contrast, the original organization had distributed over twenty thousand dollars in benefits during its nine-year existence, indicating a large and active membership. Zachary Taylor, the union's will-of-the-wisp first president, had been an activist in the original association. Union advocates may have transformed the group into a launching pad for Division 39, because many of the organization's concerns dovetailed with traditional labor demands.[37]

The company made it clear that its mutual benefit association had "no affiliation with 'union labor,' as such, and nothing in its principles or practice has any reference to wage questions, terms of employment, or any other of the numberless topics of discussion that arise between the employer and employed." That declaration did not stop the Union Railroad from using the group to undercut the union. The company hired William Abbott, the carmen's business agent, to become a director of the new benefit organization. His apparent "unfaithfulness to the union" helped demoralize Division 39. Another charter member of the union's executive board ended up as secretary-treasurer of the company's association. These turncoats followed local president Zachary Taylor, who had jumped ship earlier. Still the union held on, hosting a "grand concert" with help from Pop Spear. So great was the attendance, according to the *Providence Journal*, "that many of the floor directors unconsciously murmured 'Step forward, please,'" repeating the conductors' constant plea to passengers in crowded cars. The company's mutual benefit association retaliated with its own celebration, held in the same building. Guests wore decorative ribbons imprinted with streetcars, not unlike the trappings of a labor union.[38]

The Union Railroad attempted to match the union's cultural and economic appeal with events, regalia, and fraternal goodwill. At the same time, the company took steps to counteract a possible walkout. The Rhode Island legislature passed two "strike bills," which authorized fines and damages to anyone who vandalized or interfered with streetcar or utility service. One local literary gadfly wryly observed that the traction company made it "practically a life sentence" if you interfered with operations. Management's clout, especially in the general assembly, completely overshadowed the fledgling efforts of carmen and other labor unions in the political arena.[39]

The Panic of 1893 probably did more to discourage union activism and organization than the Union Railroad's decision to play hardball. Unemployment, wage reductions, and fear hampered the working class throughout Rhode Island and most of the country. The local Knights of Labor held their first reunion the year of the depression, marking the transition from a fighting organization to a nostalgic club. The Rhode Island Central Labor Union, formed a decade earlier by the Knights to consolidate simple trade unionism into a political force, now took the lead, especially through its weekly newspaper, *Justice*. Ironically, organized labor finally forced the state to recognize Labor Day as an official holiday in 1893, the year of the panic. Strikes, especially by textile operatives, punctuated the gloomy landscape, but the struggle of the streetcar men seemed to evaporate. Their limp embrace of the local labor movement seemed more defensive than enthusiastic. When New York state militia helped crush a railway walkout in Brooklyn in January 1895, the *Providence Journal*, which had criticized the corporate takeover of the Union Railroad, warned local crews to accept the status quo.[40]

Horsecar drivers and conductors defended their standard of living despite the inability of their union to mount an offensive against a powerful and influential monopoly. Newcomers had no such protection. The *Providence Journal* nodded its approval of employee acquiescence and company moderation: "The corporation thought better of the scheme after public opinion had thoroughly manifested its disapproval of the idea of placing cheap help upon the fast running electric cars." Earlier, when the syndicate purchased Union Railroad stock from local residents, several small stockholders feared new owners would mistreat beloved drivers and conductors. Because of this, management displayed a remarkable respect and fear of work-force and passenger resentment against a hostile takeover of a local institution by an impersonal trust. The Amalgamated concluded, "The day of the local union, as well as that of the individual among the street railway men of America, has passed and gone. . . . To-day we find the companies united from one end of the country to the other and their actions controlled and directed by the organization of the General Manager's Association."[41]

Although Providence Division 39 passed out of existence sometime in 1895–96 almost as quietly as the city's last horsecar in 1894, the conditions that created its appearance would instigate another union in just a few years, involving the public in unprecedented fashion in Rhode Island history.

THE TROLLEY HABIT

I guess it's a fact that we have got the "trolley habit" badly. In the days of the slow-going horse-car most of us preferred to walk as much as possible. . . . If we had a little journey to make—one of a quarter of a mile or so—we never thought of taking a car; now we just hop aboard an electric and are there in a jiffy.

Letter to the *Providence Journal*, 1901

We have better cars, and better motormen and conductors than any other city I know of, but we also have a line of railroads that carries us like hogs in a cattle car.

Col. Frank Arnold, Providence reform candidate, 1895

A popular uprising at the polls will convince the New York and New Jersey capitalists that a street railroad worth about five millions cannot defy the wishes of a city taxed for a hundred and seventy millions.

Providence Journal, 1895

The Union Railroad made a shrewd bargain when it compromised the employee's organizing drive with a two-tier wage system. Although the carrier continued paying premium wages to its veteran work force as a way to undermine the Amalgamated's appeal and soften public anger, the fear of technological change and the possible threat of job loss also worked as a deterrent to unionization. The syndicate wisely anticipated a surge in patronage due to the popularity of the electric streetcar and earmarked some of the increased profit to maintain the traditional rate for old-timers. Newcomers, at two dollars a day, would soon eclipse the more expensive, soon-to-retire work force. Although that policy produced short-term savings, it also helped precipitate the upcoming strike and forced the company to reevaluate its position.

Remarkably, the Union Railroad electrified its entire operation in two years. The manpower required to position thousands of poles, string miles of overhead wires, and replace lightweight horsecar rails with heavier trolley tracks engaged many a Rhode Islander during the depression years. Nor did

Streetcar track installation was as disruptive to travel in downtown Providence in the 1890s as high-way construction is in cities today.

hiring slacken after that. By the beginning of 1897 the Union Railroad employed 700 workers, including 465 motormen and conductors—a 50-percent increase in just seven years. By the turn of the century there were 1,400 employees, a reflection of an ever-expanding system that included new job classifications, such as electricians, linemen, and powerhouse workers, which more than made up for job losses in the obsolete horse stables. Management also eased construction and repair delays by hiring a permanent track crew to work nights so as not to interrupt daytime service.[1]

In the shadow of the 1893 depression, streetcar employment was as desirable as ever in a still sluggish economy. The Union Railroad reported record numbers of applicants. Despite the perils and drawbacks of a railway career, a secure seven-day workweek and a two-dollar daily stipend for rookie crews stood out in a tentative job market. According to a newspaper report, large numbers of retail clerks and factory workers "would gladly leave the bench and counter for the sake of obtaining a job on the electrics." The unemployed "lay

Electrification eliminated horses, stables, and hostlers but created hundreds of new jobs for linemen, mechanics, and pitmen.

for the general manager on the street corner, await for hours his coming at the office." As service expanded during tough economic times, management also saw an opportunity to continue and even upgrade the quality work force at a discount price. "Young men, able bodied, good appearing fellows" daily crowded the railway's waiting room armed with letters of recommendation from prominent Rhode Islanders. New employees, like horsecar crews before them, had to be bonded but no longer by a surety company. General Manager Albert Potter now required "that his men shall be well enough thought of by two responsible parties in the community to warrant signing their names to a $500 bond." Potter carried on Longstreet's preoccupation with honesty by linking an employee's reputation to city and state officials rather than to an impersonal insurance company. Streetcar workers apparently encountered few problems obtaining the required signatures, a reflection of their trusted standing as a vocational class and pillars of the working-class community. To further ensure integrity the Union Railroad—for the first time—also employed detectives to spy on conductors, who could never tell "when the eyes of a wide awake inspector" were on them.[2]

An era ended in 1894, when the last horsecars ran. The Providence Board of Trade commented: "Jack Horse has done good service. He has been beaten, overworked and otherwise abused, and cheated out of his rights yet he has been man's best friend, patient and faithful, but the time has arrived for him to step down and out of the street car service, to make room for a more powerful and rapid motor." The Union Railroad held its twenty-first and final horse auction. Most drivers and conductors made the transition to mechanical energy but always reminisced about horsepower and leisurely travel. In any case, their defunct labor union could offer them no solace or protection during this changeover.[3]

Newspaper reporters, occasionally at a loss for a story, had only to board a trolley and observe riders or an isolated locale for a quick and colorful article. Rhode Island, like most states in that period, was rife with ethnic and class prejudice. A *Providence Journal* reporter marveled at once-hidden neighborhoods and people in an 1895 article entitled "Five-Cent Journeys," describing the city's minorities in uncomplimentary terms. On an evening trolley tour, he passed through the North End, "the Russian Jew tenement quarters," where the Hebrew language filled the air. He rode past "Dagotown" on Atwells Avenue: "Here's where the I-tal-ian population lives—the land of the macaroni and the hand organ. Folks cut each other's necks here and push daggers into each other's backs." In the Pawtuxet Valley another journalist promised that trolley passengers would see "fair-haired descendants of the Vikings from Scandinavia mingle with the swarthy, degenerate offspring of the Caesars and Belgians, French-Canadians and the English speaking races, who spin and weave in the big factory under the hill."[4]

The trolley inadvertently connected places in the state that previously enjoyed only local notoriety. The streetcar to Crescent Park, the state's premier amusement center, in East Providence, passed a "district of low-down-dives, disreputable dance halls and so-called summer hotels." A group of toughs boarded a trolley there one summer and terrorized passengers and crew. Several hooligans blocked the streetcar while others dismantled the headlight and took it into nearby woods to illuminate a violent fistfight. Local residents feared the trolley would continue to bring a "horde of hoodlums" into town on weekends. Similarly, passengers on the last Broad Street nightcar in Providence became so raucous that critics suggested it carry police and nurses to protect patrons and treat the injured. And black farmhands returning home after Saturday-night celebrations in Newport caused weekly disturbances on electric vehicles there.[5]

The general public associated immigrants and minorities with this sort of violence and caricatured it into broad racial and ethnic prejudice. One historian described the streetcar as "a zone where class and racial differences could create tension and occasionally lead to open hostility." Low-ranking transit employees had no choice but to work these undesirable rough and tumble trips, earning twenty-five to fifty cents less a day than older coworkers on safer daytime lines. Several Rhode Island transit workers actually died in violent altercations with criminal passengers who challenged the crew or other riders. Despite derogatory public comment about color and national origin in that era, the usually quotable motormen and conductors kept their opinions private in order not to antagonize any group of riders and provoke further trouble.[6]

Society's class bias also rode the streetcar. Suburban mill workers packed trolleys, seeking weekend entertainment. "The person who cannot become intensely and thoroughly democratic at a moment's notice," wrote a *Journal* reporter, "has no place on these cars on Sunday." An upper-crust resident of Pawtuxet, where General Manager Potter and his neighbors sported white-duck summer outfits, explained that blue-collar workers could inadvertently dirty the clothes of other riders: "He [the anonymous rider] did not want to be construed as having a word to say against the laboring classes, the men who carry dinner pails and lunch baskets, but he thought that if—well, if they could have a car all to themselves early in the morning and again after work hours, perhaps the toilers would be better satisfied and perhaps the rich summer residents would not object." Companies around the country responded to this complaint from well-to-do patrons by requisitioning older, open cars for rush-hour industrial routes. These vehicles were nicknamed "smokers," after the habit of workers who smoked tobacco on board.[7]

When the Union Railroad completed a scenic route to exclusive Narragansett Pier in rural South County, local elites feared "early degeneration of the place" from lower-middle-class tourists and day-trippers. One merchant admitted, however, "The rich people who put up at our hotels enjoy being gazed at; they like to excite the curiosity of the middle classes—I mean the middling well off, you know." The *Providence Journal* published a popular travel guide, *Trolley Trips from Providence Out*, that described various jaunts and provided practical transit information. The booklet went through four editions in two years and spurred recreational outings by those once confined to particular neighborhoods and communities by race, class, or ethnicity.[8]

The urban riding habit, originally pioneered by omnibus and horsecar, evolved into a trolley habit in the electric period. The speed and convenience of the streetcar lured elites from carriages and workers from bicycles as a reasonable fare structure made commuting a bargain. An anonymous letter to the editor explained: "I guess it's a fact that we have got the 'trolley habit' badly.

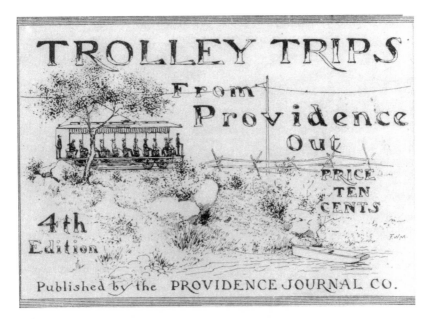

The speed, convenience, and inexpensiveness of trolley travel allowed the average citizen to break out of ethnically, racially, and economically segregated neighborhoods to see the rest of the nearby world, if only on special occasions.

In the days of the slow-moving horse-car most of us preferred to walk as much as possible. . . . If we had a little journey to make—one of a quarter of a mile or so—we never thought of taking a car; now we just hop aboard an electric and are there in a jiffy." By 1902 congested Rhode Island boasted the fourth highest number of rides per inhabitant in the United States: 145 each year, compared to the national average of 63. The high population density in the Providence-Pawtucket metropolitan corridor provided over forty-five million passenger trips that year, compared to only eighteen million twelve years earlier during the horsecar period.[9]

One group that sought liberation from home confinement by mass transit were women, especially working- and middle-class females. Suburban housewives could now make several quick and inexpensive weekly trips downtown, compared to only an occasional horsecar trek just a few years earlier. Gender-based newspaper stories poked fun at the riding peculiarities of women. Transit crews griped that ladies would often signal a car to stop, only to stand at the side of the vehicle for an impromptu conversation with a friend on board.

Other complaints centered around affluent female shoppers who took up several seats with bundles and purchases. An anonymous conductor told a reporter, "I always try to be as accommodating as possible to all women, and yet they are twice as troublesome as men." Middle-class housewives, however, helped account for increased patronage, especially during off-peak hours, when street railways were eager to fill empty trolley seats.[10]

The trolley party was another democratic and cultural spin-off of the streetcar revolution that contributed to class and ethnic segregation but ironically allowed greater group freedom. Affluent organizations could charter a single bloomer or a fleet of cars to carry members to various events and amusements. Before the popularity of this service trickled down to other groups, newspaper accounts of upper-class soirees often included a passenger list, a social register in transit. Participants lit flares and fireworks, decorated streetcars, and carried refreshments. By the late 1890s mill workers, school graduates, fraternal groups, and minority and ethnic organizations rented special cars for a night out at Rhodes-on-the-Pawtuxet, Crescent Park, or a shore dinner hall. Motormen and conductors similarly traveled in a body to annual clambakes, but only after making provisions for spare crews to replace them for the day. Each carbarn arranged its own excursion. This new mobility allowed society's underclass to break down invisible neighborhood barriers and see the rest of the world, if only on a special occasion.[11]

While transit crews grappled with the new mechanics and culture of railway service, the Union Railroad continued to battle public hostility over franchises, taxes, and labor problems. New riders boarded the trolley in previously unserviced suburbs, and casual passengers became daily commuters on older urban routes as discretionary income outpaced a stationary fare structure. Patrons developed a keen interest in railway activities. The streetcar's constituency multiplied with faster accommodations and statewide accessibility. Citizens embraced mass transit as their public transportation. Average customers could not afford a single share of high-priced stock, but each nickel handed to the conductor gave them a financial and emotional investment and the right to criticize whatever irked them about current service.

The fact that Sen. Nelson Aldrich was the president of the Union Railroad and commanded a board of directors that included the state's industrial elite was all the more reason to complain. The same group also controlled the ruling Republican Party and were easy targets of an aroused public that now scrutinized legislative activity in a personal way as it related to local service. The battle—and the stakes—over who would control urban mass transportation had come a long way since the 1860s, when opposing sides argued whether

Urban mass transportation facilitated the growth of amusement centers, parks, and sporting facilities and made them accessible to patrons.

to allow horsecar tracks to interfere with private-carriage travel. Now the issue would lace political platforms and make traction performance a partisan topic among an opposition party's rank and file. Each new route and mile of track was a link to parts of the state previously inaccessible to ordinary citizens. This expanding community grapevine, with motormen and conductors acting as spreaders of information, broadcast once unavailable news and gossip.[12]

The Union Railroad fended off criticism by playing a powerful trump card in this era: the impatient clamoring for electric car service, which temporarily overshadowed chronic antipathy toward the carrier. Virtually every Rhode Island community envisioned the benefits of a trolley route to their hometowns. Landowners and speculators predicted a period of rapid development; businessmen awaited the immigration of new customers from outlying areas; workers anticipated emigration to cheaper housing in uncongested suburbs; the riding public expected significantly faster rides. The 1893 depression, less severe in Rhode Island than elsewhere, barely crimped these dreams. Ironi-

The open car, or bloomer, operated in warm weather. The service was described as a poor person's carriage ride.

cally, railway construction employed many out-of-work laborers and may have won Senator Aldrich some local blue-collar admirers.

Several months after streetcar service began in January 1892, the Providence railroad committee noted, "Public sentiment has undergone a marked change in this city since the introduction and successful operation of the trolley electric system on the Pawtuxet line." The *Providence Journal* wrote, "The *ignis fatuus* of danger from more rapidly moving cars has vanished in the clear light of actual local experience." Downtown businessmen who did not "lightly affix their names to petitions" did so gladly to promote electric traction. Unlike horsecars, streetcars furrowed through snowbanks, providing reliable, comfortable winter travel. Even blizzards only temporarily halted the trolley juggernaut as improved plows and levelers methodically cleared tracks in short order. Motormen and conductors applauded the end of "storm time," the antiquated system of reducing wages during inclement winter weather.[13]

The Union Railroad electrified its entire horsecar system in remarkably quick fashion. Throughout the 1890s, the carrier filled in a metropolitan grid with service to new or expanding neighborhoods. In Providence, streetcars helped develop outlying sections of the city. Just as extraordinary was the railway extension into suburban and rural areas. However metropolitan Providence had become, most of Rhode Island remained a network of agricultural and mill villages connected by dusty ribbons of road. Trolleys now traveled along country trails and private rights-of-way at speeds that rivaled those of steam trains. The coming of the trolley brought rapid mass transportation, communication, utilities, and profound cultural changes to pastoral villages previously undisturbed by the march of urban civilization. Although patrons usually celebrated inaugural trips, other aspects of expansion reopened old wounds and created a new generation of grievances. Commuters lobbied for new routes and additions, but upon completion refused to let the Union Railroad run the operation without continued citizen input. Influential neighborhood improvement societies included streetcar service, transfers, and fares on their reform agendas. The battle for control of city streets and public transportation became ever more complex.[14]

Town fathers continually beseeched the Union Railroad for rail accommodations. The people of Lakewood, who lived just beyond the terminus of the first electric line in Pawtuxet, agitated for a short branch addition. Republican Charles "Boss" Brayton, a local resident himself, personally announced that the Union Railroad would build a connection. In the pouring rain dozens of residents jubilantly paraded and fired a cannon. They continued the celebration at a local hall with a collation and rousing speeches. Three cheers for the Union Railroad rattled the room. Eight months later the same celebrants gathered for an "indignation meeting" to protest the railway's decision to charge three cents for the three-fourths-of-a-mile ride. By comparison, the trip from Providence to Pawtuxet, a five-mile journey, cost only five cents. A book of twenty-five tickets sold for fifty cents on the spur, but the offer did little to stem local anger. This pattern, in varying formats, was repeated around the system.[15]

As service and grumbling penetrated into Rhode Island's hinterlands, the Union Railroad chartered separate companies to oversee suburban operations. The Pawtuxet Valley Street Railway Company began serving mill villages in the southwestern part of the state in 1894. Five years later the Union Railroad organized the Rhode Island Suburban Railway to initiate and consolidate other outlying operations, especially in southern Rhode Island. As it extended routes, the carrier redefined local geography. According to a report of the railroad commissioner, once isolated mill villages became satellites of Providence within a few years of trolley service.[16]

Where the Union Railroad lacked exclusive privileges outside of Providence, other entrepreneurs eagerly sought franchises. "There must be two dozen or more electric railroad charters somewhere in the two bodies," exclaimed the *Providence Journal* during the waning days of the general assembly. "Men who haven't an actual possession of a thousand dollars get to looking for the right to construct miles of trolley lines and bodies of citizens with large holdings of real estate in country districts work for the passage of charter rights for lines which will bring their property nearer to the city and incidentally nearer the market." The Union Railroad usually impeded such activities through legal maneuvering, stalling tactics, and legislative influence. Most of the applications went "to sleep in committee files and in the desks of clerks." The legislature did issue charters to several influential competitors or to incorporators planning to do business in seemingly unprofitable terrain. The Union Railroad managed to hold these rivals at bay, outlasting some, purchasing others, and, if all else failed, reaching some kind of financial accommodation that usually favored the veteran carrier. Management learned from the Cable Tramway experience and fought to preserve control from upstart rivals who might appeal to the public and politicians with liberal tax, franchise, and fare offers.[17]

These expanded transportation opportunities continued to enhance real estate. The street railway had a Midas touch, promoting land speculation wherever it passed. The omnibus, commuter train, and especially the horsecar had gilded suburban property with increased value. The trolley would eclipse their primitive forebears further in this realm. Even as real estate advertisements trumpeted "Horse Cars, Electric Lights and Pawtuxet Water" for Olneyville house lots in the waning days of horsepower, the streetcar soon swashbuckled through city and countryside, uplifting property values along the way. Areas not serviced by trolleys often languished. "People who owned land did not care to build houses," argued a witness at a hearing to extend a line, "because the location was not accessible by street cars." Providence issued a record number of building permits in 1892, the first year of electric operations. The 906 licenses represented more than $3 million in new property assessment.[18]

Businessmen and professionals, especially those who worked in Providence, built suburban dwellings in Cranston, Johnston, and East and North Providence. "City people with inclinations to become residents of outlying sections invariably look for home sites near a trolley car line." Industrial magnates flocked to an emerging Edgewood section of Cranston, on Narragansett Bay just north of the village of Pawtuxet. Land speculators purchased a seventy-acre farm there and subdivided it on rumors that the trolley would come. Ten months after the inaugural trip, it was observed, "Modern houses are where farms once were; streets are cut and curbed where the potato patch once throve; pretty lawns and flowers bloom where everything once was a wilderness vast." Choice lots sold for a premium fifteen cents a square foot, and the local tax assessor charted a $150,000 increase in valuation in one year. Jewelers, textile manufacturers, and other industrialists sought fresh country air close to the city. For Edgewood the "turning point in its history came simultaneously with the trolley cars, which were responsible to a large extent for the boom."[19]

Just north of Pawtuxet on Broad Street, Washington Park straddled the city lines of Cranston and Providence. Positioned for "intimate connection with the centre of the city," this neighborhood boasted sixty-two new homes along the trolley route to Pawtuxet within nine months of the streetcar's appearance. "Before that the territory was not platted," according to a contemporary article, "and was not deemed a desireable piece of real estate for residential purposes." The developers credited electric cars. As Washington Park expanded its population base, the nearby Eddy Street line was lengthened to connect to Broad Street. One thousand residents celebrated by hanging Japanese lanterns from telegraph poles and lighting fireworks. A year later another route reached Washington Park from the nearby beachfront, prompting a prediction that "shore property will rise in value like the mercury in a thermometer on a hot summer's day." A turn-of-the-century builders' prospectus described the community as a streetcar suburb and featured a bird's-eye view of a nearly deserted Washington Park in 1891 next to one of a mature, middle-class neighborhood in 1899. Suburban historian Henry Jackson commented, "By the turn of the century, a 'new city,' segregated by class and economic function and encompassing an area triple the territory of the older walking city, had clearly emerged as the center of the American urban society. The electric streetcar was the key to the shift."[20]

As land speculation gripped Rhode Island, property held by one family for a century passed through the hands of three parties in a month in rural Foster, where the state's longest trolley route would pass into Connecticut. Travelers noted the pristine beauty: "This part of the State is hilly and not thickly settled. Great, unbroken slopes of pine lands look down into valleys filled with lakes or cut in two by the north fork of the Pawtuxet; little mill villages that never heard the sound of French-Canadian since the water first ran over the dam are as purely Yankee as when they had their earliest barn raising; the village post office and grocery store have never yet surrendered those rights to freedom of speech and spit which almost every other resort of the kind in the State has given up when the new came to rule the old; and here the things

Suburban streetcar routes often terminated beyond contemporary population centers in areas awaiting future development. These cars ran on the Old Louisquisset Turnpike in Lincoln, Rhode Island. The house in the background dates from 1781. Gift of Tom Green.

the grandfather had, and did, have been the only things for the grandchildren." City chauvinism, of course, required ridicule of rustic characters. A reporter warned travelers to "be on the lookout for some of the queerest characters that [downtown] Westminster street ever squeezed between the curbing and the plate glass windows." Foster was also described as a place "where nobody dies until he is 100 or so." Passengers on suburban routes complained that motormen and conductors "talk and act at times in a way which indicates a considerable contempt for their rustic passengers," one of the few times transit crews were publicly upbraided for discriminatory attitudes.[21]

Freight, rather than passenger traffic, lured railway capital to rural Rhode Island. The entrepreneurial route to Danielson, Connecticut, initially made its profit by carrying ice from local ponds to city markets. Rural mills eagerly employed trolley services to transport raw goods and finished products. Local farmers also joined the bandwagon and dispatched sixteen thousand gallons of milk and other agricultural produce daily. The cost to haul a cord of wood to Providence fell from $2.50 to $1.00; the day-long oxen trips were trimmed to a few hours in a streetcar. Neighboring towns experienced an economic spin-off from the Danielson line as land along the route appreciated 10 percent in one year. Some residents shortsightedly complained about underwriting road improvements to send huckleberries to market.[22]

With labor relations temporarily under control and the state infatuated by the trolley habit, the Union Railroad reinforced its political position in the wake of electrification. The company's dogged determination to obtain operating concessions, however, soured a citizenry that, under other circumstances, might have appreciated the carrier's solid service performance. In 1891 the carrier had extended its franchise for twenty-five years; after a public outcry the term was reduced to twenty years, but with a new provision for a monopoly of service in Providence. Once these concessions were obtained the Union Railroad was sold to Aldrich's organization.

Now, in 1895, the Union Railroad sought another broadening of its contract for an additional twenty-five years—to 1920. Such an extension would ease the marketing of company bonds, the same argument used so successfully in the last round of negotiations. Bids currently lagged behind asking price, and the franchise expired twenty years before the bonds matured. The general assembly passed the enabling legislation "at a speed not surpassed on a trolley route" and without the camouflage of a committee assignment. While the latest extension was for only a few more years, the *Providence Journal* suggested that the proposed bill could be legally interpreted as a twenty-five-year addendum renewable for another quarter of a century; in other words, a perpetual franchise. In fact, attorney William Roelker had sent Nelson Aldrich a proof of the law two years earlier. Roelker craftily included provisions in the legislation that precluded future tampering.[23]

The stealth of the Union Railroad "created a general spirit of public antagonism to anything in which the company appears interested." Reformers, sensing a golden opportunity to harness local discontent, attempted to curtail the carrier's political influence in the Providence city council. The Union for Practical Progress, an amalgamation of religious groups, trade unions, and neighborhood improvement societies, led the charge. The nonpartisan association attracted prohibitionists, Republican mugwumps, municipal progressives organized into the Advance Club, Democrats long out of power, and small merchants in the Rhode Island Business Men's Association, an alternative to the elitist and powerful Providence Board of Trade. The *Providence Journal*, free of Boss Brayton's influence after the death of his benefactor, Henry Bowen Anthony—but still a supporter of Nelson Aldrich—called for a "house-cleaning."[24]

Disparate reform elements joined forces even though ethnic, class, and religious tensions divided them on other issues. The Union Railroad remained the spool around which all other grievances were wound. In May 1895 a front page *Journal* headline proclaimed the result of their organizing efforts: "A Tremendous Gathering at the Anti-Union Railroad Mass Meeting." Men of wealth, religion, and standing condemned the unholy alliance between the political and railway systems. Rathbone Gardner, a Yankee attorney, labeled the Union Railroad a socialist institution, "a single head controlling the whole railroad business of the city." Another speaker characterized the latest franchise bill as a Trojan horse, the first act ever constructed in Rhode Island to preclude judgment by the state judiciary. The Union for Practical Progress published a pamphlet, *The Tyranny of the Union Railroad and the General Assembly*, to protest the perpetual franchise.[25]

When the city council, in the shadow of the protest meeting, voted to nix any deals with the Union Railroad that did not include transfers, reformers redoubled their efforts in the upcoming fall elections. The *Journal* naively predicted the expulsion of "trolley agents" from city government: "A popular uprising at the polls will convince the New York and New Jersey capitalists that a street railroad worth about five millions cannot defy the wishes of a city taxed for a hundred and seventy millions." Letters to the editor throughout the summer reflected citizen outrage. One writer suggested, "To ensure a change of procedure, change representatives, retire the ringmasters, disorganize the ring." Another letter declared, "The people when aroused for the protection of their rights are invincible." During the 1895 Labor Day parade one union passed the reviewing stand at city hall carrying a banner that read, "Is Our Mayor the tool of corporations?"[26]

Throughout the fall reformers hosted numerous rallies "representing every known shade of local political opinion." A citywide Committee of Five—two Republicans, two Democrats, and a Prohibitionist—was chosen to select candidates. The coalition represented the kind of movement the machine dreaded because it fragmented Republican unity. The Democrats nominated attorney Edwin "Ned" McGuinness for mayor a third time. Independents supported him as well. McGuinness, the first Catholic in Rhode Island to hold general office as secretary of state, made railway improvement a major campaign theme: "Our citizens demand in a loud voice and no uncertain voice for transfer tickets." Col. Frank Arnold, an independent candidate for council, also raised the transit issue: "We have better cars, and better motormen and conductors than any other city I know of, but we also have a line of railroads that carries us like hogs in a cattle car."[27]

McGuinness earned an impressive victory. In the council races, progressives won several stunning contests. The *Providence Journal* headlined that aspect of the election: "Corporation Councilmen 'Transferred' to More Appropriate Spheres of Activity." Thousands stood in the evening rain to watch election results on stereopticon slides flashed from the *Journal-Bulletin* building. Perennial alderman Arthur Watson, a Union Railroad director, lost badly. The council president, accused of ties to the Union Railroad, was "the worst beaten man in the city." Mayor McGuinness, in his inaugural address, placed transfer tickets at the top of the agenda. East Providence Republicans, in the most heavily attended caucus in town history, threw out an incumbent representative for "supposed kindly feeling to the Union Railroad Company." The event was orchestrated by the Riverside Improvement Society and the local Good Government Club.[28]

A few weeks after the new mayor assumed office, the Rhode Island Business Men's Association hosted a talk by Mayor Hazen Pingree of Detroit, the nation's most outspoken critic of street railway privilege. He advocated municipal ownership and had forced Detroit's major carrier to electrify lines and lower basic fares to an unheard of three cents. After Pingree excoriated utility monopolies, Mayor McGuinness was introduced as "the Pingree of Providence." He wanted transit reform but would settle for transfers rather than radical three-cent fares.[29]

Proponents and opponents knew that something would have to be done about transfers to stem public anger, which had originated in horsecar days and intensified during the electric era. The trolley offered a greatly expanded menu of routes compared to what had been available in an earlier generation. The speed and frequency of the streetcar made switching from one vehicle to another easier and more convenient. Public and political support brought the issue to a head. The Providence city council created a special committee to hold hearings and consult with Nelson Aldrich and the Union Railroad. The carrier claimed it would lose $250,000 annually under a free-transfer system due to fraud. The company would entertain such a project only if the city waived some onerous tax obligations. The committee endorsed a simple transfer-ticket system at downtown junctures of routes, as practiced by most other American street railways.[30]

Both parties agreed to disagree once again and then headed for the general assembly for relief. The city, apparently not having learned much from previous appearances in Brayton's lair, introduced legislation for a free and unrestricted transfer system. The Union Railroad countered with a plan for a single enclosed downtown transfer station in lieu of having to perform street repairs. Trolleys would connect in this building, and passengers would switch to other cars without needing paper tickets.[31]

In a rare local legislative appearance Nelson Aldrich endorsed the station concept before the house judiciary committee. His arguments are preserved in a thirty-page pamphlet, which offers an unusual window into this brilliant

Gilded Age mind. In a no-nonsense manner, the senator got to the heart of the matter. The issue was not transfers, he argued, but "the security and inviolability of vested rights." He spuriously claimed the carrier had spent over $9 million to upgrade the system electrically. Despite this investment, he continued, shortsighted adversaries would force the implementation of transfer tickets without reimbursement. "I submit further," he growled, "that if the property or rights of the Union Railroad Company can be destroyed or confiscated in this manner, so can those of every other public or private corporation in the State." Aldrich warned that Rhode Island's reputation would be besmirched by "revolutionary doctrines." Perhaps thinking he was on the floor of the United States Senate, Aldrich boasted that the United Traction and Electric Company owned utilities in a dozen states and did "not expect to depend for its earnings upon any single road in a single community."[32]

Aldrich's denouement, like Terence Powderly's assessment of electric traction, reached beyond his legislative audience in an appeal to the American dream. The trolley made possible a suburban world of home ownership and rural pleasures. "We believe that the electric street railway is one of the great factors in modern life," he preached. "It practically annihilates distance and enables all classes of the community to live at a distance from business centers or from their place of occupation." The senator's stand against transfers eliminated any suspense about assembly action. The legislators passed the murky franchise extension but left the carrier and city to mutually agree on a transfer compromise under a threat of coercive action at the next session.[33]

Councilman P. J. McCarthy, who later rode an anti-Union Railroad animus to the mayoralty, condemned the proceedings: "The framers of the present act were practically servants, representatives and attorneys of the Union Railroad Company. They are demanding in reality favors of the city under the guise of conferring favors to the citizens and complying with a popular demand." Remarkably, even the Providence Board of Trade, once presided over by Nelson Aldrich, headlined an article in its monthly journal: "The Union Railroad Company is Evidently Killing the Goose that Lays the Golden Egg." The article stated, "It will be quite a number of years before the fingers of this gigantic monopoly can be forced to release their grip." The Outlet Company, one of downtown Providence's largest retailers and a publisher of a free weekly news sheet, continually assailed the carrier and even passed out popular buttons that boldly stated, "Transfer Tickets Or Nothing." But the Union Railroad did not issue transfers like those of most other American streetcar systems until 1902, and then only in exchange for another valuable legislative concession.[34]

The "goo-goos," as good-government advocates were sometimes deri-

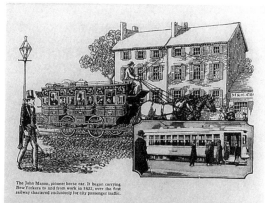

General Electric, like most utility boosters, envisioned a progressive world created by mass transportation. This magazine ad appeared in 1923.

The John Mason, pioneer horse car. It began carrying New Yorkers to and from work in 1832, over the first railway chartered exclusively for city passenger traffic.

Enter suburbs—exit slums

You will find the monogram of the General Electric Company on the motors of elevators which made possible the skyscraper, as well as on the motors of the trolleys which created the suburb. And on *little* motors, also, which do the burdensome part of housework for a wage of 3 cents an hour.

Suppose our cities still depended upon horse cars. Workers would live huddled under the shadow of their factories. Children, who can now reach the cool beaches for a few pennies, would be condemned to the hot pavements all Summer.

The trolley car has transformed the conditions of city life. With its coming the suburb started to grow and the slum to go.

GENERAL ELECTRIC

sively called during the Progressive era, could never shake a deserved elitist image. Absent from the call for representative empowerment of the capital city was a concomitant demand for liberalizing voter restrictions in council elections. Many Yankee reformers could not bring themselves to support Democrats, union workers, or the Irish. The latter groups joined the cleanup effort somewhat skeptically. Rathbone Gardner, sparkplug for the Municipal League, had recently been a lawyer for Marsden Perry's Narragansett Electric Company. Alfred Stone, the noted architect and good-government participant, was paid handsomely to draw the blueprints for the Union Railroad's proposed central transfer station. Even the political reformer Hiram Howard, who attacked railway "boodle" and corporate-controlled government in the state, asked Boss Brayton to intervene with Aldrich to secure an ambassadorship. Nor were working-class voters reassured when the Rhode Island Business Men's Association hosted Governor Elisha Dyer, Senator Aldrich, and Rep.

The Outlet Bulletin, *a free news sheet distributed by Providence's largest and most popular retail store, linked the Union Railroad to the state's political machine. The owners of this publication backed the striking carmen in 1902.*

Adin Capron, stalwarts of the Rhode Island Republican machine, at its annual banquet. The association, which only a few years before had toasted Detroit's Mayor Pingree, announced that the three politicians would address the issue of Good Citizenship.[35]

The Union Railroad displayed its resiliency by supporting a 1-percent state streetcar tax in 1898. Hidden in the revenue bill's honey was the perpetual-franchise clause. Sidney S. Rider, a prominent political gadfly and publisher, wrote that it was "conceived in iniquity, and enacted in fraud." The law passed at the anachronistic one-day Newport session of the legislature with no advance public notice and far from Providence's political reach. Lincoln Steffens, the famous muckraker, labeled it a "masterpiece of legislative treason." The act was crafted in such a fashion to virtually preclude alteration. "It is a contract between United States Senator Nelson W. Aldrich as the state," ridiculed Steffens, "and President Nelson W. Aldrich of the Street Railway

Company, by which without the consent of his company his state cannot tax his company or alter or take back its franchise."[36]

After the legislature ramrodded the franchise into law, the Union Railroad sheepishly volunteered to pay the city of Providence a full 5-percent gross receipts tax without invoking arbitration to determine the rate. Similarly, Marsden Perry's Narragansett Electric Company unilaterally agreed to cut customer prices by 15 percent. The general assembly knighted the Union Railroad with the crown jewel of railway service, a perpetual franchise that ensured uninterrupted control of city streets without council meddling. Coincidentally, the legislature, which selected the state's two national senators until passage of the nineteenth amendment, reelected Nelson Aldrich for a second term during the same fateful session.[37]

WE NEVER USED TO BE IN SUCH A HURRY

Making a car safe for a man on the track is something like lessening the destructive power of a cannon ball. . . . The persons killed as a rule were careless about
crossing the track.

General Manager Albert Potter, 1897

I could not resist the passage of the ten-hour bill, and get the other things
through that were wanted by your people the most.

Charles Boss Brayton to Sen. Nelson Aldrich, 1902

While the Association is not looking for trouble, unless the traction company
assumes a different attitude toward the union's officers and members it will
sooner or later be forced to take some radical action to adjust existing differences.

Amalgamated Association of Street Railway Employes,
Providence Division 200, May 1902

The street railway industry underwent a tremendous rationalization process
during the switch from horsepower to electricity. Novel streetcar systems in the
1890s borrowed complex organizational structure, a management dichotomy
between line and staff, and accounting and statistical controls from the railroad
experience. The new-found power of the watch manifested itself in passenger
timetables, freight schedules, urban work patterns, and the study of fares and
transfers. The drive to greater efficiency and cost containment came from the
burgeoning number of holding companies, bureaucracies, and shareholders
with a claim to Union Railroad profits. Here, too, the example of endemic
mergers and consolidations from the train world became part of the rationalization of trolley service.[1]

Some of the operational consequences of this shake-up pleased the riding
public and railway employees, but other innovations caused unintended com-
plications. These daily problems, as they evolved over the first few years of
trolley service, exacerbated labor tensions again and gave passengers new
grievances to augment a long list of political indignities on the part of the car-

rier. Patrons and crews, who had enjoyed thirty years of personal camaraderie during the horsecar era, would grow even closer in an informal political alliance against the Union Railroad and its governing syndicate, although on a day-to-day basis the old relationship was strained by the pressures of time and the sheer number of new riders. A fresh unionization drive at the turn of the century became a magnet for a large, diverse opposition to the traction company and the corrupt GOP machine that lurked behind it.

The speed and agility of the electric streetcar ensured its urban supremacy over other competitors and changed the tempo of American life. The same velocity that allowed passengers unprecedented mobility also fomented opposition because of the inherent danger in the speed itself. The Riverside Improvement Society complained about reckless celerity of streetcars to Crescent Park the first year of service there. A series of letters to the editor of the *Providence Journal* argued for and against accelerated travel. A plea for slower rides elicited a cynical reply: "We do not need for modes of transportation that will enable us to 'stop and pick huckleberries on the way' in these days." Another letter caricatured the attitude of trolley enthusiasts: "If you pedestrians and horse owners don't like it, keep off the streets, or we shall proceed to scare you off by smashing a wagon or killing a baby occasionally." One buggy driver shot at a motorman after a trolley spooked his horses. Although the city of Providence strictly limited speed to 5.5 miles per hour, the general assembly set a fifteen-mile-per-hour suburban limit. Those restrictions did not apply to private rights-of-way owned by the company. A history of the local union also noted the changes: "Cars are longer, more passengers are transported, the speed of the cars is much faster and the danger to the employes is greater."[2]

Although individual motormen regulated their speed, complaints targeted tight company schedules as the problem. Residents fretted about reckless trolleys but directed their wrath not against "the men who are obeying orders, but against the corporation by which they are controlled." Providence city councilman P. J. McCarthy claimed that crews "were afraid on every trip that they would kill somebody because the running time had been shortened." When the Union Railroad electrified its lines, ten minutes were shaved off forty-five-minute horsecar trips. Electric trolleys could complete nine trips in ten and one-half hours, compared to seven trips in twelve hours by horsepower. One motorman summarized the change in lifestyle and working conditions: "We never used to be in such a hurry because there was plenty of time and we could afford to wait a few seconds. People do not like the new schedules a bit." The carmen's union also mourned the passing of "the time when every railway man was known personally to every patron of the road." Gone were the days when horsecar drivers like Henry Olney woke passengers with a shrill whistle on early morning trips. Individual transit accommodation would eventually disappear as industrial life overwhelmed the nineteenth century's slower, agricultural pace.[3]

Horsecars, of course, had speeded life's tempo by replacing the personalized omnibus, whose operators, like a private hack, waited patiently for patrons. The Union Railroad eliminated one kind of old-fashioned courtesy by establishing trolley stops, marked by white poles a block apart. This policy facilitated service considerably by eliminating haphazard and indiscriminate boarding by riders along the route. Transit crews, not wanting to alienate faithful patrons, continued to pick up passengers anywhere, prompting management to suspend motormen who disobeyed the new policy. One veteran publicly lamented passing up "two little schoolmarms" who regularly took his car but who were not at a designated stop. Eventually, traction employees no longer used their acute peripheral vision to watch for stragglers and latecomers. A reporter who encouraged evening revelers to take a trolley home warned: "But be sure beforehand that your watch is all right, for the tides and electrics can wait for no man."[4]

Fewer trips also meant congested streetcars, a situation exacerbated by suburban trolleys that stopped for passengers inbound along city streets before the advent of express service a few years later. Although there had been sporadic complaints during the horsecar era, crowding began in earnest in the electric period despite larger vehicles. Trolleys with twenty-foot bodies replaced vintage horsecars, which measured fourteen or sixteen feet long in 1893. By the turn of the century the Union Railroad had bought coaches that measured over forty feet, weighed fifty tons, and reached speeds of forty miles per hour. These cars could seat forty-four and accommodate almost twice as many standees. These were indeed dramatic changes. Even the bloomers, the open summer cars that came in during horsecar times, expanded to fifteen benches instead of ten. In a popular move, management also voluntarily enclosed or vestibuled the entire fleet. Motormen no longer faced the elements unprotected.[5]

The Union Railroad hoped to curb labor expenses by reducing the number of trips and expanding streetcar capacity. Yet, nothing incensed passengers more than being stuffed into cars. Petitions, letters to the editor, and political outcries incessantly targeted this abuse. Standing patrons claimed they lurched back and forth in a game of human "shuttlecock." The *Providence Journal* concluded an investigation into overcrowding by admitting, "There is no question that scores of electrics in this city with the normal capacity of 40 or less are compelled to carry 'freights' of 70 or more." In one suburban town a transformed horsecar swelled to overcapacity every day with "a swaying mass, clinging to straps, to each other, to guard rails, and even hanging on with only one foot on the lower steps of the platforms." Occasionally, "boorish fellows" sexually harassed young women penned up in a jammed trolley.[6]

Such claustrophobic conditions created camaraderie among patrons. A Chalkstone Avenue trolley in Providence accommodated 102 passengers in a car designed to seat 28. A reporter overheard an embittered passenger speaking in a loud voice to share his misery with others: "That was a scorching letter [to the editor] but it hasn't made Manager Potter thin. You see him on the streets every day with the same old smile he wears, no matter what complaints are made against the company." Another indignant passenger described cars as "humanized pig pens" and moaned, "It is positively indecent the way we are forced to stand in front of the seated passengers." General Manager Albert Potter attempted to minimize problems, blaming human nature for riders' wanting to get on the first trolley available rather than wait for another. Every streetcar was in operation during rush hour, he admitted, but the company could not afford the capital investment to provide enough cars for unlimited peak-hour service and have such expensive equipment lay idle the rest of the day. He complained, "It's hard work to satisfy some of the kickers. They get an idea that the trolley incubus is tampering with their 'rights' and then every particle of reasonableness leaves their heads." As the Gilded Age passed into the Progressive era, commuters increasingly viewed mass transportation as part of the public domain. With every well-publicized legislative concession, citizens seemed more determined than ever to wring their own service adjustments and comfort from the carrier.[7]

One enterprising patron constructively turned streetcar frustration into bardic complaint:

> We were crowded on the 'lectric,
> Not a soul would care to speak;
> For thirty-three were on the car,
> Besides those in the seats.

> 'Tis a common thing in Providence
> To be packed in hard and fast,
> And to hear a big conductor shout:
> "Please let the lady pass."

So we huddled there in silence,
And the stoutest held his breath,
Fearing that to do otherwise
Might cause his neighbor's death.

And as thus we stood in misery,
Each one looking for his fare,
"Move up," the big conductor cried,
But we couldn't budge a hair.

Then spoke a maiden sweet and fair,
With hair in curly rings:
"Doesn't God control electric cars
As well as other things?"

Ah, no we said with heavy heart;
We fear from what we read
That Satan with the company
Has thus far quite a lead.[8]

The results of bigger trolleys, faster trips, and crowded cars were accidents. During horsecar days, most mishaps involved careless passengers, not collisions. In the last two full years of exclusive horsecar service, the Union Railroad reported a dozen minor injuries and no deaths. Smashups, derailments, and high-speed incidents, however, marked electric power and rivaled grim casualty statistics on steam railroads. The first year that trolleys replaced horsecars, the number of accidents climbed to 24, with 9 deaths. Towards the end of the 1890s, with increased suburban service and heavier cars, the numbers spiraled. In 1898 there were 48 accidents; two years later, 111 mishaps and 22 fatalities. In 1901 the Union Railroad and its subsidiaries experienced 140 accidents and 12 deaths. Nationally that year, 1,218 died, including 122 employees. Rhode Islanders were shocked at the local statistics.[9]

The first fatal trolley accident involving a pedestrian occurred in April 1894, when a five-year-old girl ran into the path of a streetcar. In September a seventy-year-old woman was hit by a trolley and died. In response to the carnage, Governor D. Russell Brown called for greater railway safety. A year later, three children, aged five, six, and seven, were killed in separate accidents within three weeks of each other. On June 10, 1900, a Rhode Island Suburban Railway car from Providence to Buttonwoods crashed head-on with another trolley. This, the most serious mass transportation accident in Rhode Island history,

Six passengers were killed in this rear-end trolley collision in June 1900. Popular outrage focused on unsafe operation practices established by corporate owners.

killed six passengers and seriously injured many others, including Lieutenant Governor Charles Kimball. One of the cars failed to wait at a turnout on the single-track line. "It is the desire of all motor-men to make time," explained the railroad commissioner, "and it has been a common practice with some of them when they reached a switch where they were to meet a car and it was not in sight, to proceed, hoping to get to the next switch, and to save time." [10]

On the day of the accident hundreds gathered at the Elmwood Avenue carbarn, home base for the destroyed cars, to await news. The local coroner originally announced a public inquest into the accident and then abruptly switched to a private investigation, prompting a flood of complaints that the Union Railroad was trying to orchestrate a cover-up. The coroner reversed his position and made the hearing public, as originally announced. Local interest was at a fever pitch. In downtown Providence thousands gathered to follow the affair by reading bulletins in the office windows of the *Providence Journal* building. Although General Manager Potter was described as completely shaken by the incident, the public referred to him as "Butcher Potter" after stories circulated that he entertained friends that day, unconcerned about the calamity. Only a week before the accident, the *Journal* carried a detailed article about critical operational problems on the line in question: "It is easy to understand, then, the indignation, disgust and animosity that prevails up and down the line."[11]

The coroner officially blamed the crew for the accident, but the press and the public accused management. The *Journal* cited railway parsimony: a one-track system instead of a safer two-track grid, a lack of air brakes on one car, and the absence of a signal system to warn of oncoming traffic. "The Rhode Island Suburban Railway Co. is a rich and prosperous corporation and can well afford whatever expenditures are necessary for public convenience and safety." During the inquest Rhode Islanders learned that a rookie employee had worked the route, where trolleys barreled along at forty miles per hour over private rights-of-way ungoverned by local speed limits. A few weeks after the fatal mishap, another set of streetcars barely missed colliding at the same spot. Later in the summer an East Providence car derailed with thirty passengers aboard, and every doctor in the city was summoned to assist the injured. Those not requiring medical help boarded another car and had to pay an additional fare—another example of insensitivity by the railway syndicate.[12]

Union Railroad accidents inflamed public opinion and influenced juries in liability suits against the carrier. Irish Catholic attorneys, with close ties to the Democratic Party, represented legions of clients, including disabled traction employees. After the famous Buttonwoods crash, settlement estimates ranged from $100,000 to $1,000,000. The *Journal* reported that swarms of lawyers were seeking injured clients. In another accident, Union Railroad agents were described as visiting victims to see about "healing their ailments with coin of the realm." Management employed a team of skilled attorneys, detectives, and clerks to defeat lawsuits through legal technicalities before sympathetic, machine-appointed judges. Juries, however, remained hostile, and in 1902 the Union Railroad paid $165,000 in settlements and another $212,000 in legal fees.[13]

General Manager Potter confided to a reporter, "You'd be surprised to know how many men sue for $10,000 whose lawyers would be glad enough to settle for $100." One motorman, unsympathetic to management *or* plaintiffs, claimed, "After a collision suit has been decided by a jury in favor of the plaintiff, it is astonishing how the teamsters will get in the way of a trolley car. . . . When on the other hand the jury finds for the railroad company, the drivers fight shy of the electric as if it was the Evil One." The public obviously enjoyed seeing the carrier punished in court but also feared spectacular and disabling accidents. Such sentiment soon buttressed union calls for a shorter, safer workday. State representative Lucius Garvin used the Buttonwoods accident to introduce a ten-hour law, and a reform newspaper claimed that "motormen are exhausted and sleepy from overwork." Motormen especially faced the added stress of pranksters who littered tracks with objects and occasionally dummies to frighten operators into thinking they had hit someone. Crews routinely switched positions, risking suspensions, to avoid fatigue.[14]

Concerns for safety coalesced in a demand for trolley fenders to minimize pedestrian fatalities. Providence's city clerk wrote to Nelson Aldrich advocating these safety improvements. At first, the Union Railroad seemed ready to make the investment: "This company is not only willing but anxious to adopt any safety fender or devices which will best tend to prevent injury to life and limb." Management procrastinated, testing different designs and visiting other systems to inspect bumper guards, as they had stalled when inspecting cable systems several years earlier. A letter to the editor accused the city of "a Rip Van Winkle sleep" on the matter. Even the GOP-appointed railroad commissioner alleged that the carrier had "done nothing in the way of equipping its cars with any fender."[15]

The safety issue came to a head when the general manager of the Consolidated Car Fender Company, in Providence, sent a stinging missive to the *Providence Journal*. He claimed, "The Union Railroad Co. is not willing to go to the expense of equipping its cars with a good fender, and it hesitates in assuming the responsibility of using a poor one." The locally produced bumper, according to the writer, was employed on four thousand cars in twenty-six states but cost sixty to ninety-five dollars a piece, compared to a cheap ten-dollar version the syndicate seemed to favor. In conclusion, he wrote, "The sad feature in the whole matter is that the killing will go on until something is done to influence the Union Railroad Company to equip its cars with a life-saving device." A few days later another pedestrian died in a trolley mishap, the third deadly accident in three months. Potter displayed his penchant for aggravating public relations when he said, "Personally, I believe that a competent motorman is preferable to any fender." Three years after admitting the need, the Union Railroad finally signed a contract for quality equipment. Potter could not resist one last outburst: "Making a car safe for a man on the track is something like lessening the destructive power of a cannon ball. . . . The persons killed as a rule were careless about crossing the track." He was correct, but the railway's arrogant attitude would create more animosity as the temper of the Progressive era encouraged public response to matters concerning local utilities.[16]

The issue of cold streetcars also incensed passengers. The Union Railroad ordered heating equipment for all trolleys in 1894 at a cost of seventy dollars a unit. Passengers complained that the company refused to turn them on because it was not yet chilly enough. Suburban cars were "positively frigid" on occasion, and a newspaper suggested putting straw on the floor as in omnibus and horsecar days. The carrier claimed that it often expended all available electricity to power its vehicles, leaving cars unheated. Warming the trolleys apparently took as much power as running them, and the Union Railroad wanted to curtail expenditures regardless of any public outcry.[17]

In its drive toward cost-cutting and rationalization of the streetcar system, management agitated the public in other ways. The Union Railroad eliminated the practice of color-coding cars to specific routes. Instead, all trolleys were painted the same, requiring patrons "to perform a steeplechase around the car" to read a destination sign bleached in yellow. Crosstown lines that had required only one fare and no transferring were now separated, necessitating two payments and two cars. East Siders complained that instead of a direct trip to Roger Williams Park, the new policy forced them to disembark downtown and pay another nickel on the Elmwood Avenue trolley. The company also stopped sponsoring free band concerts at Roger Williams Park, although management contributed to the event after the city agreed to host the popular concerts.[18]

In the area of fare collection, a priority and concern since Daniel Longstreet's innovations, the company instituted a new system. The Union Railroad purchased mechanical registers for the whole fleet, eliminating costly leasing for the old equipment. Conductors now twisted a brass rod that ran the length of the car, which rang a bell and tallied fares on a public dial inside the vehicle. A needle recorded each payment like the hand of a clock for all to see. Management expected the watchful eyes of riders to serve as an inexpensive deterrent to stealing. Ironically, disaffected passengers used the new system to measure Union Railroad wealth: "That dial impudently stares them in the face. Its hands tell a very interesting tale." Some passengers created tension between conductors and themselves when they avoided paying fares in a crowded car by citing the company's wealth and record of dishonesty. In some ways conductors were happy to abandon the bulky and awkward hand registers that so impugned their integrity, but allegations of impropriety persisted in the industry. In 1896 the company claimed that it fired fifty employees a year for stealing. In a work force of approximately 350 conductors, a whopping 15 percent would be terminated yearly, a figure out of line with the company's publicly avowed satisfaction with its employees.[19]

The Union Railroad augmented the new fare system by employing "spotters" to ride trolleys and secretly check collections. John T. Winterich, a Brown

University student who worked for the company during busy summer seasons and later became managing editor of the *Saturday Review of Literature,* recalled, "I would report for my equipment at the carbarn office and be told: 'On such-and-such a trip last Thursday you registered thirty-seven fares. Should have been thirty-eight. Watch it.' A sucker had turned me in. No proof whatever that the sucker was right. It was my word against his. Or hers." The company also hired inspectors to enforce daily operating rules. When Winterich improperly threw a signal light, an official was watching. "Out of the rushes at the side of the road stepped a uniform figure. It was almost as if he had been hiding there, or perhaps he had crossed the marsh by a path I had not noticed, and which the rushes concealed." He was suspended for a day.[20]

Worker turnover became endemic locally and nationally during the electric era, especially as the country recovered from the recent 1893 depression. Traction companies downplayed the skills of motormen and conductors to depress wages. Emerson Schmidt, an authority on labor-management relations in the transit industry, claimed that the increasingly thick rule books for street railway crews belied the unskilled characterization of the work. A former executive of the Philadelphia Rapid Transit Company confessed that one-third of the work force left electric railway service annually: "The conditions of employment, the hours of labor, constant friction with the public, and in short, the annoyance of platform duty appear to make it an undesirable employment from the viewpoint of the workingman." Even the national carmen's union, in a candid admission, lamented that "most men enter the occupation to tide over a period of idleness, without any idea of making it permanent. Few follow the vocation through choice." With a rebounding economy later in the decade, the legions of railway candidates who once buttonholed general manager Potter around his office sought employment in less stressful occupations.[21]

A two-tier wage system, unrelenting tension, incessant traffic, and petty harassment further tarnished railway employment and discouraged the quality applicants on which the Union Railroad had prided itself. The company publicly complained of its inability to secure superior workers. A conductor injured in a serious collision even sued the carrier for $16,000, claiming management hired an unskilled motorman to run the car. Later, in a well-publicized contract arbitration after unionization, the company asserted that the occupation called "for something less than ordinary skill, knowledge, and attendance." The union countered by pointing out that only 1,257 of 6,920 employees hired in a ten-year period still worked for the carrier "because the allurement and fascination disappeared or because the company decided they were not good railway men." The status days of horsecar employment had frayed with electric current, although the freedom of movement and outside work still appealed to many.[22]

Passengers noticed that crews were not as accommodating because of tightened rules and discipline. One patron complained, "Conductors and motormen on the Elmwood cars that run on the East Side appear to be afflicted with deafness and blindness while passing the stores. . . . They are not paid to look into space, where they can see nothing indicating [a] desire to pay a nickel for a ride." A male customer grumbled that a conductor refused to let him enter the trolley with his dog, although women were allowed that privilege. The man attacked the company's discriminatory policy but admitted that the employee politely "showed me the rules." However, during the same period another regular rider lectured a newspaper reporter: "The papers are only too willing, it seems to me, to recount the shortcomings of the conductors and motormen, and when they have the opportunity to give praise to whom praise is due, I think they ought to do so." The elderly woman continued: "I have ridden a great deal in the electrics of late, and in nearly every instance the conductor, on my leaving the car, has reached forward for my umbrella and opened it."[23]

Employees of the Union Railroad, whether horsecar veterans or novice crew members, continued to cherish friendly interaction with passengers despite tighter regulations and schedules that discouraged the personal greeting and unhurried courtesy of earlier years. Conductors, especially, still made friends with a pleasantry or joke, which eased the burden of long workdays. The number of railway workers who owned their own homes on the eve of the 1902 strike was still an impressive 70 percent, virtually the same as a decade earlier, despite the lower wages for new crews. Although rookie motormen and conductors continued to live close to carbarns, there was no guarantee of operating a vehicle in one's own neighborhood and therefore less community interaction. When the new crop of electric employees retired in the 1940s and 1950s, local newspapers honored them with complimentary stories, similar in tone to those about the horse carmen, indicating an unbroken tradition of courteous local service.[24]

Crews apparently avoided taking frustrations out on customers and instead blamed management policies, as did passengers, for the new predicaments of work life. Rationalization, deteriorating conditions, and dangerous road situations triggered the new union drive among motormen and conductors, although the wage disparity between horsecar veterans and rookie crews helped mobilize newcomers more than anything else. During the horsecar era no transit workers ever died in vehicular accidents. In the electric period several motormen perished in crashes, and several conductors were mortally struck by poles and trees as they collected fares on open cars on tracks constructed too close to impediments. Pop Spear narrowly escaped death when another trolley rear-ended his own vehicle. As the stress and strain of electric velocity took its toll, traction crews—both young and old—saw salvation in the ten-hour work-day. Passengers, whose own safety was also at stake, endorsed shorter shifts as a way to limit fatigue. The personal relationships between crews and riders was now graduating into an informal political coalition to control the details of streetcar travel.[25]

The reemerging union spirit was nurtured and spread at baseball games between teams from different carbarns. Losers usually paid for meals and drinks, during which shoptalk predominated. At times carmen played other working-class teams, further solidifying community support networks. The latest union drive went public in June 1901 when the *Providence Journal* trumpeted organization in a front-page story. Motormen and conductors had been meeting quietly for over a year to prevent any preemptive action by the Union Railroad. Some four hundred workers attended the inaugural gathering at two in the morning; three hundred paid initiation fees. Members elected strong-willed officers "despite any methods which might be used to intimidate them."[26]

The Union Railroad, fearing a supercharged, inhospitable public in the event labor troubles erupted, resurrected the old mutual benefit association, which the company had previously neglected or abandoned several times after union talk subsided. This time management also presented an eye-catching pension and life insurance plan. Hundreds of employees listened to a New York actuary explain the novel pension system until three in the morning. The retirement age was set at seventy. The Union Railroad indeed offered a liberal policy to employees—one of the first and best in the country—and paid 60 percent of the plan's cost. Depending on salaries, workers contributed between ten and twenty cents per week for life insurance that paid $500 to $1,000; an annual pension that ranged between $273 and $573.30; and, finally, a weekly sick benefit that totaled $4 to $8.[27]

The American Street Railway Association hailed the plan as a great bargain for traction employees: "the price of two or three beers." The system took effect in November, and three elderly employees took advantage of it. One retiree, Benjamin West, a Civil War veteran and former hackman, had just turned eighty and was "crippled with rheumatism" from a life on the front end of open cars. John Place, "a very feeble old man," had served as a tinsmith in the company repair shops until age seventy-three. W. E. Lord, the third pensioner, had been an operator for thirty-five years and would draw an eleven-dollar-a-week pension, more than half his take-home salary. The *Providence Journal* lauded the retirees in a prominent article featuring their photographs. "They brought their passengers home to supper, the fire and the evening paper, and jingled on into the face of the storm."[28]

Despite the progressive character of the plan and its public relations windfall, management feared to let the program stand on its own merits. The syndicate could not resist twisting the arrangement into a strategy that would undermine the nascent union drive. The Union Railroad chose the president of the new Amalgamated local, George Appleby, as a pension trustee. The carmen brought charges against him, and he subsequently resigned at a union meeting presided over by the carmen's national president, William D. Mahon. Management's brazen act undoubtedly demoralized the division's members and exposed the insurance program as a wedge between young and old employees, designed to weaken internal labor solidarity. However, most crews probably understood the connection between union activity and the company's renewed interest in assisting the work force.[29]

The carmen maneuvered around this setback, elected a new president, John Arno, and held a well-attended "First Grand Concert and Ball" to raise funds for its own benefit association. The group also forged links to other Rhode Island unions. Motormen and conductors marched in a 1901 Labor Day parade for the first time. Local union figures often addressed railway meetings. The division's business agent was elected secretary of the Rhode Island Central Trades and Labor Union. The outreach to the rest of organized labor was an admission that carmen would no longer be automatically protected simply because of their admired status. In this larger protective framework, crews rallied to the ten-hour cause as Lucius Garvin introduced legislation for the fourth consecutive year. More motormen and conductors than usual packed a committee hearing on the bill. They may have felt emboldened by the unstinting support of Pawtucket mayor and union sympathizer, John Fitzgerald, now one of the state's most influential and powerful Democrats, who testified for shorter hours again. He explained how the Union Railroad, which recently had purchased the Interstate Company road in nearby Massachusetts, had to comply with a Bay State law limiting a railway workday to ten hours on that line. The Pawtucket Street Railway, also a subsidiary, assigned employees to thirteen-hour shifts despite earlier management promises to ameliorate the problem. Overworked Pawtucket employees often talked union with ten-hour Massachusetts carmen at the intersection of state-line routes.[30]

Five hundred carmen assembled at the Labor Temple in Providence to

The labor spirit was often shared at baseball games between motormen and conductors. Here, nonunion players from Providence's Broad Street carbarn mingle with union crews from Brockton, Massachusetts.

hear from a union committee that had met with General Manager Potter. Negotiators had discussed a ten-hour day, a standard $2.25 daily wage, a union shop, and binding arbitration. "There are numerous other complaints," the *Providence Journal* reported, "of a nature best understood by the employees and which would probably not be understood by the public." Members seemed pleased at the cordial treatment accorded their representatives. Potter had supplied chartered trolleys for the 1-A.M. meeting and agreed to bring their demands before the company's directors. Division 200 also hired the former mayor of Pawtucket, Republican Henry Tiepke, to lobby the general assembly and influence GOP machine leaders. The union presented a petition for a ten-hour day signed by almost seven hundred employees. At the senate judiciary committee, advocates argued that a shorter day would prevent accidents and enrich a carman's family life. The Union Railroad claimed that such a bill would force it to hire more employees and cut daily wages for existing workers.[31]

Nationally, the American Street Railway Association seemingly endorsed a shorter work week: "Better service and more alert attention to business can be secured by making it convenient or compulsory for the men to take regular days of rest rather than have them taking days off at irregular times." William Mahon, leader of the Amalgamated, injected leisure time into a larger public debate in a speech to one of the union's local women's auxiliaries: "It is a struggle for the fireside, a struggle in the interests of wife and children; the world will never be free, man will never be civilized, until the fireside is made sacred."[32]

While the legislative debate over the ten-hour day continued, the Union Railroad announced in late March that it would not recognize the union or accept its contract proposal. Potter, in a chilly change of attitude, fumed, "Not only is it proposed to submit all differences between the company and its employees to arbitration, but by the terms of the agreement, the operation of the road is practically taken out of the hands of the company and placed in the hands of the association." He further asserted that "an outside and irresponsible authority" would force the syndicate, under terms of a standard Amalgamated contract, to dismiss many old-timers who might refuse to join a union. The *Providence News* suggested that the United Traction and Electric Company, on reflection, feared that a union beachhead in Rhode Island might spread to its other properties, especially the sprawling Philadelphia system, where labor-management relations were always volatile.[33]

Privately, the company promised to honor the ten-hour law, if it passed, and agreed to consider a wage increase. The Union Railroad also consented to meet union negotiators again, interpreted by some members as de facto recognition of the union. In return, Division 200 pledged to act conservatively so as not to jeopardize public support. At one of the union meetings, "the mere mention of the word 'strike' was met with derision." The company, meanwhile, received a "flood of letters" from strikebreaking firms seeking employment in case of a shutdown. Potter claimed that job applicants once again jammed his new office in Marsden Perry's Union Trust Bank building after the Union Railroad took its hard line against labor demands.[34]

In April the state legislature, under the thumb of Boss Brayton, surprisingly passed the ten-hour railway bill and a fifty-eight-hour workweek for women and children. Republicans, who usually opposed these reforms, introduced their own versions of Democratic bills "to catch the labor vote at the next general assembly." Carmen were jubilant. The same session also authorized free transfer tickets after years of contentious debate. These concessions did not signal a liberalized policy toward or concern for consumers, despite their increasing hostility to the Union Railroad. Rather, these statutes were a ploy to defuse public anger over the passage of an act to join the Rhode Island Company, an amalgamation of the Union Railroad, Narragansett Electric Company, and Providence Gas into one corporate body. Privately, Brayton apologized to Aldrich for having to link popular issues to corporate ones: "I could not resist the passage of the ten-hour bill, and get the other things through that were wanted by your people the most." The senator understood. He had been counseled by Rhode Island GOP congressman Adin Capron that the 1902 election might be decided by the "class of working men upon whom so much depends in this campaign."[35]

Despite labor reforms and transfer tickets, opponents inside and outside the general assembly hammered away at the act to incorporate the Rhode Island Company. Hostile witnesses testified against further corporate empowerment. Democrats tried to shackle the bill with obstructive amendments, arguing for increased state taxes, minority stockholder rights, and stricter leasing agreements. Lucius Garvin led the attack, citing out-of-state control. Although the legislation passed the house forty-two to fourteen and the senate twenty-five to ten, Republicans tacked on several changes to assuage public opinion and placate worried utility stockholders. The assembly imposed a gross tax of 1 percent on the new entity, to increase to 2 percent over four years, and allowed minority stockholders a court appeal. The *Springfield Republican*, a reformist newspaper in neighboring Massachusetts, declared: "The syndication of the state of Rhode Island has finally been perfected, and its sale to monopoly for private profit is complete."[36]

First-term Republican senator Robert Treat of Warwick, risking the wrath of Brayton and Aldrich, condemned the merger: "This act I consider a prostitution of the rights of the people of the State, and I do not believe this General Assembly has the right to give to any corporation its power." Treat was not nominated for reelection by the party. The *Providence Journal*, about to undergo a secret takeover attempt by Nelson Aldrich, continued its retreat from any confrontation with the carrier. It endorsed the utility merger plan, citing tax revenues and better facilities: "There is no danger that the community will suffer from any deterioration in the quality of the service rendered it."[37]

Management at the Union Railroad, Narragansett Electric Company, and Providence Gas took remedial action to pacify dissident stockholders. Although stock prices soared for these three major utilities in anticipation of consolidation, officials at each concern guaranteed rate returns and offered additional stock in the parent company if the merger was consummated. The newly formed Rhode Island Company became part of the United Gas and Improvement Company, another holding company, with a stable of over three hundred other utilities scattered throughout the United States. Marsden Perry would manage the local enterprise. Street railway combinations mimicked the initial mergers between the nation's railroads a decade earlier.[38]

Regardless of the new corporate structure, members of Division 200 rejoiced at passage of the ten-hour law and viewed management's refusal to recognize the labor body as necessary public posturing. However, during the ten-hour debate the Union Railroad fired the Amalgamated's vice president because of a series of minor accidents and passenger altercations. The union muted its protest. Then management suspended John Arno, the union's new president. Arno, a motorman, had an accident with a wagon that broke a wheel and threw the other driver from his seat. After a two-day investigation by the company's claim adjustor, former city clerk Henry Joslin, the Union Railroad fired the union president despite evidence the trolley in question had a history of brake problems. The local division sarcastically claimed that the carrier was trying to decapitate the union: "The first president is gone. The vice president is gone. Get rid of Arno, and you will weed out the leaders."[39]

In a publicly released letter, Arno stated that he never received a reprimand during a five-year career as a motorman and cited several instances of outstanding service that reflected the traditional attitudes of horsecar workers a generation earlier: "I performed my duties with as much interest and promptitude as if I owned the road and operated it for my own personal interests." He contended the company fired him in retaliation for passage of the ten-hour law just four days before his suspension. "I still retain the respect and confidence of my fellow workmen," he continued, "which is much dearer to me than any position that I ever held with the traction or any other company." Division 200 then hired their dismissed president on a full-time basis at his motorman's salary. The local issued an ominous warning: "While the Association is not looking for trouble, unless the traction company assumes a different attitude toward the union's officers and members it will sooner or later be forced to take some radical action to adjust existing differences." With a majority of the work force signed to the union, the carmen voted to hold the charter open until June 10, after which time new members would have to pay three dollars rather than a one-dollar initiation fee.[40]

As the two sides hardened, the stakes became higher. The first decade of electric streetcar service had increased the number of routes, miles traveled, and passengers significantly (see Table 6.1). Nationally, the industry employed

Table 6.1. The Rhode Island Railway Industry's Transformation from Horse-power to Electricity, 1892–1902

	1892	1902
Total assets	$2.5 million	$9.4 million
Salaries	$483,000	$747,000
Passengers	18.6 million	44.6 million
Electric cars	27	462
Horsecars	302	0
Miles of main track	45	125
Employees	1,000	1,581
Taxes	$10,170	$120,000

140,000, owned 22,000 miles of track, and carried almost five billion riders in 1902, seven times the passenger traffic on the steam railroads that year.[41]

As mass transit evolved into public transportation, foes of the Union Railroad and the GOP machine behind it complained about riding conditions. The shrill chorus was joined by upset traction workers with their own set of grievances. That standoff might have festered without resolution, but the appearance of a galvanizing personality would soon bring the battle to fruition after ten years of hostility and offer the public an opportunity to recapture lost prerogatives.

I BELIEVE IN USING HEROIC METHODS

Governors may come and go, but General Charles R. Brayton never loosens his grip on the trolley.

Springfield Republican, March 1900

I believe in using heroic methods with these companies, who feel that they are so strongly entrenched behind the unjust privileges granted them by past servile Legislatures and contracts made by negligent City Councils, that they can defy the people and refuse them their just rights.

John J. Fitzgerald, reform mayor of Pawtucket, December 1900

There is a cohesion of organization and "community interest" that is of a strength and co-operative nature far exceeding any that has ever before existed in this city [Pawtucket] and vicinity. The disposition of every labor organization to assist in any way possible the welfare of its fellow organizations, is so marked as to deserve more than passing notice.

Providence Journal, May 1902

As the dawn of a new century rose over an integrated streetcar system that cobwebbed the state, the heyday of the trolley was still in the future. Despite this impressive transportation grid, Rhode Islanders continued to be subjected to disagreeable traction contracts and company misconduct. The Union Railroad, in its drive to maintain a monopoly, seemingly usurped the streets and dictated riding conditions. As restiveness grasped the state in the waning years of the nineteenth century, political scandals and injustices upset the community's sense of fair play. The dramatic controversy over the ten-hour workday, unionization, and incorporation of the Rhode Island Company took place within this corrupt framework. Although the GOP addressed these concerns with halfhearted reforms, the festering street railway situation would trigger a major political uprising.

Charles Boss Brayton carried the incubus to a new generation of "machine" operatives, and Sen. Nelson W. Aldrich and Marsden Perry brought the legacy of political debasement into the realm of twentieth-century finance capitalism. Brayton was not a one-dimensional messenger between eras, but a dynamic emissary with imaginative plans to strengthen GOP power. The old ring had institutionalized a nearly impregnable system of minority control. David Graham Phillips, an incisive muckraker, wrote, "The Aldrich machine controls the legislature, the election boards, the courts—the entire machinery of the 'republican form of government.'"[1]

A majority of the state's thirty-eight cities and towns, sometimes representing less than 10 percent of the population, controlled the general assembly through a vetolike lock on the powerful senate. A local political science professor characterized the state's governing body as "the most undemocratic and most unrepublican legislative organization in the United States." Each municipal entity, regardless of size, wealth, or population, elected only one senator. This rotten-borough system placed major cities on the same senatorial level as tiny hill towns in rural sections of the state. Furthermore, even in the house of representatives, Providence was limited to a maximum of twelve of the seventy-two seats. The capital city reached that plateau in 1850 and remained there through the rest of the century, despite a population that swelled from 41,000 to more than 175,000. The capital city, with a preponderance of the state's wealth and population nestled within its borders, was partially disenfranchised, while the Union Railroad was perpetually enfranchised.[2]

When the state's Irish Catholics raised large families of voting-age, native-born Americans, Brayton backed the constitutional Bourn Amendment in 1888 to end voting restrictions for naturalized and poor citizens. The Republican Party hoped to offset the growing influence of Irish Democrats by an about-face championing of the voting rights of immigrants and by accentuating cultural and religious tensions between the Irish and newcomers, especially French Canadians. Although the GOP lifted the real estate requirement for gubernatorial and mayoral races through the Bourn Amendment, it substituted property qualifications for city council elections, in which financial matters, favors, and patronage were determined. This crafty maneuver prevented working-class and ethnically based control over local municipalities; an occasional Democratic mayor or figurehead was the price Republicans had to pay for continued dominance. The malapportioned general assembly, ruled by rural towns through a complicated and endemic system of voter bribery, similarly ensured virtual Yankee dominance.[3]

The boss crowned his dictatorial achievements with a law that bore his name in 1901. The Brayton Act, anticipating an eventual Democratic victory at the gubernatorial level, stripped the chief executive of budgetary and appointive powers and vested them in the ironclad Republican senate. As "Mr.

Inside," Brayton manipulated the daily chores of the machine; "Mr. Outside," Senator Aldrich, brought respectability and national political influence to bear in his home state; and, as the *Providence Journal* put it, the "inevitable" Marsden Perry, with a far-flung financial empire, masterminded large-scale financial machinations among a supportive Rhode Island business community. One local historian pinpointed the source of control: "As the power of the public service monopolies increased, Brayton's grip on the General Assembly tightened." This oligarchy and its successors ran the state nearly unmolested into the mid 1930s. Institutional gerrymandering outlasted by years the deaths of both Brayton and Aldrich.[4]

Edward Lowry, a reporter for the *New York Evening Post*, wrote a series of articles about political corruption in Rhode Island including a candid, blockbuster interview with Brayton. "As every one knows," the boss casually admitted, "I act for the Rhode Island Company and . . . have had connections, not permanent, with various companies desiring franchises, charters, and things of that sort from the Legislature." Although Brayton received a sizable $10,000-a-year retainer from the New York, New Haven, and Hartford Railroad, he did so with the proviso, according to Lowry's interview, that "the street-railway people are to have first call on his services." When the reporter asked Brayton if Marsden Perry took an active role in transit legislation, the Boss acted surprised: "Good Lord, why should he? Hasn't he got everything he wants? Hasn't the Street Railway Company got a perpetual franchise? Do you think they want the earth?"[5]

Another exposé, in the *Springfield Republican*, declared: "Governors may come and go, but General Charles R. Brayton never loosens his grip on the trolley." Lowry named fourteen purchasable small towns in his *New York Post* articles. He also singled out twenty others that possessed a political influence disproportionate to the size of the population. The nation marveled at the state's backwater political system, while local citizens, especially a sensitive middle class, recoiled at the negative publicity and impudent confessions of the Boss. Lincoln Steffens claimed that Rhode Islanders were addicted to corruption as a way of life.[6]

There were reformers outside of Providence, but rural Rhode Islanders enjoyed unrepresentative power at the capital's expense and went along with the system. A crusade to democratically empower Providence, which contained 40 percent of the state's population and paid 47 percent of all taxes, meant weakening the influence of rotten boroughs. Yet the capital city had only 16 percent of the state representatives and 3 percent of the state senators. Another impediment to reform centered on mass transit itself. As a hub of trolley service, downtown suffered from what one writer described as "municipal appendicitis": lines of streetcars bound for innumerable destinations clogged thoroughfares. Suburban villages, on the other hand, petitioned the Union Railroad for a single lifeline. Local politicians often delivered these requests personally to transit management. Residents probably feared that any show of independence from the machine might jeopardize proposed trolley routes.[7]

Near century's end, a reform leader finally emerged who strategically exploited the railway question within the political framework and used his political power base to reshape the equation of street control, not unlike mayors Hazen Pingree in Detroit and Tom Johnson in Cleveland. John J. Fitzgerald was born in 1871 in the mill city of Pawtucket, birthplace of the American industrial revolution. He attended local public schools and was one of the first Irish Catholics to graduate from Brown University. He received a law degree from Georgetown University a few years later. Fitzgerald joined the Rhode Island Bar Association and opened his own practice. He also represented Pawtucket in the house of representatives, where he actively opposed the Union Railroad and championed free transfer tickets and the ten-hour day. James J. Higgins, Fitzgerald's law partner, attended the same schools and was the other rebel representative from Pawtucket. He later succeeded Fitzgerald as mayor of Pawtucket and became the state's first Irish Catholic governor.[8]

At the time Pawtucket was a spindle city, whose manufacturing wealth and employment came from a century of cotton production. Like Providence, it hosted a large immigrant population of English, Irish, and French Canadians, with sizable pockets of Portuguese, Italians, and Syrians arriving after the turn of the century. Unpropertied voters could participate in mayoral and gubernatorial elections, but not in those for council seats, where financial power was vested. In 1890 the city celebrated the Cotton Centennial and its industrial legacy. With an area of nine square miles, Pawtucket was only half the size of neighboring Providence and had a population of 32,000, compared to the capital city's 145,000. But because of its manufacturing importance, it was a key player in the Rhode Island political scene.[9]

After finishing his first legislative term, Fitzgerald ran for mayor of Pawtucket in 1899. The twenty-eight-year-old novice quickly displayed his societal prejudices: "I believe in justice to all classes, special favors to none. I believe and will act on the belief, that the man who handles the pick and shovel, or who toils in the factory, is entitled to as much consideration as the man who sits in an easy chair in his office and clips coupons from his bonds or draws the interest from his investments." He assailed the local and state railway system and promised to force the transfer issue. Fitzgerald's prolabor stance uncannily

Pawtucket's mayor, John Fitz-gerald, mobilized citizen discon-tent and turned it against the Republican ring and the Union Railroad. He provided unstint-ing assistance to striking car-men in 1902.

anticipated a union upsurge in this blue-collar town. Unlike some opportunists who superficially championed workers' rights in that era, Fitzgerald's commit-ment would be unswerving. His opponent, Henry Tiepke, was the Republican incumbent. Tiepke was commissioner of industrial statistics, compiler of the state census, and a rising star in the GOP. As evidenced by his support for the carmen in their legislative battle for the ten-hour day, Tiepke was not insensi-tive to the changing demographic and electoral patterns in the state. He fit the Roosevelt model of the party rather than the Rhode Island brand and was a formidable officeholder.[10]

On November 7, 1899, Pawtucket voters gave Fitzgerald a plurality of 395 votes over the popular Tiepke, another urban casualty of the Bourn Amendment, which, a decade earlier, had extended the ballot to unpropertied voters in mayoral contests. A new era began in Rhode Island politics as Irish Catholic voters began the political ascendancy that Brayton, Aldrich, and the GOP machine had long feared. In his inaugural address Fitzgerald reiterated proworker sentiment and antirailway animus. The mayor also testified before the house of representatives in favor of the ten-hour law for railway workers, introduced by Lucius Garvin and endorsed by the state Democratic committee, which hoped to attract propertied railway employees to the party. He spoke to six hundred union members in Providence: "You must unite and present a solid front, and by force of numbers, demand from the government you create, your rights." In Pawtucket, he clashed with both Democrats and Republicans on the city council over appointments, patronage, and voting lists. Fitzgerald also set a record for vetoes, including one that blocked the city from constructing a road for a local corporation at public expense.[11]

In May 1900 Fitzgerald commanded state attention when he reassigned a police lieutenant from strike duty at the Lorraine Manufacturing Company after picketers complained about the officer's unfriendly behavior. The Republican board of aldermen countermanded the mayor and ordered the Pawtucket police chief to reinstate the lieutenant to his original assignment after company officials protested. Fitzgerald then suspended the chief for disobeying his orders. The textile company called on Hunter C. White, high sheriff of Providence County, to furnish deputies to escort scabs. White provided immediate protection for "property or to persons engaged or desiring to engage in their lawful occupations." A graduate of the United States Naval Academy, he was a textile manager in Providence and had held the appointed position of sheriff since 1891. White was also chairman of the Providence Republican Party. Charles Boss Brayton worked directly out of White's statehouse office. The sheriff was widely considered to be Brayton's lackey and a key individual in the ring's power structure because of the intimidating power of his position.[12]

The *Providence Journal* sensed trouble in Pawtucket. The newspaper endorsed a threat by the general assembly to deprive Fitzgerald of "every vestige and shred of authority and control over the police department, and in their action they will probably be supported by the overwhelming sentiment of the entire State." The conservative editors believed that Fitzgerald's support of the picket line jeopardized industrial law and order. The mayor answered the *Journal* in a balanced letter revealing that the alderman who requested police protection was an employee of Lorraine Mills. Fitzgerald defended the strikers as "an orderly body of men and women" and felt they deserved "great credit for the peaceful and law-abiding manner in which they have conducted the matter so far." He concluded: "All attempts to stir up trouble and cause them to lose the respect and sympathy of the public will not be countenanced or abetted by the Mayor." The legislature retaliated by stripping Rhode Island mayors of police powers and empowering aldermanic bodies with that authority. Not coincidentally, most mayors in the state were Democrats, chosen by a broad electorate. City councils, elected by a disproportionally small number of voters, remained heavily Republican and more powerful than the chief executive.[13]

Fitzgerald staged a rally to protest the assembly's action divesting mayors of police powers. Referring to rotten-borough power in the legislature, he declared that small suburban districts in the state would not dictate how to run the city of Pawtucket. Two thousand supporters, "frequently interrupted with shouts of approval and vociferous cheering," denounced "political leeches" at the general assembly. The crowd, by formal resolution, censured restrictive voting in city council elections. At the same time, Fitzgerald began a sustained attack against the Union Railroad over transfer tickets and procured the backing of the Pawtucket Retail Merchants' Association.[14]

The Union Railroad had plans to modernize the narrow-gauge track system in Pawtucket to intersect with newer routes featuring standard gauge in northern Rhode Island and neighboring Massachusetts. Fitzgerald saw an opportunity to leverage a transfer system as well as break Pawtucket's railway isolation, caused by the incompatibility of its rails with those of other lines. Pawtucket residents debated the carrier's proposal to double-track Main Street and build a central transfer station like that proposed for Providence. However, laying two sets of rails on Main Street entailed a major construction project to widen the city's main thoroughfare.

The Union Railroad offered to contribute one-fifth of the purported $125,000 cost of the project, a portion generally unacceptable around town. The twenty-year franchise agreement between the city and railway provided a meager one-half-percent gross receipts tax the first five years and an additional one-half percent every succeeding five years to a maximum of 2 percent. Furthermore, there was no legal way to verify the carrier's figures. Agitation in Providence for higher franchise fees put pressure on Republican officials in Pawtucket to do the same thing. The city solicitor wrote privately to Nelson Aldrich: "The recent action of the Railroad Company with reference to the demands of the city of Providence has stirred up our Railroad Committee and they think that something should be done without unnecessary delay in the matter of adjusting the claims of the City of Pawtucket." The local Business Men's Association, an organization of wealthy manufacturers, voted to authorize only one track, perhaps fearing higher taxes. The Retail Merchants' Association, on the other hand, endorsed double-tracking to enhance local downtown commerce. As in Providence, a stalemate soon ensued.[15]

Fitzgerald continued to channel local anger against the company through a broad coalition of minority supporters. In Pawtucket he advocated an eight-hour day for city workers, local band concerts, and a public park. In his drive to unite diverse working-class constituencies, Fitzgerald addressed the town's small black population on Emancipation Day. He represented, *pro bono,* a Chinese laundry owner to secure voting privileges for him, and the mayor was the only non-Italian guest to speak at the organization of a Pawtucket branch of the Societa Di Mutuo Soccorso, a mutual aid group. He also belonged to several Irish organizations and fiercely supported Irish independence from England. Later in his career he brought that issue to the floor of several national Democratic conventions and allegedly harbored Eamon De Valera, revolutionary and future prime minister and president of Ireland, at his Pawtucket home. Fitzgerald championed the very ethnic groups often ridiculed in stories about trolley rides to ethnic neighborhoods.[16]

The mayor became president of the Blackstone Valley Democratic Club. In that capacity he and long-time reform representative Lucius Garvin held a series of "cart-tail meetings" in the area to denounce imperialism and industrial trusts in support of the presidential bid of Democrat William Jennings Bryan. He also assembled a militant youth group known as Fitzgerald's Guards, who turned out regularly to intimidate opponents. In November 1900 the mayor won reelection by over nine hundred votes, eclipsing all other mayoral majorities in Pawtucket history. He took votes on his political left and right, which the year before had gone, respectively, to the Socialist Labor and Republican parties. The Lorraine Mill episode and the assembly's police action motivated a large turnout. Although Republicans maintained a firm grip on the common council and the powerful aldermen's chambers, Fitzgerald mobilized a volatile public to pressure them to back his programs.[17]

After the election Fitzgerald began a concerted effort to confront the Union Railroad and bring the issue of transfer tickets to a resolution. A subcommittee of the Business Men's Association issued a report claiming that the city's railway contract indirectly provided for transfers. The agreement stated that "the fare for one person for one continuous passage from one point to any other point . . . within said city . . . shall be five cents." The mayor decided to test that interpretation and had two supporters ride a streetcar and refuse to pay a second fare when transferring from one line to another. He had two others repeat that action on the following night. Both sets of passengers were ejected. Fitzgerald then initiated a breach of contract and trespass action against the Union Railroad. Like the Lorraine Mills incident, the transfer suit and most of the mayor's other initiatives received prominent and suspicious coverage in the statewide columns of the *Providence Journal.*[18]

In a strongly worded letter to the city council, Fitzgerald threw down the gauntlet: "I believe in using heroic methods with these companies, who feel that they are so strongly entrenched behind the unjust privileges granted them by past servile Legislatures and contracts made by negligent City Councils, that they can defy the people and refuse them their just rights." The Pawtucket Street Railway paid only $900 for use of city streets, while gas and electric monopolies contributed a paltry $269. In Providence those three utilities paid $108,000, a tribute considered just as niggardly, but substantially larger by any formula. Despite these meager tax payments the council approved rail construction on four streets under old franchise provisions. Fitzgerald vetoed the ordinances. In a stinging inaugural address, the second-term mayor challenged the Pawtucket city council: "If . . . your only object in seeking the office, is to have people point you out as Alderman so and so or Councilman so and so, to pay some fellow a grudge you owe him, to have a grab at the political pie counter, either in the form of jobs for yourself or for friends, then it were better for the city that you had never been elected."[19]

Fitzgerald's characterization of the Republican council received an unusual second from an unlikely source during the same period. Lyman B. Goff, prominent Pawtucket businessman, GOP stalwart, and a director of the local street railway, wrote to Nelson Aldrich, "There are no competent men in the City Council. But being elected has given them the big head." Goff resigned from the Pawtucket Street Railway's board of directors because he was kept uninformed about decisions: "There has been any quantity of consultation however, but it has been with those who are working for what they can get out of the Railroad, without any regard for the interest of the city." Like most Republicans disenchanted by machine policies, Goff kept his feelings private and addressed Aldrich as if the senator was innocent of any complicity.[20]

The general assembly, in an embarrassing turnabout, surprisingly restored police powers to local mayors. Fitzgerald's convincing victory in Republican Pawtucket had galvanized support even among GOP members there. By rescinding the bill, the assembly gave Fitzgerald an even greater triumph. Pawtucket residents celebrated in a parade to the mayor's home for an "enthusiastic ovation." The *Providence Journal* predicted that Fitzgerald's forces would attempt a full takeover of the city council in the next election.[21]

The mayor meanwhile continued his efforts on behalf of organized labor. He testified before the state legislature once again on behalf of a shorter workday for motormen and conductors, noting that most railway employees feared to speak publicly on the subject. In the previous session fifty-seven Pawtucket carmen had supported ten-hour legislation. They distributed a "round robin" petition, signed circularly to prevent detection of the instigators. Officials of the Pawtucket Street Railway, a subsidiary of the Union Railroad, had temporarily reduced hours to between ten and eleven. Despite this concession, local transit employees had joined Division 200 of the Amalgamated with assurances of legal assistance from the mayor.[22]

When Fitzgerald spoke to members of the carmen's union who attended a "smoker" at the Providence Labor Temple, he placed their struggle in the larger framework of Rhode Island political reform: "The railroad company that you work for can go up to this State House . . . and can dictate to the Legislature just what laws shall be passed." Dr. John A. McLaughlin, a Providence veterinarian and close associate to peripatetic reformer Lucius Garvin, told union members that when the assembly surrendered public highways to the Union Railroad, "it gave you away also." Garvin and other speakers emphasized the need for leisure time to ensure good citizenship and a quality family life. The careers of John Fitzgerald, Lucius Garvin, and members of the carmen's union were about to be inextricably linked.[23]

John Fitzgerald and workers at the Union Railroad Company warily eyed management as the syndicate prepared to create the Rhode Island Company. Tense labor relations existed elsewhere in the state that year. Demands for shorter hours, better working conditions, and union recognition came from the backbone of the local working class. Weavers spearheaded a nine-month strike in a tumultuous attempt to abolish the two-loom system throughout New England. Team drivers sought wage increases and union shop provisions during a sometimes violent month-long walkout. Brewery workers gained a nine-hour day after long negotiations marked by strike threats. Skilled journeymen in the construction trades shook the establishment with successful agitation for an eight-hour day. The commissioner of industrial statistics exclaimed in 1902: "Probably never before, with conditions so prosperous and work so abundant, has there been so intense a spirit of unrest among the wage earners."[24]

The bleak years after the 1893 depression gradually gave way to better times. Labor agitation, which historically has been dampened by economic downturn, was now fueled by returning prosperity. Rhode Island workers, like their counterparts elsewhere, clamored to raise their living standards. They joined unions in unprecedented numbers and became politically active. The *Journal* unenthusiastically reported "waves of trades unionism . . . sweeping over the city of Providence" as union membership in the capital city reached an all-time high of approximately fifteen thousand in 1902. That energy found political expression in the local Trades Union Economic League, fashioned after similar organizations elsewhere, especially in Hartford, Connecticut, which had just elected a labor leader as mayor. Property qualifications minimized the number of voters for city council and general assembly seats and curtailed political activity by labor, but trade unionists pushed ahead with an eye on the governor's office because registry voters could participate regardless of personal wealth.[25]

There was a tension between labor advocates and Democratic Party partisans in this new electoral impulse. Rather than collaborate, both sides seemed intent on capturing one another. League members complained of being "tails for the Democratic kite," while party officials envied the registration apparatus of the unions. Labor activists sent hundreds of new voters to statewide canvassing boards, establishing branches of the league in Providence, Pawtucket, Newport, and Woonsocket. Democrats likewise stepped up enrollment activities, offering free baseball tickets in Woonsocket and signing up the first Chinese American voter in Providence history. Venerable Episcopal bishop Thomas Clark endorsed voter registration as a balance to a growing American plutocracy in a widely reported pastoral letter read to parishioners throughout the state. Enrollment, according to official canvassers, was running three to four times the 1901 pace.[26]

Union representatives hoped to influence the Democratic platform by endorsing initiative and referendum. These popular constitutional devices were also embraced by Lucius Garvin as a way to sidestep the suffrage-abbreviation clause in the state constitution. Garvin also organized the Constitutional League to push these measures and pry open the political system through citizen mobilization. He thought conservative lawmakers might capitulate to an aroused electorate in this fashion. While there was an element of capitulation by the Brayton machine to emerging Progressive-era sensibilities, the GOP saw it more as a simple tradeoff to obtain the lucrative but pressure-packed incorporation of the Rhode Island Company.[27]

The labor juggernaut appeared so formidable at the time that ward politicians tried to join unions to influence the labor vote. In an effort to maintain independence, the Rhode Island Central Trades and Labor Union, predecessor to the state American Federation of Labor and parent to the league, refused to recognize the credentials of a local union delegate who was chairman of the Providence Democratic Party. Some labor leaders counseled against any political involvement, while left-wing activists pushed a socialist strategy. A letter to the Sunday *Journal* fearfully predicted a union takeover of Providence through registration and naturalization drives; other opponents derided the prospects of a working-class "hoodlum government." The *Journal* reported that the Economic League was making inroads among conservative, skilled Germans, Swedes, and English union members, who ordinarily voted Republican.

The carmen's union was actively involved in registering its own rank and file as part of this solidarity movement.[28]

Although the Democrats and the labor community harbored differences, both groups shared similar goals, at least in politically repressive Rhode Island. Neither side could afford to alienate the other and dilute their campaign against corporate rule. Two well-respected politicians forged a coalition of workers and Democratic partisans, more by action than design. For a generation Lucius Garvin had carried the workingmen's banner as an often lonely sentinel at the statehouse. John Fitzgerald, although a political newcomer, spoke boldly and achieved municipal reform in formerly Republican Pawtucket. Garvin was more the theorist, and Fitzgerald the implementer. Together they welded Democrats and trade unionists in common cause. In the fall of 1902 both stood for the Democratic nomination for governor atop a movement each had helped to fashion.

The legions of organized labor had experienced a resurgence in the Blackstone Valley, especially Pawtucket, about the same time John Fitzgerald became mayor in 1900. His sympathies did not create the labor renaissance, but his bold demeanor, genuine concern for the common person, and disdain of the state's restrictive political system imbued him with the spirit of the age. As mayor and lawyer, Fitzgerald offered workers a municipal base of operations and legal protection. Unions grew, according to a *Journal* correspondent, "spontaneously" as the cost of living rose dramatically in that period. "Not for 20 years or more has the labor movement in this city and State assumed such a numerical importance and cohesive strength as now." Union leaders no longer operated secretly but organized publicly.[29]

Fitzgerald won the admiration of labor when he backed strikers at the Lorraine Mill and later forced the legislature to return police power to urban mayors. He solidified blue-collar support by instituting the first eight-hour day in the state for city workers with no loss in pay. The symbolic reduction from a ten-hour day was not lost on the carmen. After the Republican-controlled city council passed the measure under strong public pressure, Fitzgerald ran into opposition from the new Democratic majority in the aldermen's chambers. Several questioned the wisdom of such an ordinance during austere times. On a tie vote, the mayor cast the deciding ballot: "Corporations which do not pay one-fiftieth of what they should for the privileges they enjoy," Fitzgerald argued, "can come before the City Council and get anything they want, whereas any measure in the interests of the people is met with the stand that the city cannot afford to make a change." The measure affected 208 laborers in the public works department and cost $65,000 a year to implement.[30]

Pawtucket became a union town. Between February and May at least eight nationals established local branches: teamsters, retail clerks, machinists, stationary engineers, farriers, barbers, bartenders, and textile workers. Many trades banded together into the Pawtucket Central Labor Union, a confederated city body designed to enhance local, grassroots activism. Workers in older, more established organizations like the typographers and cigar-makers guided the effort. Craft associations also sent delegates and formed the separate Building Trades Council to address construction issues and the eight-hour day. The Pawtucket Central Labor Union grew to represent four thousand members.[31]

The *Journal*'s Pawtucket correspondent displayed alarm and amazement: "There is a cohesion of organization and 'community interest' that is of a strength and co-operative nature far exceeding any that has ever before existed in this city and vicinity. The disposition of every labor organization to assist in any way possible the welfare of its fellow organizations, is so marked as to deserve more than passing notice." When newly formed Local 533 of the Retail Clerks' National Protective Association pushed for early store closings on several weekday evenings, it received labor support for a boycott of stores open on Tuesday nights. When small businesses agreed to Tuesday closings during slower summer months, the union pushed for year-round curtailment. The clerks numbered about three hundred in Pawtucket, evenly divided between men and women; they would be a force in discouraging all services to strikebreakers in the fast-approaching trolley strike.[32]

When twister tenders walked out at the J. & P. Coates Thread Company in Pawtucket in May, labor solidarity and a sympathetic mayor forced a quick settlement. Other textile operatives in the city joined the protest against a wage reduction when the state-mandated fifty-eight-hour work week—one of the tradeoffs for incorporation of the Rhode Island Company—took effect for women and children. Management cut salaries accordingly, although legislators reluctantly viewed the law as a primitive and indirect way to establish minimum-wage standards. The newly formed Pawtucket Central Labor Union spearheaded the fray as hundreds of striking mill workers joined the local textile union. Within a week the company, almost apologetically, agreed to reinstate the old wage scale despite the shorter work week. In stark contrast, the earlier Lorraine Mill walkout and controversy had sputtered for months and ended with a union defeat during Fitzgerald's first term. The city's political and economic mood had changed dramatically.[33]

Fitzgerald continued to engage the Union Railroad in and out of the courtroom, attempting to procure higher franchise fees and taxes. The mayor's intrepid case against the carrier's transfer policy was silenced when the assembly authorized stationless transfer tickets, but Fitzgerald's energetic prosecution of the issue was widely admired. He continued to turn up the pressure when he questioned the previous year's decision by a then-Republican city council to allow the Pawtucket Street Railway to build a new local route. The old council authorized this action after 10 A.M. on January 6, 1902. At that time, according to the city's charter, power was to be transferred to the newly elected council. Although the meeting in question started before the ten o'clock deadline, Fitzgerald claimed the act was improper and unconstitutional. He petitioned the state supreme court for a decision.[34]

The railway, sensing trouble, worked feverishly to finish the line before a decision could be rendered. Spectators crowded the street to watch the progress, including a contingent "whose hobby seems to be hostility to the railroad corporation." In March an appellate court issued a preliminary injunction against the railway. Fitzgerald notified the company to cease construction on another line because it had failed to complete that job in the contracted time period. Work stopped. The mayor humbled the mighty Union Railroad, and by implication, the machine behind it, an accomplishment no one else had ever achieved.[35]

Fitzgerald now rekindled opposition to the transfer situation. He assailed the lack of connections between the lines of different companies that intersected in Pawtucket. The mayor intervened in railway affairs again when he overruled his own public works commissioner and stopped the Pawtucket Street Railway from temporarily laying rails across Main Street. The mayor appeared at the scene with the police lieutenant he had suspended earlier at Lorraine Mills and threatened to arrest anyone using the unsanctioned tracks. He relented ten days later, but only after his authority had been recognized by all in the incident.[36]

The *Journal*'s Pawtucket correspondent was a fierce partisan of the Union Railroad and a bitter detractor of Fitzgerald: "The vast majority of the people simply want the new railway lines, and they don't care a fig whether the arrangement whereby they get them is one-sidedly in favor of the street railway company or not." The Union Railroad called Fitzgerald's bluff by refurbishing narrow-gauge tracks, already in use, as a subtle threat to keep Pawtucket's system antiquated and unable to interconnect with new, standard-gauge routes. In May the supreme court ruled that the old city council violated the city charter by enacting ordinances after its term had legally expired. Fitzgerald ordered the once-suspended police chief to force the Union Railroad to ignominiously rip up four hundred feet of illegally installed rails. He warned the carrier there would be no new tracks until an agreement was reached to pay a 3-percent gross tax to the city and to institute an adequate transfer system suitable for Pawtucket's unique layout.[37]

Fitzgerald had triumphed against the hated railway monopoly, employing legerdemain often used by the carrier. The *Journal* carried a statewide picture showing rails being torn up as the mayor's popularity and notoriety skyrocketed in Rhode Island. Fitzgerald's triumph was fraught with danger, however. He anticipated that Pawtucket's key position as a way station for connecting routes into northern Rhode Island and nearby Massachusetts would force the Union Railroad's directors to sue for peace so that the company could mine this lucrative trolley crossroads. The syndicate was torn between compromise and intractability: any perceived weakness on their part might spread the mayor's activism to city officials elsewhere, while further battle with the wily chief executive might bring more humiliating defeats. Both parties realized that the larger issue of political reform lay just beyond the railway issue. The citizens of Pawtucket, while ostensibly behind the fighting mayor, might prove fickle if the railway decided to stonewall and indefinitely delay improvements. The *Journal*'s Pawtucket reporter claimed that Fitzgerald and his supporters "almost fear that in their 'fight for principle' they have retarded, and sacrificed for years to come perhaps, a large portion of the material interests of the city." Events in Providence soon interceded and changed the course of action for both sides in the Pawtucket confrontation. The battle for control of the streets was about to become physical.[38]

FITZGERALD'S REBELLION

This strike has been brought about by professional agitators who go from city
to city sowing seeds of discontent, endeavoring to create dissatisfaction between
the employe and the employer, and then injecting themselves into the situation
as arbitrators, that they may become dictators later. They have no interest in
the community, and no stake in our common welfare.

Marsden Perry, state utility king, June 1902

Prosperous looking men who under ordinary circumstances would not be seen
talking to a poor driver, filled with a desire to sympathize with the strikers,
came down to the plane of social equality and halted the wagons in the middle
of the track to carry on an impromptu conversation with the drivers. The sole
object of this was to impede traffic on the cars.

Providence Evening Telegram, June 1902

Our police force is not at the beck and call of any man, men or corporations
who feel that they are entitled to special escort service, nor is it large enough to
spare men for ornamental purposes on street cars.

Pawtucket mayor John Fitzgerald, June 1902

Rhode Island's ten-hour railway law was to take effect June 1, 1902. The evening before enactment, carbarns were crowded with motormen and conductors as "everyone was watching for the new time tables to be posted." Superintendent Albert Potter had told the *Providence Journal* on May 16 that the Union
Railroad would shorten the workday and keep the present wage scale. "As fast
as it becomes necessary to change the schedules on these lines before June," he
informed a reporter, "they will be made to conform with the new law." That
declaration and its reiteration on several occasions cooled any strike sentiment
and earned respect for the local division, according to a history of the ensuing
walkout by two union executive board members. "Men that would not join the
union, now came to the hall after they were assured of the ten hours with
the same pay and signified their intention of maintaining the organization
which had procured for them better conditions."[1]

Management startled everyone at 6:00 P.M. on May 31 by posting a notice that rejected the ten-hour law as unconstitutional for penalizing those who wanted to work more hours. There were no adjusted timetables, but the notice stated, "All conductors, motormen and gripmen who wish to continue work under their existing contracts are free to do so; and those who wish to reduce their time to 10 hours per day, with proportionate reduction in pay, are equally free to make their choice." The company also promised to protect employees opting to stay at work under the old arrangement. Potter waited to retract his original statement about legislative compliance until the middle of the month, although the union and the *Pawtucket Evening Times* cited his reversal on several occasions.[2]

The unanticipated turnabout by the Union Railroad caught the local unprepared. John Arno, president of Division 200, promised swift retaliation but admitted his surprise: "This is entirely unexpected to us. We had no idea that such a notice was to be sent out by the railroad company." The union's strike account wistfully lamented, "The action of the company destroyed all the good feeling that had been brought about by the ten-hour law." The local and just about everyone else in the state failed to anticipate the traction company's decision to buck the legislature. With so many resources invested in its sophisticated lobbying program, the union had not formulated a backup plan.[3]

Division 200 was in a quandary. Management's double cross created intense bitterness, prompting a disgusted rank and file to clamor for more traditional labor action against the railway. "From what could be observed," reported the *Journal,* "it was evident that the employees of the company were aroused as they had not been since the organization was started." A protest meeting netted seventy-five new members, a surprising majority from the ranks of the higher-paid old-timers, who, in retrospect, did not foresee the direction of the controversy.[4]

A. O. Vetter, the local's business agent, wired two telegrams to Amalgamated headquarters in Detroit on June 2. The first mentioned the company's refusal to abide by the ten-hour law and inquired about accepting a slightly lower wage scale. Vetter pleaded, "The situation is getting critical so you had better send some one here immediately." The second telegram, later on the same day, demonstrated how fast things were moving in Rhode Island: "Have given company until six P.M. today to grant demands. We are ready to go out. Do you endorse?" International treasurer Rezin Orr wired back the next morning that he would arrive in Providence on June 4 but warned the local, "If company has refused demands do not take final action until I arrive."[5]

The strike began at midnight, June 4, and Orr arrived later that morning.

The local had announced that union benefits would be $5 a week and would increase to $7.50. Orr stayed for several weeks but notified the strikers immediately that there would be no benefits. "I informed them that under the constitution, according to their actions, they were not entitled to it from the international." The Amalgamated Association of Street Railway Employes of America, like its parent body, the American Federation of Labor, frowned on unauthorized strikes and generally withheld funding to unsanctioned walkouts to dampen spontaneous, poorly planned, and damaging wildcat strikes. Orr eventually loosened the Amalgamated's purse strings for a mere two hundred dollars during the ensuing five-week strike by seven hundred carmen. That parsimony, however justified, seemed petty in the heat of battle and belittled the national union and its Providence affiliate.[6]

The decision to strike was as astonishing as the company's refusal to abide by the new state law. The *Journal* expected negotiations and complimented street carmen as a conservative and law-abiding group. The division's attorney, Henry Tiepke, the former mayor of Pawtucket, counseled moderation and couched the conflict in the language of public safety issues. However, the majority of motormen and conductors, who toiled for two dollars a day next to horsecar veterans making up to 25 percent more for the same work, became militant. That wage disparity, and the sense of political betrayal after two years of hard work at the statehouse, exploded into the most momentous civil disruption in Rhode Island since the Dorr War in 1842. The strike would detonate a generation of pent-up political frustration among a citizenry who enthusiastically supported the labor action as a way to indirectly attack Brayton's machine and the Union Railroad.[7]

The walkout began peacefully, although the *Journal* printed an incendiary front-page headline: "Fight to the Finish is Expected." The union represented approximately 750 of the 1,000 motormen and conductors, including some horsecar veterans like Ben Jepson. Potter claimed the loyalty of 300 senior employees who earned premium wages. On June 1, 1902, a few days before the strike, the division augmented its strength by organizing 100 skilled shopmen, about half the number employed by the railway. Last-minute attempts to sign up electricians, firemen, and engineers at the company's critical power facility failed because the twenty-seven workers there felt miffed that no special demands, like the eight-hour day enjoyed in similar crafts, had been formulated for them. Recent efforts by the International Brotherhood of Electrical Workers at the power station resulted in the enrollment of only two members. Despite rhetoric about the righteousness of the strikers' cause, electricians stayed on the job.[8]

"We Walk!" Striking carmen march from the industrial village of Olneyville to the downtown Labor Temple on June 5, 1902. Providence's worst civil riot occurred that evening in support of transit crews.

The Union Railroad immediately announced that no strikers would be rehired and all employees who continued to work would receive police protection. Each barn superintendent intimidated motormen and conductors by inquiring individually whether they would work the following day. They also contacted carmen's wives, informing them that their husbands might be fired. Management notified all strikers to turn in badges and punches on payday and receive back wages, and Potter advertised for replacement workers in front-page advertisements in local newspapers. The Providence police department deployed overnight officers, assigning two to a carbarn and a special detail at the powerhouse. Marsden J. Perry thundered to the press, "This strike has been brought about by professional agitators who go from city to city sowing seeds of discontent, endeavoring to create dissatisfaction between the employe and the employer, and then injecting themselves into the situation as arbitrators, that they may become dictators later. They have no interest in the community, and no stake in our common welfare."[9]

The first full day of the strike was a standoff as both sides waited to see how many would show up for work. There was little service disruption in the morning, because most early runs were operated by old-timers. Many of these veterans continued their runs after quitting time, somewhat camouflaging the effects of the strike. That night, however, only 24 of 137 trolleys ventured over normal routes. The *Providence Evening Telegram*, sympathetic to the carmen, estimated that only half the usual streetcars ran all day; the *Journal*, on the other hand, implied that the railway had the upper hand.[10]

On the evening of the second day of the walkout, a riot in support of strikers rocked Rhode Island's capital city and changed the nature of the contest altogether. At 6:00 P.M. hundreds of striking motormen and conductors marched from downtown Providence to Olneyville and back. A military band led the procession. Twenty thousand supporters cheered the carmen in the city's center, while thousands more applauded along the parade route. Strikers carried signs that underscored the political nature of the conflict: "Now, Gov. Kimball, show your hand and straighten matters out"; "Ten hours are enough"; "We are out for a just cause"; "The Union Railroad Company has the people by the throat, Will you stand it?" The *Journal* claimed that only 356 union men participated in the procession. The *Evening Telegram* wrote that 700 marched.[11]

When the parade disbanded downtown, strike supporters appeared to "come out of the ground," precipitating a number of incidents. Frustrated teamsters, who had just concluded an unsuccessful strike, blocked streetcars with their vehicles. Demonstrators hindered police patrol wagons. Soon, a fusillade of rocks and other objects pelted strikebreakers and law enforcement personnel. The *Journal* summed up the mayhem in a sensationalized headline: "Streets Filled with Rioters, Cars Destroyed, the Switches Plugged, Motormen and Conductors Terrorized and the Police Officers Stoned." The newspaper blamed striking railway workers from Pawtucket and a few anarchists for instigating the turmoil.[12]

The *Evening Telegram* reported that "enthusiasts jammed the business section of the city and gave to an outburst of popular feeling that has no parallel in the city's history." Even the police commissioner expressed amazement: "I don't think that anyone in the city dreamed that such a thing would occur at that time and place." The *Journal* described the rioters as strikers "or, at least, union men." However, students from Brown University also joined their generational peers from local mills in fueling the disorder. Participants sang:

> We are, We are, We are, We are, We are
> the union men,
> We won't go back till doomsday,
> and maybe not go then.

Other young protestors with no kindred affection for horsecar veterans carried threatening signs: "Kill the scabs"; "Hang the Traitors"; and "Yank them off the car." Potter feared that strikers would destroy expensive electrical equipment.[13]

Local newspapers headlined the ongoing strike for weeks. The Providence Journal *took the side of management. Notice the $500 reward notice for conviction of trolley vandals.*

The riot, which ebbed and flowed throughout the evening hours, finally subsided at midnight as police gained the upper hand. "The sound of night sticks falling across the parts of bodies most easily reached was like the sound of flails on a barn floor in harvest time," wrote the *Journal.* The police arrested dozens of workers and revelers. The *Evening Telegram* noted one group of law-breakers who gingerly joined the fray: "Prosperous looking men who under ordinary circumstances would not be seen talking to a poor driver, filled with a desire to sympathize with the strikers, came down to the plane of social equality and halted the wagons in the middle of the track to carry on an impromptu conversation with the drivers. The sole object of this was to impede traffic on the cars." Such middle-class sentiment, probably more against the political establishment and the Union Railroad than for labor, would generate an important undercurrent in the strike and bear fruit in the fall general elections.[14]

Local labor unions, including Division 200, condemned the violence. But the riot served a purpose: all car service was discontinued the night of the upheaval. Superintendent Potter sadly admitted, "Three hundred men whom we have engaged and who have never run a car are afraid to venture out." The company posted front-page reward notices promising $500 for any information leading to the arrest of those who violated a state law prohibiting physical interference with street railways. Aldrich had sanctioned the bill during the last organizing efforts. The controversial statute called for fines of up to $3,000 or two years in prison.[15]

Despite widespread public enthusiasm for the strike in Providence, police vigilance and stiff sentences and fines quickly ended popular disturbances, although individual acts of violence and vandalism were endemic for a month. Plainclothes detectives and mounted officers patrolled the downtown area, and squads were organized to respond to any carbarn within minutes. Officers with experience in breaking textile strikes were given free rein. Patrolmen, toiling double shifts, rode streetcars and were empowered to arrest anyone speaking loudly, swearing, or uttering the word "scab." Overzealous officers mistakenly beat an undercover detective in a crowd when he failed to obey orders to move. Saloons were arbitrarily closed. The police chief announced that anyone arrested for reveling would be jailed until a hearing rather than released on bail, as was common practice. Many justices imposed maximum penalties. One judge sentenced a lunch-cart driver to thirty days in jail for obstructing trolley tracks. Such a violation usually cost twenty dollars, and the harsh judgment sent "a breeze of astonishment" through the courtroom. Another judge fined five youngsters the maximum twenty dollars each for yelling "scab" at strike-breakers. The Union Railroad hired an undetermined number of private detectives to augment local police, who were indebted to the traction company for a generation of free-ride tickets.[16]

The carmen's union, despite an impressive membership roster on paper, suffered from the old-timers' fifth column and "weak-kneed" younger members who deserted the organization in response to the company's "carrot and stick" approach. Forty-two veterans from the Olneyville carbarn, seedbed of the union, sent a five-man committee to visit Potter. They complained that "they were ridiculed by the public." The *Evening Telegram* reported, "The word 'scab' was hurled at them with a regularity which must have been especially humiliating." One "cried like a baby," and another left service due to "nervous prostration" after being tormented for several days. Potter told them "not to get discouraged, for the company appreciated the trouble the men were having and would always remember it." Surprisingly, strikers and rioters showed no bitterness toward old-timers who stayed on the job, recognizing just how much these employees, who had pioneered the union just a few years earlier, stood to loose: higher wages, seniority, and an upcoming pension. The veterans, many of whom joined Division 200, could not bring themselves to jeopardize long-standing careers and break out of a nineteenth-century deferential mind set. When push came to shove, old-timers rode out the storm and allowed younger, Irish workers to continue the union's mission. One retiree, who worked during the strike, said the division "did not put me out. I didn't belong . . . but that didn't seem to matter."[17]

Albert T. Potter was no workplace mountebank. He had saved the higher $2.50-a-day wage scale for horsecar veterans when Aldrich originally purchased the system. Since his employment in 1866 he had risen through the ranks as helper, hostler, switch boy, and driver to vice president of the corporation—the same career path as his mentor, Daniel F. Longstreet. He had hired many horsecar employees personally, sometimes offering work to a man on the street after observing some exemplary personal quality or civic act. He occasionally lent money to workers to shield them from "loan sharks." His son, Albert E. Potter, on a fast track to superintendent of transportation, personally directed operations the night of the Providence riot despite being manhandled by the crowd. An unequivocal testament to the elder Potter's diplomatic skills as an employee advocate appeared in the strikers' souvenir history: "A. T. Potter was one of the boys, and he is one of the boys today . . . working for the interest of the railroad men." His occasional criticism of personnel was seen as posturing and part of his managerial duties.[18]

Potter also understood generational tension between railway employees and was not above exploiting that division among old-timers and new carmen—interlopers who never experienced the tug of a "hoss" and who took for granted the speed, power, and convenience of an electric streetcar. The veterans' work life had revolved around horsepower, now the symbol of a passing age and the object of derision among contemporary crews. Some novice motormen even enjoyed scaring horses with noisy air brakes, to the chagrin of older peers. Horsecar drivers had been skilled practitioners who nimbly worked brake and steed on inclines and strained muscles with a multihorse team in the snow. Some of them protested the installation of modern shielding vestibules, preferring to face the elements unprotected. Electric motormen were trained in a few days and, without a longer apprenticeship, made equal to the most skilled veteran. Furthermore, the Amalgamated by this time was a militant, industrial-style union that enrolled all workers regardless of skill or craft and appealed to a younger generation of Irish carmen hungry for advancement. In this respect the national union resembled Eugene Debs's radical American Railway Union rather than the earlier Amalgamated, which had mirrored the conservative railroad brotherhoods and the cultural moderation of horsecar workers. In 1926 a retiree still chided the younger men: "Think of it boys, with your vestibuled cars, and your little 'La De Dah' seats to sit in. We never sat down during business hours."[19]

Imbued with a strong sense of personal loyalty to Potter, and with too much to lose, the old-timers stayed on the job and provided the manpower to defeat the organizing drive. The veterans cordially received a union delegation that tried to capitalize on their discontent, but they politely refused to join the strike. Potter's genuine deference to these popular employees returned a huge dividend to the corporation. Although he often fumbled public relations assignments, solicitous behavior toward his own generational peers shielded the syndicate from a unified work force.

Except for sporadic incidents, the decline of violence against railway operators in Providence after the police crackdown emboldened "weak-kneed" union members and scabs to operate streetcars. According to the *Pawtucket Times*, "They believed there was no danger of violence and therefore went back again." Potter, despite his earlier fulmination not to rehire strikers, reengaged a couple of hundred union renegades that first week, although these carmen forfeited their seniority. Local and out-of-state strikebreakers filled remaining positions. Militant opposition to the Union Railroad quickly shifted from the capital city to Rhode Island's two major industrial valleys—the Blackstone and Pawtuxet. The anger followed recently installed trolley tracks to suburban and rural areas.[20]

The same night that the riot exploded in downtown Providence, a similar demonstration jolted Pawtucket. Although pale in comparison to events in Providence that evening, rowdy public behavior toward scabs led the *Journal* to comment: "No such scenes were ever witnessed [before] on the streets of Pawtucket."[21]

The Pawtucket Street Railway, although a corporate part of the Union Railroad, retained a distinct identity. No other part of the transit empire faced such a hostile citizenry and chief executive. Paltry tax payments, inferior equipment, uncoordinated track gauges, and poor service forced Republican politician Edward L. Freeman, the machine-appointed railroad commissioner, to admit: "The people are obliged to ride in vehicles which are a disgrace to any civilized community; not only uncomfortable, but absolutely injurious to health and morals." The 125 employees of the Pawtucket Street Railway, while members of Division 200 in Providence, also enjoyed a camaraderie separate from their colleagues in the capital city. Unlike their neighboring peers, they forged a solid phalanx of union solidarity that remained unbroken throughout the entire strike, although they had joined the parent organization later. Seven of them returned the second day of the strike; none afterward. Transit service within Pawtucket had not been established until 1886, so there were few real old-timers and therefore less generational conflict.[22]

Pawtucket strikers hosted a parade the night after the Providence tumult. Some five hundred carmen from around the state marched to adjacent Central Falls and back for a mass meeting. Protestors carried signs that implicated the Union Railroad and the state's corrupt political system: "The railroad company means to rule or ruin"; "The legislature makes laws to suit the U.R.R. Co."; "If the workingman breaks the law he is arrested; tis different with the railroad company"; "This is the people's fight as well as ours"; "The legislature and the Union R. R. seem to be one company." Labor and political figures addressed the militant but peaceful gathering.[23]

Although the rally proved tranquil, the Union Railroad sent a letter to Hunter C. White, sheriff of Providence County and now chairman of the state Republican Party, requesting marshals to guard traction property in Pawtucket. Potter complained that Mayor Fitzgerald had removed patrolmen from carbarn duty despite pleas for such protection. White, perhaps itching for another confrontation with Fitzgerald, whom he had faced in the Lorraine Mills affair, apparently got the go-ahead from Brayton after intervention by Marsden Perry. White assured Potter: "I shall answer your letter in the same terms which I used in replying to a similar one several years ago." He assigned two sheriffs to ride every car in the Pawtucket system.[24]

Fitzgerald, bristling at the intrusion of state sheriffs in response to a situation that was a shadow of the one in Providence, defiantly declared: "Our police force is not at the beck and call of any man, men or corporations who feel that they are entitled to special escort service, nor is it large enough to spare men for ornamental purposes on street cars." The Pawtucket city council concurred and passed a resolution that labeled White's actions "at least a breach of official courtesy, if not an insult to the city" and demanded immediate withdrawal of the sheriffs. Local citizens, treated to years of railway indignities and tired of waiting for transit and political reform, turned to guerrilla progressivism by taking matters into their own hands. A sustained riot kicked off a month-long series of widespread, popular assaults against the railway company, strikebreakers, and deputies.[25]

Protestors formed a two-mile human chain that intermittently stretched down Broad Street through neighboring towns and harassed sheriffs in streetcars. Demonstrators blockaded rails, hurled objects, and viciously attacked scabs. Twenty deputies with drawn revolvers rescued three of their colleagues from a crowd of two thousand that surrounded a car in Central Falls. The next day four marshals were assigned to each trolley. Mayor Fitzgerald, meanwhile, transferred five patrolmen who tried to interfere with the rioters. On the other hand, officers sympathetic to the mayor arrested several strikebreakers and deputies, and on one occasion later in the dispute, even harassed militiamen. During the walkout Fitzgerald appointed an auxiliary patrol, including three strikers! With a small force of forty-four officers, there was one policeman for every one thousand residents. In Providence, on the other hand, there was a professionally trained body of three hundred, one for every five hundred citizens, although the capital city was twice the geographical size of its next-door neighbor. Commanders were chosen by Brayton's machine.[26]

The contrast between law enforcement in the two cities was graphic. Crowds often gathered on North Main Street in Pawtucket, just beyond the car barn in Providence. Both municipalities stationed officers on their own side of the city limits. Pawtucket police made no attempt to control demonstrators who harassed strikebreakers operating out of the nearby facilities, but protestors carefully avoided crossing the line into Providence. On one occasion, however, a railway crew, unfamiliar with the area, inadvertently ran into Pawtucket by a car length. Rioters broke nearly every window in the vehicle before the trolley reversed direction. Pawtucket officers did not intervene, while their counterparts on the Providence side stood and watched impotently.[27]

Ironically, the disturbance seemed to mobilize the frustrated residents of the state and Pawtucket into performing some kind of daily strike duty, virtually eclipsing the role of the carmen in their own job action. After the initial riot in

Pawtucket demonstrators often gathered downtown. The "scab" sign stretched across Main Street, and an effigy of a strikebreaker can be seen hanging from a pole to the right.

Providence, authorities never accused strikers of fomenting trouble. Average citizens assumed the role of instigators once the norms of ordinary civil behavior crumbled.

Violence escalated in the Blackstone Valley over the next few days as crowds continually forced the operators of passengerless trolleys to run a gauntlet of physical and psychological abuse. Unlike in Providence, the few culprits arrested in Pawtucket, especially, received light fines from locally appointed judges. White and the *Providence Journal* correctly accused Fitzgerald of directly interfering with police to secure the discharge of offenders. The newspaper decried incidents of "pluguglyism" and editorialized that "Pawtucket is being disgraced by manifestations of mob rule and anarchy."[28]

On June 11 a dozen deputies discharged live ammunition into the air to keep an angry crowd at bay. Eighteen sheriffs were subsequently injured that night by bricks and rocks while escorting a trolley. One marshal removed his uniform coat and quit on the spot but was pursued through backyards by demonstrators. Townspeople reacted to the influx of deputies and outside strike-breakers as an invading force bent on taking away any local prerogatives that remained independent of the state's political machine. The city council of neighboring Cumberland blamed constables for "inciting the people to disorder and disturbances." Fitzgerald claimed the police were "intruders in the community and a taunt to the city." Effigies of scabs and sheriffs hung indiscriminately from poles around the valley, and a permanent banner stretched across Main Street in downtown Pawtucket asking people to stay off the trolleys. In the southwest corner of the state, Republican George H. Utter, former state representative, speaker of the house, and secretary of state, attacked the mayhem in the columns of the machine's *Westerly Daily Sun.* "The deputy sheriffs at Pawtucket made a serious mistake yesterday when they fired their revolvers over the heads of the mob," he intoned. "There is just one place to aim a revolver under such circumstances after the mob has been warned, and that is where the bullets will take effect."[29]

On the evening of June 11, Governor Charles Kimball, apparently at the urging of Marsden Perry, mobilized the Rhode Island militia for Pawtucket duty. For the first time since the Dorr War sixty years earlier, local troops would engage fellow Rhode Islanders. The modern state militia had never been called to active duty. While Providence police had recent experience handling strikes and riots, the militia practiced but once a year in the traditional art of military combat. The first five hundred soldiers, including a cavalry battalion and a Gatling-gun battery, arrived in Pawtucket on June 12. The ill-prepared troops nearly joined the demonstrators.[30]

The national guardsmen's compassion for the strikers is not surprising. Regiments contained many workers, including a sizable number of union members and even a few striking carmen! The *Journal* fumed, "Some of the militiamen, while they do not refuse to obey the order given, openly expressed their sympathy with the mob and the strike which is back of all the present trouble." Thirty-five soldiers from the Second Regiment forced a scab crew to carry them across the city line to Pawtucket and refused to pay fares. A lieutenant threatened the carbarn superintendent and held a rifle in his face. When a *Journal* reporter queried an infantry sergeant about the lack of security, he replied, "Well, the cars weren't protected, were they? . . . And you can bet your life they won't be." The journalist wrote that a number of ranking officers heard the threat but made no comment. One guardsman was overheard telling demonstrators, "Never mind, boys, we are with you. We have to do this." Troops openly fraternized with protestors and friends in the crowd. Two soldiers yelled "scab" as they passed by the Pawtucket carbarn. A livid *Journal* railed against a breakdown in military discipline, calling the troops farcical and a catalyst for anarchy. The *Westerly Daily Sun* concurred: "It was not until the afternoon that the militia seemed to realize that it had been called out to suppress disorder."[31]

The day the troops arrived, sheriffs shot into a crowd, seriously wounding a fourteen-year-old boy, who later sued the Union Railroad for injuries. (A deputy was indicted for the shooting after the strike but was released for lack of evidence.) Marshals underwent such harassment that they eventually refused to serve. Almost all of them sustained injuries during their hectic tour of duty. Strikebreakers, too, suffered: seventeen of fifty-one were hurt the first week of the walkout. Local mill workers allegedly carried out many hit-and-run attacks. Brig. Gen. Herbert S. Tanner saved face for Hunter White by diplomatically offering to relieve the beleaguered deputies. The sheriffs left a day after troops arrived but not before a crowd dismantled their headquarters and forced them to flee ignominiously. In a public letter printed on the front page of the *Journal*, White bemoaned that his force had "to face a mob as vicious as any which ever assembled in an American community." He placed the blame squarely on Fitzgerald. A similar statement by Perry, implicating Pawtucket's mayor, also appeared on page one. A letter to the *Journal*, displaying a flair for ancient history, targeted Fitzgerald too: "As the ancient clay of Assyria and Babylon has been perpetuated in quaint cuneiform on lasting clay and stone, so should an imperishable record be made of Fitz's war, done in brick and hand tooled—and bearing the union label." In fact, the feisty mayor was so closely identified with the uprising that many participants and observers called the incident Fitzgerald's Rebellion or Fitz's War.[32]

The militia, still unsure of its legal role in Pawtucket, acted cautiously at first. General Tanner addressed an unruly gathering in downtown Pawtucket in a conciliatory fashion: "We are with you, boys, and we don't want to have any trouble whatever. We are sent here by the State of Rhode Island to maintain the peace, and I call upon you all to disperse and go quietly to your homes." The crowd, by and large, welcomed the troops as a liberating, neutral unit replacing the hated sheriffs, who were seen as the machine's private police force. Demonstrators, however, still refused to budge and resisted several infantry charges, despite having guns shoved in their chests. Soldiers had to brandish bayonets to move the protestors. Such courage by the citizenry was turned inside out in the official military report, which repeatedly depicted them as cowardly in the face of military determination.[33]

Just hours after the militia arrived in Pawtucket, Governor Kimball issued an awkwardly worded proclamation forbidding "riotously or tumultuously as-

The Rhode Island militia leaving the Pawtucket Armory for strike duty. Mobilized for the first time in modern state history, the soldiers harassed strikebreakers and company officials. Many union members and even a few strikers were in the guard.

sembling." The act fell short of a declaration of martial law but protected the government from liability. "The state of affairs in Pawtucket is so unwonted for a Rhode Island city," explained the *Journal,* "that ignorance as to the details of the two is excusable; since the Dorr War there has been nothing like it on Rhode Island soil." The manifesto empowered the militia to restore order but not interfere with civil rule, which would require an act of the general assembly. The governor publicly endorsed the use of live ammunition.[34]

At 7:00 P.M. Tanner led his troops from the Pawtucket Armory, the militia's largest facility in the state, "with the object of making a demonstration in force throughout the infected portions of the city." Troops removed all signs and effigies and ordered residents to close all windows and doors along main avenues. Anyone arrested was prosecuted by the military commander or bound over to a grand jury. The *Journal* happily informed its readers, "The infantry was instructed to use musket butts should resistance be encountered, but bayonet and bullet were also to be called into play should there be occasion for their

145

use." Four Gatling guns and a number of cannon were also put in place, "ready to sweep the streets if a rush should be attempted."[35]

The troops made a show of it in Pawtucket for two weeks before pulling up stakes. At its peak the force numbered 641, almost half the state's organized and uniformed militia. The ranks eventually included two Newport naval battalions—strangers to the people of Pawtucket, but trained in suppressing street riots. Despite this firepower, the militia contained outbreaks only in the center of town. Riots flared along all car routes, especially during evening hours. By the time troops arrived, crowds melted into familiar neighborhood terrain not wishing to engage or antagonize soldiers directly. In marked contrast to the injuries sustained by despised scabs and deputies, no militiamen were harmed during the entire fray. Denizens of adjoining towns, where troops were not empowered to enter, kept up the protest in these municipalities.[36]

With the militia shackled by a hit-and-run foe that, according to the *Evening Telegram,* practiced guerrilla warfare, the soldiers proved embarrassingly impotent. State authorities watched helplessly at a strike that now assumed the guise of a political conflict. Furthermore, the daily cost to sustain a small army was prohibitive, and officials feared that it might become an electoral issue in such a tax-conscious state. Troops also chafed at enforced absence from work, skimpy meals, and inferior accommodations in an unpopular campaign. A number of employers, "showing much feeling against the service," groused about the loss of skilled employees and actually fired absent militiamen, to the chagrin and embarrassment of the *Journal* and military authorities.[37]

Once again the Republican power structure, under the prodding of Marsden Perry and the leadership of Hunter White, had tried to embarrass and defeat Pawtucket's wily mayor. Once again, John Fitzgerald had pulled the tiger's tail. Most of the militia left Pawtucket on June 26, and, in a final gesture of solidarity with the strikers, a band of soldiers purposefully left a Providence-bound trolley run by scabs and boarded a union-operated steam train. The troops not only failed to tame the mayor or his constituents, they empathized with them. If only for a few tumultuous weeks, the people of Pawtucket had taken control of the streets from the Union Railroad and the GOP establishment.[38]

WE WALK

Mothers take unruly children to the front door and threaten to put a boycott on them instead of scaring them into good behavior by asserting that the bogey man will get them if they don't watch out.

Providence Journal, June 1902

During the past month, the paper had been through a crisis unequalled in its history. It had stood for law and order, as in 1842, while its contemporaries had espoused the cause of the trolly [sic] railroad strikers. A systematic boycott had been brought against the circulation and advertising, threats made to destroy the building, and one of the reporters had narrowly escaped with his life, at the hands of a mob, in Pawtucket.

Richard Howland, *Providence Journal* editor, July 1902

It is about time for the workingmen to stand shoulder to shoulder and register so that by the time another year rolls around we will have men in office that will serve the public and not be at the beck and call of Marsden J. Perry and Co.

Pawtucket Evening Times, June 1902

Throughout the walkout the union and its supporters employed a devastating tactic—a publicly enforced ban on streetcar riding. In 1902 the Pawtucket Street Railway was the only line in the state to lose money due to the five-week strike and boycott. Although the militia cited fear as a reason for the public's shunning trolleys in the Blackstone Valley—and certainly that was a partial explanation—most citizens voluntarily and enthusiastically punished the hated railway and the political machine behind it. The carmen's union, saloon keepers, and local entrepreneurs printed badges, pins, and other ornaments that proclaimed, "We Walk." One bartender distributed embossed ribbons in support of the strike, which made "a greater hit than a trading stamp scheme in his business."[1]

A massive crowd of French Canadians that turned out in Pawtucket for the annual St. Jean Baptiste Day on June 24 sported "We Walk" badges—

Small businesses in Pawtucket outfitted antique omnibuses to provide rudimentary service during the strike. Strikers staffed the vehicles and kept the fares for the union.

another example of broad and diverse ethnic support. The railway wisely suspended all service as a precautionary measure. Mayor Fitzgerald opened a rally sponsored by the Trades Union Economic League in Providence by hollering, "We walk!" as fifteen hundred supporters yelled their approval. Even as the strike petered out, the *Journal* marveled that the boycott had succeeded "to an extent that can hardly be conceived to be possible." There was a rumor that the company paid three dollars a day to a few riders just for show. Of course, the close proximity of steam railroad service, especially to Providence, made the boycott less onerous for some commuters. Inner-city Pawtucket routes were also shorter than those in the capital city, allowing former passengers to walk manageable distances. The introduction of primitive, but convenient, omnibuses by the union and local businesses also ameliorated the transportation problem.[2]

The boycott affected anyone assisting strikebreakers. "The terrorism . . . is such that no one having facilities to furnish board and rooms for one or all of these men would dare do it," commented the *Journal*. Parents encouraged their children to harass teachers who took a trolley; a businessman whose wife rode suffered retaliation; police who arrested rioters were shunned by neighbors; and a boardinghouse keeper who rented to scabs had his windows broken. The militia found it almost impossible to secure horses for strike duty, and the few liveries that would rent charged exorbitant rates. Any union members observed on streetcars were fined or expelled from their locals. Pawtucket merchants declined service to scabs and instructed employees to stay off cars for fear of incurring union wrath. A young bootblack even refused to finish a shoe shine when a customer asked when the next trolley arrived. According to the *Journal*, "Mothers take unruly children to the front door and threaten to put a boycott on them instead of scaring them into good behavior by asserting that the bogey man will get them if they don't watch out."[3]

Unions and fraternal groups took positive action by hosting statewide fund raisers. Retail clerks, textile workers, and building trades members all made donations. Community-based organizations and ethnic societies with no direct connection to organized labor like the Modern Woodmen of America, Chevaliers Canadien Français, and the Young Irelanders Association all actively supported the strike. There were picnics, sporting contests, and other entertainments. Small businesses in Pawtucket outfitted eighteen omnibuses operated by strikers who kept the modest fares. The *Evening Telegram* initiated and advertised a subscription service for the carmen, raising over $1,400, including a five-dollar gift from Buffalo Bill, whose Wild West show was in town. Donations came from employees in both union and nonunion firms. Small businesses took out hundreds of advertisements in the union's souvenir history book. Despite these efforts, Pawtucket and Providence carmen raised only enough cash, above and beyond organizational needs, to provide strikers with one five-dollar stipend during the course of the walkout.[4]

The *Journal* editors credited the unions with spearheading the boycott and solidarity campaign in the Blackstone Valley: "The air is surcharged with the organized labor spirit, which during the last few months has experienced a renaissance a little less than wonderful. It has spread and taken possession of one form of skilled labor after another, until there now exists a well nigh perfect and unbroken solidarity of laborers, craftsmen, and salespeople whose numbers run into the thousands." The carmen's strike galvanized this evangelical labor army into a unified body. "In their inflamed imagination," the *Journal* wrote, "the traction company became the incarnated foe of union labor, the embodiment of capitalist oppression."[5]

Most observers agreed on labor's key role in the entire affair. There was more to the story, however. The *Evening Telegram* perceived, "There is no apparent dissatisfaction at the tie-up by the traveling public, whose sympathy is all with the men, and they accept the situation philosophically." The same paper also reported that prosperous businessmen impeded car traffic during the Providence riot. Even the *Journal* noted with perplexity that "respectable persons" joined the ranks of demonstrators, if only out of curiosity. Although the editors tried to suggest an anarchist influence on several occasions, the unfounded red-baiting fell flat. At least one letter writer, however, forwarded an ethnic interpretation to the unrest by asking: "Are we in Ireland, where the shillalah grows indigenous to the soil and where the rock and the bullet are a part of the air we breathe, or mayhaps in Italy, the home of the bright shining stiletto." In an ironic way this stereotyping, and the disenfranchisement that accompanied it, underlay the troubles and the prejudice evident in articles about trolley trips to immigrant neighborhoods.[6]

The *Journal* itself became a target of protestors who rightly saw the state's premier newspaper as a stalwart defender of the political status quo. In Lonsdale, residents hanged a likeness of a scab complete with a *Journal* in his pocket, while protestors in the Pawtuxet Valley strung up an effigy of a local reporter there. The newspaper was roundly denounced at a solidarity rally in Providence, and Rezin Orr called it the "capitalist's paper." The Pawtucket Central Labor Council condemned the publication because it "hideously distorted and misrepresented the true state of affairs in this city." The same labor body joined its Providence counterpart in placing the newspaper on a boycott list. A conductor remarked that the editors "hated unions like the devil hated holy water." Journal management privately growled that "during the past month, the paper had been through a crisis unequalled in its history. It had stood for law and order, as in 1842, while its contemporaries had espoused the cause of the trolly [sic] railroad strikers. A systematic boycott had been brought against the circulation and advertising, threats made to destroy the building, and one of the reporters had narrowly escaped with his life, at the hands of a mob, in Pawtucket."[7]

During the strike, the owners of the Outlet department store secretly "lent" the carmen's union $200. The retailer's full-page advertisement in the strikers' souvenir booklet read: "The *Outlet Bulletin* extends its support and sincerely trusts the Conductors and Motormen will win their just cause." The company's influential weekly handout, allegedly with the largest circulation of any periodical in Rhode Island at the time, continually linked the *Journal*, the Union Railroad, and the state's corrupt political system.[8]

The walkout ignited more opposition against the political establishment

than any event since the Dorr uprising. Several Protestant ministers ser-
monized in favor of the strike, and the *Providence Visitor*, official organ of the
Catholic diocese, defended Fitzgerald, proclaiming: "It is neither Christian nor
human to ask men to work fourteen or sixteen hours a day for the pittance a
conductor earns." An official of the Providence County Savings Bank, a leader
of the state's influential Prohibition Party, also backed the strikers. Others, if
not wildly prounion, were enthusiastically antirailway. For example, small businesses, especially in Pawtucket, felt the pinch of lost trade as the walkout
dragged on and impatiently urged the governor to test the constitutionality of
the ten-hour law. One local merchant branded the pushy militia "more exas-
perating than the hoodlum element." A tired Providence police officer even
confessed to a reporter, "If any of us men had our way about it we would haul
in every scab at work on general principles."[9]

That attitude also found expression outside of the Blackstone Valley. In
Rhode Island's other industrial center, inhabitants clamored for justice. The
Pawtuxet Valley, southwest of Providence and still heavily agricultural but hon-
eycombed with industrial villages, hosted support events. The railway terminated all night service there to avoid vandalism and violence. Warwick police
feared to arrest demonstrators and winked at behavior considered punishable
in Providence, "shouting and yelling not constituting revelling as an offense in
the country villages." Local officials initially deputized several strikers, as in
Pawtucket, and eventually had to reorganize the entire police department to
restore order. Thousands turned out in these rural areas to cheer carmen at
boisterous rallies. The *Journal* suggested sending the militia there too. When
the strike sputtered out in early July, railway officials asked the town to lay off
twelve extra patrolmen, prompting the *Journal* correspondent to reveal that
"they were in the employ of the Traction Company, not of the town, and that
the former expects to pay for the service rendered." Fitzgerald had pointedly
accused sheriffs of working for the Union Railroad.[10]

Regardless of statewide solidarity, the strike had to be won in Providence,
although the union felt for a time that a suburban strategy employing a public
relations pincer campaign in both valleys would win the day. Labor in the capital city lacked the messianic quality of the recently organized Blackstone Valley,
nor was it a monolithic working-class town like Pawtucket, with "occupational
homogeneity." Business interests ruled the roost in Providence. Mayor Joseph
Grainger, although a Democrat, owed his election to other groups. He therefore kept aloof from the troubles while allowing police to maintain law and
order. Public sentiment against the Union Railroad, especially among daily
commuters, withered somewhat in the face of the inconvenient and prolonged

pedestrian life. The union was unable to mobilize enough transportation alternatives despite deploying some "antiquated arks" in the early days of the conflict. The Providence Central Labor Union championed the strikers by distributing support leaflets in working-class neighborhoods, but its recently developed political arm was still in a pioneering stage.[11]

Fitzgerald enlisted the lukewarm support of Mayor Grainger and several other chief executives and council presidents to pressure Marsden Perry into a compromise agreement with the union, but to no avail. Attempts to pass ordinances in these towns requiring motormen and conductors to have prior streetcar experience never reached fruition. Earlier, the carmen's union influenced Governor Kimball to arrange a meeting with Perry, but the traction king refused to see the committee because two union members were on it. Kimball softened his own involvement by explaining: "I suppose that people will think I was trying to settle the strike, but all I desired to do was to see what could be done toward bringing about a meeting."[12]

Failure of a suburban strategy to force the Union Railroad Company to the bargaining table left the union one last hope—a favorable ten-hour ruling from the state supreme court. Albert Potter had arrogantly challenged the act when he said, "The right of every man to sell his labor at such price and upon such terms as are satisfactory to him must and will be maintained in the State of Rhode Island in the future, as it has been in the past." The company legally avoided forcing anyone to work longer, but given the circumstances it would have taken a brave soul to insist on a shorter workday. Ironically, the first challenge came from a disgruntled stockholder of the independent Woonsocket Street Railway, which had obeyed the ten-hour statute. A wealthy investor asked the courts to overturn the law on constitutional grounds and prohibit the carrier from limiting the workday. The carmen's union, partially through the hesitancy of counsel Henry Tiepke, who hoped to fashion a political solution, failed to act quickly. Tiepke waited for the state's desultory attorney general to initiate proceedings.[13]

Railway and elected officials whined endlessly about law and order during the strike while mobilizing police agencies against local citizens. The public fumed at the corporate and political hypocrisy in disregarding the ten-hour law. The *Springfield Republican* tweaked the local power structure when it reasoned, "The good citizens of Rhode Island should not forget that the anarchy has not been exhibited solely on one side." The union constantly underscored the double standard. Lucius Garvin, the bill's originator, complained publicly, and the Cumberland town council denounced the double standard: "The United Traction Company . . . has demonstrated its ability to secure whatever legislation is beneficial to itself, and prevent the passage of any act that did not meet with its approval in the past, thereby setting the public an example of what a powerful corporation may do in setting aside legislative enactments and judicial opinions that do not satisfy its interests." A letter to the editor reflected popular opinion: "The Union Railroad Company to-day deliberately defy all law and obedience, declaring by their acts and declarations that they will not recognize the authority of the Legislature and moreover are importing and arming aliens [scabs] from other States to come here and help them in their struggle for supremacy." Even party stalwart and state railroad commissioner, Edward L. Freeman, admitted, "There is no doubt but that the great majority of the people of the State believed that it was the duty of the railroad corporations to obey the ten-hour law, so called, until it was declared unconstitutional or was repealed."[14]

On June 26 the Rhode Island supreme court finally rendered an advisory opinion, requested by the governor, upholding the law's constitutionality. It cited a 1898 United States Supreme Court decision in *Holden* v. *Hardy*, supporting an eight-hour day for miners in Utah. Five of the justices signed the decision, one abstained, and the seventh released a dissenting opinion. The Union Railroad still refused to comply until the issue was reviewed by a federal appeals court. Even the *Journal* editors, bitter detractors of the strike, recoiled at this obduracy: "The railroad management, evidently indifferent to popular feeling in the matter, proposes to fight it out on its own line if it takes all summer." The cleavage among GOP factions was widening.[15]

On June 28 a circuit court also upheld the law in response to the suit by the Woonsocket Railway shareholder. The state attorney general immediately announced there would be no legal action until the fall term. A speaker at a labor rally in East Providence ruefully commented, "When the Court gives its decision some years from now these motormen and conductors will be all dead." The union, however, finally found a working motorman to contest toiling more than ten hours, and a sheriff issued a citation to the railway. That case went to a grand jury but was held over until September as well. Meanwhile, Marsden Perry's Union Trust Company, acting as trustee for bondholders of the Rhode Island Suburban Railway, furthered the Byzantine drama by asking for an injunction against the attorney general to prevent enforcement of the act.[16]

Strikers had long since returned to work in Providence; union members in the Pawtuxet Valley threw in the towel on June 23. Pawtucket carmen were disheartened. At a union meeting in late June, a passing streetcar in the midst of a rousing speech brought an unrehearsed and eerie moment of silence from the speaker and his listeners, as if they sensed it was finally over. Union officials tried to get Potter to take back all the strikers. He eventually allowed most to come back, but without seniority. Returnees also had to sign a "yellow dog" contract, promising never to join a labor organization while working for the Union Railroad. Division 200 officially ended the strike after a four-hour meeting in Providence on July 5. The vote was 141 to 47.[17]

The few Pawtucket men in attendance returned to the Blackstone Valley, where they voted 41 to 10 to continue the walkout independent of Providence. A waiting crowd cheered the decision, and children were sent through town with placards announcing the outcome. Strikers balked at returning as junior employees. Some old-timers would lose fifty cents a day. "The men feel that they couldn't, with honor, submit to such humiliation," a union spokesman announced, "and they refused to call the strike off. They have done all they could without absolutely grovelling at the feet of the company, to settle this matter, but they believe that they owe it to their manhood and to the public to act as they have."[18]

Henry Tiepke, the union's lawyer, met with Potter after the Pawtucket vote and tried to arrange a better deal. On July 8, five weeks after the strike began, Pawtucket carmen voted to return. The company agreed to rehire all but five of the local strikers, but without seniority. Most scabs left town immediately, mitigating the loss of rating but not the question of wages. The union secretary announced the decision from a window at strike headquarters on Main Street. He virtually apologized to the hostile throng, who had adopted the walkout and political battle as their own. He explained that the strikers had no alternative once the Providence-based union had capitulated. Carmen also wished, he commented defensively, to avoid further damage to local businesses that had been so supportive. After jeering the announcement, supporters lowered the union banner over Main Street in a dramatic act of surrender. At least a dozen bombings and shootings occurred in the waning days of the strike as frustrated followers vented their anger.[19]

The authors of the strike history, both of whom returned to work through Potter's largesse, ended their short chronicle on a lyrical note: "The battle has been fought and lost, but with defeat comes the thought: Honor and fame from no condition rise; / Act well thy part, there all the honor lies." Ironically, during the Amalgamated's next foray, in 1908, several strikebreakers from the 1902 walkout joined the labor fold. Both sides finally negotiated a contract in 1913. As late as 1920, however, new employees were warned by union members to shun the few remaining outside scabs from a generation earlier. The carmen may have been defeated in 1902, but the issues raised regarding corporate and boss rule in Rhode Island took on a life of its own. The strike triggered a larger conflict that played out in the general elections that fall and influenced political battles for the next three decades.[20]

The subtitle of the souvenir history published by Division 200 read, "Showing the Difference between the Organization of Capital and Labor." Despite that heading, the chronicle was not a sophisticated, socialist treatise about strengths and weaknesses. Rather, the pamphlet narrowly compared the power of the Union Railroad and that of the street carmen's union. During the walkout, the carrier became part of the much larger Rhode Island Company, Marsden Perry's amalgamation of local utilities controlled by a Philadelphia syndicate. The strikers' memoir reasoned that "by perfect organization the managers or leaders were enabled to form what has become one of the most powerful corporations in this part of the country." Against this financial and political behemoth, the carmen fashioned an impressive organizational solidarity but one internally undermined by several hundred old-timers and inexperienced younger members.[21]

The carmen's history pessimistically bemoaned the union's showing. In a larger context, which the title suggested but never addressed, Rhode Island labor organized a most sophisticated campaign in view of limited time and difficult circumstances. Although the Union Railroad and its successor, the Rhode Island Company, came packaged in the latest corporate wrappings, it was local capital that fragmented. There was a breakdown of unity within Brayton's inner circle; small business chafed at dominance by big business; and the middle class, usually a reliable bulwark against labor violence, turned against the state's political leaders and briefly encouraged labor turbulence as a sign of collective disenchantment with the corrupt system. Despite this fractured ruling sector, even an unblemished union operation might not have been enough to defeat a dominating enterprise backed by repressive governmental machinery. Still, the labor juggernaut, accelerated by support from thousands of disgruntled Rhode Islanders, reached dizzying political speeds. The 1902 carmen's strike was the first important labor leg on the road to Democratic Party suzerainty in the state, accomplished by weaning conservative skilled workers and minority newcomers from the Republican Party fold. The emergence of capable, well-educated Irish Catholic Democrats like John Fitzgerald and James Higgins gave the middle class new options in the voting booth despite lingering ethnic and religious prejudice.

In retrospect, Division 200 committed several fatal but seemingly unavoidable mistakes given the complexity of the political landscape in Rhode Island. Inexperienced union officers failed to harness seething employee anger when the Union Railroad disobeyed the ten-hour act. The precipitous strike, called out of enraged exasperation rather than calculated strategy, was premature by a few weeks. The local division should have waited for Rezin Orr and gained official Amalgamated sanction and requisite strike benefits. In the interim, the union could have given management a deadline to comply with the law and channel a fathomless discontent with the Union Railroad into positive prounion insurgency. This disaffection included a reform sector of the Republican Party that was embarrassed by noncompliance with GOP-sponsored ten-hour legislation. The carmen similarly failed to formulate a comprehensive strategy for a political settlement by further isolating the railway and Marsden Perry in the eyes of the community and legislators. The union also needed to arrange for alternate transportation, however limited, to assist middle-class supporters in Providence who wanted to boycott streetcars but had no other way to travel. Large downtown retailers, like the Outlet, might have been willing to help.[22]

The Outlet Company was not alone in its animosity to the Union Railroad. Community-based merchants, whether in towns or rural areas, harbored grievances against the traction company. Route selection meant the difference between customers' trading at a neighborhood shop or making a trip to a larger store elsewhere. Bypassed retailers, like those in Olneyville, cursed the railway for waylaying shoppers. Downtown commercial businesses, on the other hand, wanted lower fares, free transfers, and better service to attract more suburban shoppers. Outlying markets, now thoroughly dependent on rapid but monopolized trolley freight service, complained of high rates. In Pawtucket, where the Merchants' Association felt alienated from the exclusive ranks of big capital's Business Men's Association, local store owners bristled at the political power wielded by factory magnates. Furthermore, the strike itself dampened commercial activity throughout the state as stores, entertainment facilities, and amusement parks felt the boycott's indirect pinch. Most small businesses probably shared their customers' distaste for a scofflaw railway and its long-time arrogance. For a decade the Union Railroad blatantly manipulated all levels of government and soured Rhode Islanders toward the traction system and its political handlers.[23]

The state labor movement, affiliated with the American Federation of Labor, desperately needed to coordinate strike activity between several important unions. Walkouts by textile workers, teamsters, and street carmen in 1902 all overlapped, however briefly. The railway commissioner labeled the traction insurrection "the most formidable strike that ever occurred in the history of the State." Henry Tiepke, with a less parochial vision because he compiled the state's comprehensive industrial statistics, branded the weavers' nine-month walkout against the gargantuan American Woolen Company as the "most important and wide reaching" that year. Militant team drivers, miffed at the failure of their own job action, took out their frustrations on the Union Railroad Company, long after their own strike ended. Only an occasional socialist like Dr. James Reid, an Olneyville dentist, ever addressed the need to integrate these disparate actions into a coordinated force. The A. F. of L., representing mostly skilled, English-speaking workers, was indifferent and at times hostile to organizing the unskilled or assisting new immigrants from eastern and southern Europe—rapidly becoming key players in Rhode Island's industrial work force and ethnic neighborhoods. A harmonized strike command might have empowered labor to a greater degree. Both socialists and mainstream unionists advocated political action during this period but wasted valuable organizational energy bitterly contesting one another for leadership of the state's working class.[24]

The carmen also held a wild card that, if played differently, might have made a difference in the state's Machiavellian framework. The Republican legislature, in the waning days of the 1902 session, watched with fear as organized labor, especially in Providence, entered the political arena. "To catch the labor vote at the next general assembly" and take the sting from unpopular legislation to incorporate the Rhode Island Company, the machine passed a fifty-eight-hour-a-week factory law and the ten-hour traction statute. At the time, organized labor was unwilling to associate itself too closely with either major party, so GOP maneuvers kept the union from tilting too closely to kindred Democrats. Dr. Lucius Garvin, who had annually sponsored the ten-hour law since 1898, ruefully watched Republicans amend that bill into their own: "At the last session they passed two labor measures before they adjourned," he commented, "because they thought the labor people were waking up and taking an interest in politics."[25]

The *Springfield Republican,* always a keen observer of the Rhode Island scene, admitted, "It is a mystery that this [ten-hour] bill should have been permitted by the boss to pass." In a rare gesture of bipartisan support, the assembly had unanimously ratified both labor statutes. Although there is no extant source material that proves the Union Railroad agreed to obey the law beforehand, it stands to reason that the GOP would never have entertained such a law without the explicit prior consent of Nelson Aldrich. On April 5, one day after the ten-hour ordinance passed, Brayton wrote to the senator informing him that he "could not resist" the measure and still ensure legislative approval to incorporate the Rhode Island Company. Superintendent Potter gave a public impression of compliance for eight weeks, until the eve of the strike. Edward L. Freeman, Republican insider and railroad commissioner, indirectly confirmed the railway's concurrence in his annual report: "It was generally understood that the law would be obeyed by the several street railroad corporations."[26]

Lincoln Steffens claimed that the Philadelphia holding company negotiated to buy an eleven-hour road that paid two dollars a day in wages, not a costlier ten-hour one. The *Pawtucket Times* cited a rumor that the same syndicate stopped implementation at the last minute for fear that a shorter day in Rhode Island would spread demand for the same to their other properties. Marsden Perry had protested that union demands would "make it impossible for the company to pay any dividends for a series of years." The utility king predicted that the enterprise's strong stand would "certainly be a lesson in the future for unions and agitators to look for a more favorable field of operation than the street railroad system of the United Traction and Electric Company."[27]

Perry, after masterminding formation of the Rhode Island Company, may have felt powerful enough to buck even the legislature to protect his gingerly assembled utility realm. Three days into the strike, with the Rhode Island Company about to take form, Nelson Aldrich suddenly resigned as president of the Union Railroad, an action the *Outlet Bulletin* characterized as "a great bluff on the public" and another example of devious "Aldrichism." The company was becoming a serious political liability, so the senior senator ducked out of the traction limelight, kept his valuable stock, and left his financial henchmen in control.[28]

Perry, who now openly commanded the empire, had just built a spacious bank building for his Union Trust Company in downtown Providence that signaled his ascension to the pinnacle of financial power in the state. He moved the street railway hub from one location to his new edifice, bringing "all of Rhode Island to the Union Trust's doorstep." The Union Railroad relocated its offices there as well. Perry took control of the strike and seemed to enjoy using his influence to ensure law and order. He helped break the walkout but unleashed an unexpected political backlash. Lincoln Steffens and others also theorized that Brayton occasionally threw a monkey wrench into GOP affairs just to prove his indispensability to Aldrich and Perry. The Boss was allegedly indignant about Perry's embarrassing, last-minute double cross on the ten-hour bill. The carmen could have mobilized public support, untainted by Democratic partisanship, to influence Republicans outside the inner circle to force the railway to toe the line. That window of opportunity opened briefly during the split between Brayton and Perry's Union Railroad.[29]

While news of civil disorder dominated the front pages of all Rhode Island newspapers for almost the entire month of June, less eye-catching but no less significant intelligence was buried in back pages and short paragraphs. The first day of the walkout, 150 strikers marched to Providence city hall to register to vote. Earlier in the year, Republicans had extended enrollment an extra month through June, thinking such action would enhance a GOP turnout. Democratic operatives initially worried that a lengthened period would dilute any urgency among their supporters. By early June, statewide registration had already eclipsed the 1901 total.[30]

Democratic, socialist, and labor forces had in fact long been active in registration drives, especially in the effort to qualify so-called registry voters. These citizens were eligible to cast ballots in mayoral and gubernatorial races but not council elections because of property restrictions. Only those voters who paid taxes on $134 worth of real or personal property had an unencumbered franchise. Registry voters had to remit a dollar to qualify—a practice that often led to party operatives paying the fee for prospective voters and providing a little extra to each as an incentive for future party loyalty.

By the middle of June more than 10,000 such voters qualified, compared to 7,729 the year before. Canvassers toiled evenings the last week of June and enrolled about 1,000 electors a day. When registration ended, some 80,000 voters were eligible to cast ballots. Fifteen of the state's thirty-eight municipalities set records, and most of those were in working-class areas in Democratic strongholds like Pawtucket, Woonsocket, and Providence, where an astonishing 19,000 enrolled. State historian Charles Carroll remarked: "Seldom in Rhode Island's long and unique political history had an issue reached a crisis at the period for registration." He called the showing "without precedent" and "most extraordinary for other than a presidential year."[31]

Near the end of the walkout, a speaker at a mass demonstration in East Providence challenged listeners: "To-day on the labor question we are on a sleeping volcano. You must send workingmen from all the towns in the State to the Legislature." East Providence registration shot up more than 15 percent, and a *Journal* writer estimated that almost half the town's voters were trade unionists. The GOP had successfully enticed workers, both locally and nationally, with the politics of prosperity and the imagery of a full dinner pail. Now, the reporter concluded, "A good many men, who have hitherto been considered staunch Republicans, are said to be Union men." During another strike rally in Olneyville, socialist speakers urged the audience to vote "on election day with united class consciousness." Providence tallied 1,866 more registrants in twenty-two Democratic districts but only 346 more in thirty-four Republican ones. Observers credited similar increases in North Providence as a consequence of the railway strike. "Labor troubles [in Warwick] are expected to have a great influence in behalf of the Democrats," wrote the *Journal*'s correspondent there. Pawtucket achieved an enrollment record. The *Providence Evening Telegram* concluded that a "great stimulus to registration was the series of labor troubles affecting and afflicting the city and state." The Trades Union Economic League began training members in the art of party caucuses. The issue of street control had left the physical realm and entered the polling booths.[32]

Rezin Orr characterized strike violence as "the people uprising in their wrath against a corporation which had apparently up to the present time owned them." Fitzgerald said the "We Walk" campaign must be used to dispatch entrenched assembly representatives. The *Pawtucket Evening Times* editorialized: "It is about time for the workingmen to stand shoulder to shoulder and register so that by the time another year rolls around we will have men in office that will serve the public and not be at the beck and call of Marsden J. Perry and Co." During the summer of 1902, fall election fever already gripped a still restive population ready to deal another blow to the state's industrial and political leaders.[33]

THE UNION RAILROAD IS OUR SUPREME COURT

The feeling against the Ten Hour law has been very strong in the Blackstone Valley and the Republican party has been blamed for this fact. . . . While Mr. [former governor] Kimball may not have been to blame for any of the trouble incident to the recent strike among the street railway employees, he was identified with the party which passed the legislation and then did not enforce the law. This fact was, I think responsible most largely for our victory.

Lucius F. C. Garvin, governor elect, November 1902

The Democrats didn't do anything but elect a governor who can't do anything but sign notaries' commissions and a lieutenant-governor who can't do anything.

Charles Boss Brayton, March 1903

That a Legislature should enact a [ten-hour] law by unanimous vote, witness its high-handed infraction for six months, and then turn tamely around and change the law at the behest of its violators, will be cause for deep humiliation to every citizen of the State.

Lucius F. C. Garvin, governor-elect, December 1902

Although the carmen's strike failed as a labor-relations tactic, the political ramifications achieved a partial victory. During this period of unprecedented upheaval and opportunity, state Democrats faced the prospect of internal divisiveness when two strong candidates vied for the gubernatorial nomination. In addition, Providence trade unionists fielded an independent slate of aspirants for mayor and city council. Democrats had sent Lucius Garvin as their sacrificial lamb against Brayton's candidates in 1901. The physician, whose integrity even the Republicans never questioned, lost by over sixty-five hundred votes to William Gregory, who died in office and was succeeded by Charles Kimball, the lieutenant governor. Garvin seemed the likely party candidate again in 1902, an eventuality enhanced by his long association with the ten-hour law, an issue on everyone's mind at the time. The railway strike, however, also brought to statewide prominence the "beau ideal of the young Democracy," Mayor John Fitzgerald of Pawtucket.[1]

Speculation about Fitzgerald's intentions began in earnest during the railway strike, although his bold actions and confrontational demeanor had always marked his mayoral style. During the first week of the walkout, Pawtucket crowds had spontaneously chanted his name for governor. The *Providence Journal* charged the mayor with exploiting the turmoil for his own political advantage: "The situation in Pawtucket has narrowed down to a political issue, pure and simple, and to that end is being worked to the limit by cheap politicians who have not so much the interests of the strikers at heart as they have the belief that it will make political capital this fall."[2]

Fitzgerald may have been the "beau ideal" of a resurgent Democratic Party, but Lucius Garvin had legions of influential and dedicated supporters who admired his relentless toil for the organization during the lean years. On Labor Day 1902, Rhode Island unions hosted the largest parade in their history, with four thousand nattily attired marchers organized by crafts. Iron moulders, carrying signs demanding political representation and an end to boss rule in the state, warned, "Watch how we vote next November." The parade turnout was particularly impressive in view of the fact that Pawtucket did not participate but held its own Labor Day observance for the first time. Similar events were hosted by other decentralized labor councils in Woonsocket and Newport. Forty thousand jammed Crescent Park after the Providence procession—the biggest crowd ever assembled at the amusement center. The two main speakers were Fitzgerald and Garvin.[3]

The master of ceremonies confused six hundred listeners at the park's amphitheater when he announced that the next governor of Rhode Island would speak. No one was sure who would answer the call, Pawtucket mayor or Cumberland legislator. Fitzgerald went first, attacking monopoly and saying that Independence Day celebrated freedom from external enemies, while Labor Day commemorated freedom from internal ones. Garvin emphasized education, cooperative enterprises, and working-class legislative reform.[4]

Although there was no outward animosity between the two candidates, Rhode Island historian Charles Carroll saw one major difference. He characterized Fitzgerald and his law partner James Higgins as the "Younger Democrats," well-educated, aggressive, third-generation immigrants schooled in the art of local politics. That analysis was corroborated in a contemporary letter to Nelson Aldrich by Joseph P. Manton, Republican activist and owner of a Providence engineering company: "The Democratic party are raising up a large number of bright young men who scent the battle and are eager to fill positions." Garvin and other senior party stalwarts belonged to the old school of patrician, mostly native-born Rhode Islanders, who wielded considerable influence in the Democratic Party long after the Irish came to dominate its rank and file. This benign generational disparity underscored the dividing line between the two camps. Labor Day officially kicked off this novel campaign season.[5]

Fitzgerald continued his intrepid, post-strike, political campaign by giving Garvin "a terrific black eye." Fitzgerald's slate beat Garvin's team in the physician's home town of Cumberland during party caucuses. The mayor then scored an expected clean sweep in Pawtucket several days later and seemed poised to grab the bulk of a large delegation in Providence and other urban centers. Labor mirrored the fissured Democrats; older leaders favored a trusted ally, Garvin, while younger activists hooked onto the rising star of the charismatic Fitzgerald.[6]

As the Democratic state committee met to choose a ticket, both candidates claimed enough support to win the nomination. "Honest" John Davis, the only Rhode Island Democratic governor since the Civil War, was elected symbolic chairman of the gathering. Speakers assaulted the Union Railroad's lawlessness and compiled a platform that encompassed a host of Progressive-era reforms, including shorter working hours and a local three-cent trolley fare. Garvin's nominator trumpeted his candidate's creative action, pointing out that without Garvin's ten-hour law there would have been no railway strike and, by implication, no Fitzgerald candidacy. He emphasized a controlling majority in the legislature rather than election of a ceremonial chief executive.[7]

James Higgins, whom the *Journal* ridiculed as "Fitzgerald's residuary legatee," did honors for the mayor. He asserted that years of Republican rule required heroic leadership. Higgins directly attacked the theory that Fitzgerald was too radical and therefore unelectable. He reminded listeners that the mayor had dismantled an entrenched Republican machine in Pawtucket and built a Democratic majority of one thousand voters in three years. The fiery Higgins, who succeeded his law partner as mayor of Pawtucket that fall and later became the youngest governor in Rhode Island history, exclaimed that Governor Fitzgerald would never call out the militia "at the behest of a party leader to shoot down peaceable and unoffending citizens who were battling for their rights."[8]

Delegates voted 119 to 101 for Garvin, although Providence electors gave the mayor an 18-to-8 advantage. Fitzgerald moved Garvin's nomination by acclamation and stated: "Let the enthusiasm of all those who fought for me be passed over to Dr. Garvin's standard." He promised a large plurality for the party nominee in Pawtucket. Garvin then excoriated the shadowy, extralegal legislative body in Rhode Island controlled by local corporations in league with the Brayton-Aldrich machine. He promised to retake control of local government, not with exploited labor arrayed against honest capital, but by linking the two together against a common enemy: unnatural monopoly and its agents.[9]

The larger issues of the trolley walkout were still foremost in people's minds. Throughout the campaign, candidates from both parties continually peppered the electorate with weekly reminders of the strike. The *Journal* editorialized about a militant Amalgamated action in nearby New Haven, Connecticut, and advised authorities there to "begin at the beginning and arrest every man who cries 'Scab' and break up crowds of loiterers even if a few heads are whacked in the process. Providence adopted that policy. Pawtucket did not." Railway officials also made good copy when the Rhode Island Company announced retroactive daily raises to the lowest-paid employees. "This increase in your wage," Marsden Perry wrote, "is intended to recognize those of the $2.00 men who remained loyal to the Company during the recent attempted strike."[10]

The following spring the railway shocked everyone by instituting, "without solicitation," a standard $2.50 wage for all employees. Pay differentials between motormen and conductors, horsecar veterans and electric crews, and strikers and strikebreakers were eliminated over a five-year period. The company expected the raise to be "an incentive to co-operate with the management in such improvements of the service as may be introduced from time to time for the safety and better accommodation of the public." The Rhode Island Company realized it needed to soften the impact of rationalization with higher wages to prevent the crews' alliance with patrons. Furthermore, the *Journal* reported that when the premium horsecar salary had been in effect, "the men employed on the cars were largely recruited from the trades and were noted as being far superior in general personnel to the conductors and drivers employed in many other places." Management expected the increase to draw a "better class of help, although the change of pay was not made for this purpose, but for the betterment of the conditions of the men." The long shadow of Daniel Longstreet, still active in railway affairs in Colorado, and the contemporary lobbying of Albert T. Potter with current owners paid dividends for the work force once again, although the strike's impact made the largesse necessary. The workday remained at eleven hours until 1907.[11]

Meanwhile Perry dismantled two colonial homes on Providence's fashionable East Side to make way for a princely stable to service the recently purchased John Brown House, the city's most genteel real estate on College Hill.

At the same time, Nelson Aldrich bought a mansion several blocks away to complement his Warwick home, said to be the "grandest country estate" in New England.[12]

In September 1902 a Providence County grand jury tackled one of the largest caseloads in its history because of twenty-four strike-related incidents. Due to a lack of evidence, a judge released a deputy sheriff who had been accused of shooting a boy during the riots. And in Pawtucket the former union secretary challenged the Pawtucket Street Railway for violating the ten-hour statute. He was represented by the irrepressible Henry Tiepke, who was contemplating another run for mayor of Pawtucket.[13]

A few days after the strike ended, the Rhode Island Company finally instituted the long-awaited and controversial stationless transfer plan, which had been postponed for a month because of the walkout. Within a day of implementation, the city of East Providence prepared a damage suit over transfer restrictions; the *Journal* wrote that fall elections in Warwick would turn on the question of narrowly drawn fare zones; passengers complained of inequities; and it was reported that conductors were "intensely and thoroughly disgusted with the transfers." By the end of the month, management established more changeover points. In a peace gesture to the Blackstone Valley, the company made Pawtucket and Central Falls one transfer zone, a concession not required in enabling legislation. Before the election, the *Journal* carried at least a half dozen negative stories about other aspects of Rhode Island Company operations.[14]

The Philadelphia-based United Gas and Improvement Company similarly made the news with plans to merge all utilities in its own home town, consolidate Connecticut railways, and make further acquisitions in Rhode Island. The U.S. Department of Labor and Commerce, in discussing the financial arrangement among Rhode Island carriers, called it "peculiarly complicated." United Gas and Improvement owned most of the Rhode Island Securities Company, which held title to the Rhode Island Company, which, in turn, leased all railway property from the United Traction and Electric Company and the Rhode Island Suburban Railway. Burton J. Hendrick, muckraking chronicler of the nation's urban traction systems, stated, "An attempt to trace the convolutions of America's railway and public lighting finance would involve a puzzling array of statistics and an inextricable complexity of stocks, bonds, leases, holding companies, operating companies, construction companies, reorganizations, and the like." These agreements may have been state-of-the-art financial wizardry, but they loomed as one more conspiracy to suspicious Rhode Islanders.[15]

Once Democrats ended an exciting caucus period and nominated Garvin, Republicans finally chose a slate only a month before the general election. The *Journal* headlined it as "The Same Old Ticket." Joseph P. Manton, who exchanged twenty letters on a variety of topics with Nelson Aldrich during the senator's career, criticized local GOP officeholders as "fossils who are no earthly good." He observed, "Dry rot has control of the Party in the state, and unless something is done to change the condition, the Party is gone." Whereas the Democratic platform emphasized state issues, Rhode Island Republicans highlighted national topics, especially economic good times. The GOP shamelessly took credit for the ten-hour railway law and other labor legislation that Democrats had introduced and championed for years. Brayton touted generous franchise taxes to cities and state; commended the Providence Police Commission for upholding law and order during the carmen's strike; and praised Governor Kimball, the Republican standard-bearer, for mobilizing the militia. The two party platforms were antithetical and offered voters a clear ideological choice.[16]

As expected, the Providence Trades Union Economic League bolted from the Democratic Party and ran an independent legislative ticket after negotiations broke down over a compromise slate. The league also fielded a mayoral candidate, an officer in the highly politicized Iron Moulders Union. In a private letter to Nelson Aldrich, Joseph Manton characterized the league as consisting of "cranky and Independent Democrats." He advised the senator to infiltrate the organization with Republican operatives, "smart, smooth talking men, to insist that they must be independent, not be an annex to the Democratic Party."[17]

The incumbent Democratic mayor, Daniel Granger, decided not to seek reelection in Providence after compiling a lackluster record on transit and workers' issues. In Pawtucket, on the other hand, Republicans named four labor candidates to a seven-member assembly ticket in an attempt to regain power by upstaging the local Labor-Democratic alliance. In what must have been a rebellious act against Brayton and Perry, Republicans there chose the former secretary of the Pawtucket carmen's union, the plaintiff in a ten-hour suit, as one of the nominees. Henry Tiepke, however, apparently foresaw no chance against James Higgins in the race for mayor and went on a fact-finding mission to Pennsylvania as a nationwide coal strike pinched Rhode Island's main energy source. Pawtucket Democrats, who had worked hand-in-glove with the local labor movement, avoided any Economic League disaffection, despite the lack of exclusive union candidates. John Fitzgerald, who ran for his old assembly seat after his defeat in the party caucuses for governor, lambasted workers who ran on a Republican ticket.[18]

Members of the state's minority party cautiously sidestepped internal discord and hammered away at the election's paramount issue, the insolence of the Union Railroad–Rhode Island Company. Garvin ridiculed skimpy franchise payments, praised railway strikers, and suggested that Governor Kimball had changed from being a Mugwump reformer to Brayton's lackey. By and large, Garvin took the high road in the election, leaving assault duty to other candidates and party officials. Dennis Holland, for example, seeking the office of attorney general, decried the dilatory prosecution of ten-hour law violations and advocated revoking the railway's charter.[19]

Democratic Party chairman and former Knights of Labor official Patrick H. Quinn started a publicized imbroglio when he accused Governor Kimball of being a secret stockholder in the Rhode Island Suburban Railway, a Rhode Island Company subsidiary. The governor and his wife had been injured in the spectacular Warwick trolley crash in June 1900, which killed six passengers. Quinn charged that Kimball, who was lieutenant governor at the time, dropped a lawsuit in exchange for $40,000 in trolley stock. The governor denied the accusation vehemently. Although Republicans tried to contradict Quinn's shaky evidence, the indictment probably rang true to a cynical public, ready to believe any account of traction malfeasance.[20]

Unions hosted a rally for Garvin at the Providence Labor Temple, where the gubernatorial candidate was glowingly introduced by John Fitzgerald. The physician cautioned his listeners not to divide votes in Providence between the Democrats and the league. At a separate gathering later in the campaign, Providence unions attacked both major parties and trumpeted their own slate in the capital city, a tactic not unlike the stance of the socialists. They also took credit for the voting registration increase, "brought about by the efforts of labor men, following the strike of the team drivers and the street railroad employees." Of course, traction management received a verbal swat: "When the 10 hour law was passed, they appealed to the Supreme Court, and then we found that the Union Railroad Company is our Supreme Court." One letter to the editor warned the league not to assist "Trolley Government" in Providence by siphoning away votes from the Democrats.[21]

The GOP held a series of well-attended noontime rallies in downtown Providence featuring different candidates. Charles Stearns, the sitting attorney general, who had won the 1901 election by nine thousand votes, defended his desultory actions in the ten-hour controversy, claiming no plaintiffs had come forward to press charges. Henry Tiepke disingenuously defended Stearns's actions as "prompt, vigorous and fearless." He also hailed the transfer bill: "This single act of legislation is of sufficient practical value to the traveling public to entitle all of the candidates of the Republican party to their hearty support and endorsement." The GOP stuck to its guns in an election-eve advertisement that almost swallowed the entire front page of the *Journal*. Republicans reiterated pride in the railway franchise tax, transfer tickets, and labor laws. One bold statement distilled the entire GOP campaign: "Police Commission laws vindicated, as shown by order and safety in Providence and mob violence in Pawtucket."[22]

Voters went to the polls on November 4 with a clear choice of issues and candidates. Garvin won big, beating Kimball by over seventy-seven hundred, a remarkable turnaround from 1901, when he had lost to William Gregory by over sixty-five hundred. The turnout for governor eclipsed that of 1901 by more than twelve thousand votes, a 25-percent increase. Almost sixty thousand electors participated. The *Springfield Republican* wrote that the results "emphatically condemned the course of the street railroad corporation and has sustained the law by . . . ballots; for no one can doubt that the strike entered largely as an issue into the state campaign." The *Boston Herald* noted: "Rhode Island's Democratic Governor-elect looms up like a headland in a fog," the only head of state in his party elected east of the Mississippi. Despite the dramatic increase in registration, those who voted straight Democratic barely outdistanced those who voted strictly Republican, 21,991 to 20,890. Crucial independent voters, or those who split their ballots, endorsed Garvin 10,288 to Kimball's 3,651.[23]

Garvin's running mate, French Canadian Adelard Archambault, also won but by a slender margin. Republican attorney general Stearns was reelected, but his earlier plurality shrank from over nine thousand to a mere twelve hundred. In Pawtucket James Higgins became the youngest mayor in city history, compiling a huge victory margin of fifteen hundred and even earning a handful of Republican votes. Garvin eclipsed even Higgins in Pawtucket, scoring a lopsided plurality of eighteen hundred in Fitzgerald's stronghold. The former mayor was easily elected to the general assembly. In Providence the Economic League's mayoral candidate received a respectable 10 percent of the vote, but only those league candidates for the legislature endorsed by both unions and Democrats won. Edward L. Freeman, the Republican railroad commissioner, whose political career began in 1868, lost his first election ever by a large margin. Despite their euphoric victory, the Democrats failed to win the house of representatives, trailing thirty-seven to thirty-five; in the senate, the GOP margin was twenty-seven to eleven because of that party's strength in country towns.[24]

The *Journal* blamed the GOP loss on boss rule, not on Kimball's unpopular strike stand: "The Brayton machine came pretty near being thrown into the junk heap on Tuesday," the editors wrote. Garvin offered an evenhanded assessment: "The feeling against the Ten Hour law has been very strong in the Blackstone Valley, and the Republican party has been blamed for this fact," the newly elected governor explained. "While Mr. Kimball may not have been to blame for any of the trouble incident to the recent strike among the street railway employees, he was identified with the party which passed the legislation and then did not enforce the law. This fact was, I think responsible most largely for our victory."[25]

The Republicans wasted no further sentiment on progressive labor law. Governor Kimball reconvened the old legislature in a lame-duck session in December 1902. Brayton instituted this postelection gathering a few years earlier to remedy any hostile developments in the general elections. The Boss arranged a "disemboweling" of the shorter workday for railway employees at this conclave. Judge Elmer J. Rathbun, a West Greenwich representative, introduced the amendment to emasculate the ten-hour law by allowing individuals to contract separately for longer work hours. It passed the house, forty-three to twenty-two, but not on a strict party vote, because some Republicans were embarrassed by the about-face. A livid Garvin, only a representative in the rump session, assailed this hypocrisy: "That a Legislature should enact a law by unanimous vote, witness its high-handed infraction for six months, and then turn tamely around and change the law at the behest of its violators, will be cause for deep humiliation to every citizen of the State." Rathbun, who once worked summers on the Crescent Park line for the Union Railroad to earn college tuition money, declared, "Any strong and vigorous man can work 10 hours a day if he sees fit." When the bill came before the senate, Democrats fought it "tooth and nail," and Garvin even entered the senate chambers and defiantly sat next to Kimball during the debate. The lame-duck senate voted, twenty-five to six, in favor of the amendment and then adjourned.[26]

Garvin served two one-year terms as a figurehead. Brayton had initiated another act limiting the governor's budgetary powers and transferring almost all appointive authority to the Republican senate. The "Blind Boss," now losing his sight but not his insight, remarked: "The Democrats didn't do anything but elect a governor who can't do anything but sign notaries' commissions and a lieutenant-governor who can't do anything." In private, the Boss nervously confided to Nelson Aldrich, "We are holding our own in the legislature very well but our majority is so slight in the House that it is with great difficulty that we can always have enough members present to hold the minority in check." He also groused about poor legislative attendance by ungrateful GOP lawmak-

Governor Lucius Garvin, who served from 1901 to 1903, was a follower of the single taxer, Henry George; a fierce opponent of political corruption; and a physician, delivering most of the babies in his representative district. In the state legislature, he initiated the bill establishing a ten-hour workday.

ers. Brayton was already making amends for the election debacle by registering voters in thirty-one of Rhode Island's thirty-eight cities and towns, but he expressed disappointment that "nothing is being done" in seven Democratic strongholds.[27]

Garvin won a second term in 1903 and continued to use the office as a bully pulpit to champion a progressive list of reforms, including a bona fide ten-hour law. In the 1904 campaign, Aldrich took control from an allegedly ailing Brayton and spent $200,000 to regain the governor's seat as well as secure his own reelection to a fifth consecutive term in the United States Senate. Garvin lost to George Utter, Republican operative and owner of the *Westerly Daily Sun*, whose columns had advised the militia to shoot rioters during the railway strike. Utter barely outdistanced Garvin by 856 ballots, riding the coattails of Republican Theodore Roosevelt's dramatic sixteen-thousand-vote presidential plurality in Rhode Island. An anonymous union broadside attacked Utter during the campaign for his earlier remarks and asked, "Is the man who holds the views set forth in that editorial the proper person to be elected commander-in-chief of the forces of the State of Rhode Island?" A similar flier indicted Aldrich for twenty "crimes," including four related to his railway deals and the 1902 strike. A poem in an opposition newspaper decried Perry's role as well:

Who was it made the carmen strike?
Most of you well know;
Who saw the men do lots of work
For small amounts of dough?
Who does not try to arbitrate?
Who uses all his "grease,"
To have capital and labor
At anything but peace?[28]

The senator's active involvement was unusual in this election. Edwin Lefevre, who popularized Aldrich's unofficial title, "General Manager of the United States," in a friendly magazine article, commented: "At home he merely bosses Boss Brayton as Boss Brayton bosses—or bossed—the bosslets. He takes no interest in local issues, and comes to life politically only during national elections—or when his own reelection to the United States Senate is at stake." Besides temporarily pushing Brayton to the sidelines, Aldrich and Perry also replaced Hunter White as Republican state chairman. Dumping the sheriff may have won back some disgruntled Republicans, who still chafed at the party's inept performance during the ten-hour controversy and the railway rebellion. Joseph P. Manton, GOP stalwart, who continued to support Brayton, criticized White: "The Chairman of the State Central Committee is filled by a man who draws the largest salary in the state, and showed his inefficiency at the riot in Pawtucket, who instead of leading his deputies in number sufficient himself, and properly so, sent an inefficient deputy with arms concealed. The Brigade Commander took his troops without ammunition thus inviting assault, and addressed the rioters as friends."[29]

When Garvin lost, Fitzgerald was the only Democrat elected to the assembly from either city, an incredible turnaround from two years earlier and a testament to the GOP machine's resiliency, Aldrich's tenacity, and continued ethnic and religious fragmentation. It also underlined the strike's galvanizing effect, if only for a couple of years. Garvin, on the other hand, received some solace and recognition for his efforts. William Jennings Bryan mentioned him as presidential timber, and muckrakers like Lincoln Steffens used the governor's pronouncements to attack municipal corruption. Nevertheless, Rhode Island's national black eye was worn as a sign of courageous combat by Brayton's defiant machine.[30]

CONCLUSION: ANOTHER DORR WAR

At irregular intervals what might be called the strike bacillus takes serious hold of the employes of street-car companies in various parts of the United States and strikes follow. The fever rages in one city and then in another. It starts suddenly, as a rule, and runs its course, with violence to mark its frequent changes. Inasmuch as it begins with almost no warning, it is difficult to foretell when the next attack will occur.

Harper's Weekly, 1899

The small business man is the most heavily oppressed man there is to-day, for capital grinds him on one hand and labor on the other.

Providence Journal, 1903

Old Providence turned with a gasp and pinched itself to see if it was awake . . . when the old familiar tinkle of a horse car bell and the shrill whistle of the conductor was heard.

Providence Journal, 1912

Despite years of daily, hands-on, quality personnel management from Daniel Longstreet and Albert Potter, Rhode Islanders debated the volatile railway issue as part of the era's larger and hostile contest between private trusts and public interest. Criticism of corporate ownership and influence, rather than operational questions, triggered a violent response in the framework of labor unrest against monopoly. The period's controversy between weal and wealth overwhelmed the legacy of polished employee relations at the Union Railroad–Rhode Island Company. Notwithstanding the widespread discontent by crews and riders, unionization required four different organizing drives to overcome the liberal and paternal policies of two outstanding managers. The Amalgamated assigned division numbers in chronological order—39, 200, 504, and 618—all chartered to Providence carmen between 1894 and 1913.[1]

Local historian Patrick Conley, in his account of the Dorr uprising, characterized nineteenth-century Rhode Island as a "democracy in decline." In some ways, the Union Railroad's imperial owners stretched the political de-

When young Irish and Italian transit workers finally established Division 618 of the Amalgamated in 1913, after three previous attempts, they maintained solidarity by engaging in social and cultural activities with men of similar ethnic background.

cline into a longer retreat. Within two generations of the founding of mass transportation in the state, Rhode Islanders lost the right to control routes, fares, transfers, and franchises. At the same time, local politicos used the traction company to enrich themselves and perpetuate machine rule. The Union Railroad became a conduit for legalized state corruption. Traction employees had inadvertently confronted the whole rotten system over the right to organize but lost.[2]

Governor Lucius Garvin was an admirer of Thomas Wilson Dorr, the legendary political reformer who gave his name to the local mid-nineteenth-century upheaval. The physician told an instructive and ironic story during his first term. A trolley conductor for the Rhode Island Company, discussing the futility of electoral change in the state, declared that "reform could not be gained except by another Dorr War." Fitzgerald's Rebellion, as many observers–both friend and foe—had noted, was a related twentieth-century version of that earlier struggle for political rights. The conductor, without a historical perspective and with the bitterness of defeat so recent, failed to appreciate his role and those of his fellow workers in striking a blow for justice. The Progressive era was a new kind of Dorr War, although the state's liberation was further postponed until New Deal forces finally broke machine control in the 1930s.[3]

The striking street carmen comprehended the dual nature of their walk-out. On the one hand, they instituted an ordinary job action to ensure a better way of life, as did workers throughout the nation in this period. On the other hand, motormen and conductors recognized the inherent lack of probity in Rhode Island's political system. The machine had victimized them by passing, and then not enforcing, the coveted ten-hour law. Their righteous response, publicly exposing the corrupt machine through symbolic slogans on picket signs, galvanized thousands of citizens to perform actions that cut deeply across class lines: rioting, reveling, boycotting, or making contributions in support of labor, all aimed at humiliating the railway and the ring.

Like other transportation workers in different sectors, the carmen under-stood a community's pulse from daily social intercourse. Mutual kindness and favors between transit workers and riders fashioned an unusual personal alli-ance in which an injury to one became an injury to all, a bonding unduplicated in scope in most other American industries. No other class of worker was the subject of so many human-interest stories in the local press, usually combining humor and respect for a vocation always in the public eye. Passengers, in gen-eral, supported carmen's demands for better wages, a shorter day, and safety improvements; in return, motormen and conductors attacked the hated rail-way and the state political regime that nurtured and protected it. The riding public, like the striking employees, gently tolerated the old-timers who stayed on the job, saving their wrath for unfamiliar strikebreakers and Sheriff White's deputies in Pawtucket. Commuters, some of whom traveled with the same transportation crew for decades on stagecoaches, omnibuses, horsecars, and trolleys, sympathized with the veterans' dilemma and turned the other cheek, even though their stance crippled the walkout.[4]

These same citizens went to the polls in record numbers that fall, probably realizing that even a dramatic victory by Garvin could not really undo the institu-tionalized tyranny of local political life. There was some satisfaction in saddling Brayton, Aldrich, and Perry with the bosses' arch-enemy as governor, but the real psychological release came in the strike's guerrilla progressivism. Rhode Island-ers repaid the Union Railroad and boss rule in a sustained and violent mayhem aimed at the carrier and its elite supporters. The attacks may have provided more gratification than any venomous release in the polling booth.

The walkout in Rhode Island thus effected a vendetta against a corporate ruling class that cut across two generations. "For years Rhode Island has been a sort of feudal state," author Mary Cobb Nelson asserted, "with the mill owners ruling their operatives as surely as medieval landlords ruled their serfs. The interests of the manufacturers were well taken care of by the legislature, and the first duty of the senators and congressmen was to represent Rhode Island's industry." To dislodge such an entrenched machine would take a sustained effort, a relentless drive that could expect no dramatic, rapid settlement. Historian John Buenker commented, "On the surface, at least, Rhode Island was little troubled by the reformist turmoil which elsewhere characterized the Progressive Era." However, he uncovered considerable reform activity beneath the exterior calm and lionized the "urban, foreign stock, working class and their representatives" as historiographically unappreciated and unrecognized shock troops for liberalization in the state.[5]

Rhode Island Democrats, ethnic communities, labor unions, and even small businesses forged an informal pluralistic coalition to lobby for progressive issues at the same time that the nation's two major political parties suffered a weakening of rank-and-file loyalty. Even before the 1902 strike wave, several unions joined forces with the Rhode Island Woman Suffrage Association to back a local constitutional initiative at the general assembly. The sixty-member Providence Retail Cigar Dealers Association met at the local Labor Temple to coordinate strategy against the tobacco trust over several issues, particularly the employment of children. Labor delegates attended, and the group received strong union backing. Similar concerns about school-aged children working in textile mills drew the influential middle-class and female Rhode Island Consumers' League into the labor orbit as well by jointly criticizing weak enforcement of state factory laws.[6]

The railway strike's ramifications were not unique to Rhode Island, although few other states outside of the South were so politically debased. When the chronic labor battles on the nation's steam railroads receded after the Pullman strike in 1894, that vacuum was filled by the new railed juggernaut in urban transportation. The Amalgamated Association of Street Railway Employes resurrected transit strife by engaging in more than two hundred strikes during the Progressive era. These "car wars," as they were colloquially known, engulfed small and large cities alike and resulted in close to one hundred deaths. Only the country's coal wars claimed more victims. Legal historian Sidney Harring recounted that the carmen's union "took advantage of the social costs of massive urban violence, and used the public character of these strikes to generate support for settlement." The union officially excoriated dynamiters "as the enemies of our association" but used the fear of such unbridled passion to forge compromises. These conflicts were often remembered as the most momentous in a city's history.[7]

Ubiquitous railway walkouts had different consequences in various times and places but shared a similar anatomy: tax and franchise controversies, politically influential owners, labor unrest, a strike, boycott, and popular upheaval. The larger the system and number of strikers, the greater the turmoil. General union organizing, especially teamster activity, gave a boost to the carmen's cause. The presence of a city labor council also acted as a contributing factor. On the other side of the ledger, a well-heeled management with connections to the political establishment produced a united front of judicial, police, and military powers. The strikers counted on assistance from the Amalgamated, although the limited resources of the parent organization did not seem to deter action. The introduction of professional, outside strikebreakers mobilized citizens of all stripes to support their beloved motormen and conductors. The progressive temper of the times also meant that newspapers, retailers, religious groups, and middle-class elements would, out of character, swing to the side of labor against the railway and its benefactors. In these promethean battles the appearance of a political champion who engaged a corporate carrier seemed to make the most difference in whether a walkout succeeded. Fitzgerald in Pawtucket; Pingree in Detroit; the mayors of Bridgeport, Connecticut, and Portland, Maine; the Saint Louis city attorney; and aldermen in Waterbury, Connecticut, gave sustenance and encouragement to strikers and their supporters. Such political sympathy, combined with popular violence, often forced traction owners to compromise quickly—giving the strapped crews a respite from the owners' superior resources, which usually overwhelmed them after a few weeks. Although sustained mayhem eventually alienated middle-class sympathizers, a local chief executive with police powers seemed to legitimize the community's right to protest militantly, if only briefly.[8]

As organizing campaigns continued, the casualties mounted. A railway rebellion in Saint Louis in 1900 ended only after the deaths of sixteen and the wounding of hundreds. A trolley strike in Albany, New York, a year later triggered the mobilization of three thousand militiamen. The same year as the Rhode Island conflict, a clash in Terre Haute, Indiana, exposed class division in a city once known for its intraclass solidarity. Eugene Debs's personal intervention did nothing to soften the stance of an out-of-state corporation. Traction troubles in Houston, Texas, in 1904 followed a similar scenario, but initial public support eroded during a five-month walkout that ended with a backlash against labor anarchy. In San Francisco a decade-old drive for municipal ownership exploded in a fray that left two dead and twenty injured.[9]

The culmination, in intensity anyway, occurred in Philadelphia in 1909. A city-wide railway eruption rocked that bastion of finance capital and touched off a general strike, sympathy walkouts along the East Coast, and a call for national action. For a thin moment, organized and unorganized labor, union members, and large segments of the public shared one objective: conquest of the hated enemy who owned the right to travel.[10]

In a way, control and use of the nation's streets became a metaphor for control of society, and the combatants often chose to fight it out on the very thoroughfares in question. The Amalgamated complained, "Mediation, and conciliation were tried and arbitration was offered, but in every case the companies refused and the only resort left to our divisions was to strike or surrender their rights as an organization." The national union, one of the earliest and most vociferous proponents of industrial refereeing, found a receptive audience in a reform-hungry public. Once rebuffed in their efforts, striking carmen found militant allies, whose violent mischief along miles of unpatrolled railway tracks did not usually seem to harm their cause. A writer for *Harper's Weekly* conceptualized these walkouts: "At irregular intervals what might be called the strike bacillus takes serious hold of the employes of street-car companies in various parts of the United States and strikes follow. The fever rages in one city and then in another. It starts suddenly, as a rule, and runs its course, with violence to mark its frequent changes. Inasmuch as it begins with almost no warning, it is difficult to foretell when the next attack will occur." Unlike other labor disputes, trolley wars were highly visible and touched the lives of much of the population. Rank-and-file members and leaders of other unions sometimes viewed a transit conflict as more deserving of support than their own workplace confrontations.[11]

The generic street railway strike, often more decisive in the political realm than in the field of labor relations, exposed sores in the body politic as the battle unfolded in the anxious confines of the American city. Strike supporters integrated their own frustrations with those of the union and transferred the anger from the narrow confines of a local carbarn to the larger urban context. A transit imbroglio allowed the community to demonstrate its displeasure against an alien company that valued profit above public comfort. Trolley strife had an immense effect on the wider culture and polity of the city.[12]

Traction owners understood these dynamics but refused to change their ways until the Amalgamated's scorched-earth policy forced them to negotiate. "Some wonder has been expressed at the prevalence and extent of strikes on street railroads during the present time of prosperity," the industry's journal wrote, and "the sympathy of the public, either by countenancing acts of violence, by boycotting the cars or by supporting retaliatory measures in the Municipal Court. This tendency indicates a serious condition in municipal and industrial affairs, being a direct attack on order and the rights of property and in favor of confiscation." Despite such concern, only a few municipalities ever appropriated traction systems—and they paid dearly for the privilege. Other local governments were content with smaller concessions and riding improvements. By the time the entire industry realized that "the accretion of small troubles" could no longer be allowed to explode into populist revolt, the progressive Brown system of discipline used on the railroads was making only small progress on urban railway systems. Eventually, hostile riders clamped the industry under an ever-tightening regulatory harness that froze the five-cent fare for decades and indirectly led to the underfunding and decline of mass transit.[13]

The traction question was a great cross-class connector and the lowest common political denominator of the age. The Amalgamated wistfully scented the era's perfume: "Let the battle cry be, 'Municipal control of all these monopolies,' and let us not be satisfied until every street railway in the country is in the hands of the municipality, for then, and only then, will we be safe and out of the reach of the greedy, grasping hand of inhuman avarice." Such a stance allowed the labor movement to become a partner with the middle class and western agrarians, who also experienced a collective vulnerability to railroad and utility monopolies. The fear that railway bribery and influence would further undermine community values and government honesty only increased urban malaise. Genteel reformers also looked to organized labor, perhaps unrealistically, as a mighty force to be directed by their betters. A local muckraking newspaper idealistically portrayed unions as the tip of a working-class iceberg: "Although they include within their ranks only a minority of wage-workers, yet they are the leaders and the representatives of the unorganized as well."[14]

Of course, many businesses felt equal antagonism toward both labor and capital and would gravitate to one side or the other depending on the issue at hand. A local grain dealer unintentionally captured the spirit of the age during the local teamster strike in 1902, when he lamented, "The small business man is the most heavily oppressed man there is to-day, for capital grinds him on one hand and labor on the other." Still, during much of the Progressive era, commercial interests tilted in favor of striking workers—who patronized their stores on a regular basis—against the forces of monopoly.[15]

In no other arena did the tensions in progressivism play out so clearly and explosively. The employer-employee dichotomy held firm in most labor conflicts, but not in the street railway industry. Motormen and conductors avoided the public's "plague on both your houses" mentality by guarding public access to affordable street travel. Although horsecar veterans and electric crews had different historical orientations, they and their passengers sided with each other in a mutual-admiration society. Industrial relations in the streetcar industry were no longer a simple standoff between labor and management, but a complex political balance between city councils, state legislatures, and thousands of daily commuters who now believed that public transportation was indeed public.

In 1911, the year Nelson Aldrich retired from the United States Senate after twenty-nine years in office, horsecar veterans began an annual reunion that dripped with public nostalgia. Clarence "Pop" Spear, who masterminded the event and was still working as a motorman, arranged for a horsecar filled with disabled pensioners to pass through downtown Providence. Their advancing age did not dull the veterans' love of detail and accuracy. The vehicle was pulled by "a finer pair of horses than were ever seen in the old days," and when the antique reached a slight incline, an elderly participant attached an extra steed, symbolizing days when the men had apprenticed as hill boys. William Vinton, who had retired only a year earlier, was the honorary conductor on the trip. Although the sentimental journey was unannounced, hundreds of spectators quickly lined the streets, applauded spontaneously, and threw paper streamers from building windows "as the shadow of the past flit by." After parading through town, the 250 horsecar veterans eligible to attend the reunion reassembled and boarded a small fleet of modern electric trolleys. Pop Spear drove one of the streetcars to a rural clambake. "The big shore dinner attracted added interest," according to a newspaper report, "because of the abundance of lemonade—the old-fashioned drink of the old horse car men."[16]

For a couple of years the parade became a formal event with bands and larger crowds. But the advent of World War I and the deaths of number of participants put an end to the festivities. While they lasted, "Old Providence turned with a gasp and pinched itself to see if it was awake . . . when the old familiar tinkle of a horse car bell and the shrill whistle of the conductor was heard." Reporters used the occasion to take stock of progress and the state's well-being. Retirees did not require such formal analysis. A placard on the side of the horsecar said it all: "The Good Old Days."[17]

The veterans' final requiem came in 1920, when Albert T. Potter died after more than a half century with local transit operations. He had served the riding public since 1866. Although he mastered the intricacies of electric traction, he, like his aging colleagues, lamented the passing of horsepower. By the time he retired, he was affectionately known by his initials, A. T., just like his

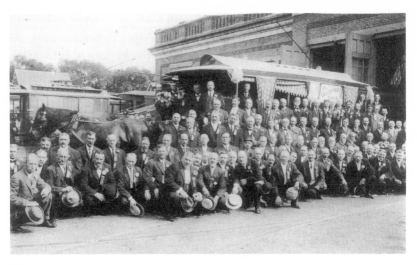

In 1911 veterans of horsecar service began an annual reunion that included a ride in a vintage horsecar. The sign on the side of the car reads, "The Good Old Times."

predecessor, D. F. Longstreet. Time and again he argued for better employee working conditions and higher wages before the tight-fisted Nelson Aldrich and Marsden Perry. After the 1902 walkout he rehired almost every one of the seven hundred strikers, bonding young and old transit workers. He introduced the liberal pension system and equalized wages after the conflict. As a management official he fought the introduction of the union but was an amicable negotiator once the Amalgamated was recognized in 1913. At his funeral hundreds of coworkers gathered to look "for the last time upon the face of the man who for years had been their friend and associate." Eight of the oldest pensioners served as ushers, and, at exactly twelve noon, every streetcar in the state stopped for a minute of respect. His son, Albert E. Potter, succeeding him as general manager, was every bit as popular as his father. His tenure reached into the era of bus service.[18]

As the conventional polity of the Gilded Age collided with the new sensibilities of the Progressive era, it created a riptide of generational friction and a clash of deference and ethnicity between horsecar and trolley crews. On the other hand, the machines they operated—horsecars and trolleys—make nice images for the two periods. In a way, the vehicles glide across invisible barriers that historians erect to demarcate one span from another. Although the technological changeover from horsepower to electricity helped set the stage for citizen and workplace unrest in the industry, Pop Spear whisked away the horsecar veterans in an electric trolley after paying homage to the past in the downtown parade. The old-timers may have been sentimental, but they were also pragmatic and wanted to arrive at the cookout in timely fashion. They longed for the good old days and lamented the uncomfortable and dislocating change they helped usher in through railed transit, but they grudgingly accepted the new way of life with its speedier pace and softer amenities.

Notes

PREFACE

1. Since that time a group of labor activists has established a labor archives at the society's library in Providence.

2. Scott Molloy, "Collecting Labor," *Labor's Heritage* 2 (spring 1990).

3. Scott Molloy, *Division 618: Streetcar Employees Fight for a Union in Rhode Island* (Providence: Division 618, 1977). Scott Molloy, "Rhode Island Communities and the 1902 Carmen's Strike," *Radical History Review* 17 (spring 1978).

4. Scott Molloy, "Motormen, Moguls, and the Machine: Urban Mass Transit in Rhode Island, 1864–1902" (Ph.D. diss., Providence College, 1991).

INTRODUCTION

1. One of the few academic exceptions is Joshua Freeman, *In Transit: The Transport Workers Union in New York City, 1933–1966* (New York: Oxford University Press, 1989).

2. John Gilkinson chose Providence for a study of middle-class formation because it represented a "medium size industrial city" (*Middle-Class Providence, 1820–1940* [Princeton: Princeton University Press, 1986], 7).

3. Undated letter to the editor. The late Dick Wonson, scheduling supervisor at the Rhode Island Public Transit Authority, collected several turn-of-the-century scrapbooks filled with clippings from many different newspapers about local transit history. Although not paginated, they are very valuable. They are hereafter referred to as "Scrapbook."

1. THE PEOPLE'S CARRIAGES

1. Quoted in Welcome Arnold Greene, *The Providence Plantations for Two Hundred and Fifty Years* (Providence: J. A. & R. A. Reid, 1886), 127.

2. *Providence Journal*, 3 Feb. 1876, 29 Jan. 1882, 6 July 1902.

3. "The Journals of Lucy A. L. Howlett, 1848–1852," unpublished diary, kindly

lent to me by Thomas Green of North Providence, R.I. Scott Molloy, "Motormen, Moguls, and the Machine: Urban Mass Transit in Rhode Island" (Ph.D. diss., Providence College, 1991), chap. 1. Henry C. Binford, *The First Suburbs: Residential Commuters on the Boston Periphery, 1815–1860* (Chicago: University of Chicago Press, 1985), 85, 90, 98. Rider Broadside Collection, Brown University.

4. *Providence Journal*, 11 Apr. 1921.

5. *Providence Journal*, 17, 18, 20 June 1864.

6. *Providence Journal*, 10 Sept. 1901. Obituary in "Scrapbook."

7. *Street Railway Journal*, June 1889, 131. Maury Klein and Harvey A. Cantor, *Prisoners of Progress: American Industrial Cities, 1850–1920* (New York: Macmillan, 1976), 20. Charles Carroll, *Rhode Island: Three Centuries of Democracy*, 4 vols. (Lewis Historical Publishing, 1932), 1:521.

8. Peter J. Coleman, *The Transformation of Rhode Island, 1790–1860* (Providence: Brown University Press, 1969). Patrick T. Conley and Paul Campbell, *Providence: A Pictorial History* (Norfolk, Va.: Donning, 1982), 86.

9. *Rhode Island Manual* (Providence: State of Rhode Island, 1988), 722–26. Corrected figures are in Conley and Campbell, *Providence*, 226. The rankings are in William Harrison Taylor, ed., *Legislative History and Souvenir of Rhode Island, 1899 and 1900* (Providence: E. L. Freeman & Sons, 1900), 389.

10. Patrick T. Conley, *Democracy in Decline: Rhode Island's Constitutional Development, 1776–1841* (Providence: Rhode Island Historical Society, 1977), 159; see especially chap. 6.

11. Klein and Cantor, *Prisoners*, 58.

12. Daniel Longstreet, "Events Which Led Up to the Formation of the American Street Railway Association," *Street Railway Journal*, Nov. 1892, 655–59; Oct. 1893, 656.

13. Henry V. A. Joslin, "Street Railway Lines of Rhode Island," in William T. Davis, ed., *The New England States: Their Constitutional, Judicial, Educational, Commercial, Professional and Industrial History*, 4 vols. (Boston: D. H. Hurd, 1897), 4:2518. "The Union Railroad: Development of Street Car Lines in Providence," *Providence Journal*, 19 Nov. 1877. This long, charmingly crafted account of horsecar development in the state is an important, detailed source for understanding the transit story.

14. *Providence City Documents*, "Newspaper Reports" (June–Dec. 1862). This series of valuable scrapbooks at the Rhode Island Historical Society Library in Providence contains newspaper clippings, flyers, and documents from the 1860s and 1870s. *Providence Journal*, 18 June 1862.

15. *Providence Journal*, 21 June 1862.

16. *Providence Morning Star*, 8 Jan. 1882. *All Aboard*, 1 May 1927. Superintendent of hacks, *Annual Report*, in *Providence City Documents, 1866–1867* (Providence: Providence Press, 1867), 77. *All Aboard* was published sporadically in the 1920s and 1930s by the United Electric Railways, successor to the Rhode Island Company and the Union Railroad.

17. *Providence Daily Post,* 13 May 1863. *Providence Evening Press,* 12 May 1863. *Providence City Documents,* "Newspaper Reports" (Jan.–June 1863). *Providence Journal,* 9 May 1863. *Providence Sunday Journal Magazine,* 16 Nov. 1930.

18. *Providence Evening Press,* 12 May 1863. *Providence City Documents,* "Newspaper Reports" (Jan.–June 1863). *Providence Journal,* 13 May 1863.

19. *Providence Journal,* 2 June 1863. *City Documents,* "Newspaper Reports" (Jan.–June 1863). "The Union Railroad," *Providence Journal,* 19 Nov. 1877. *Providence Journal,* 4, 5 Feb., 18 Apr., 5, 31 May, 2 June 1864. *Providence Evening Press,* 3, 7, 11, 14, 24 May 1864. Carroll, *Rhode Island* 2:830. Edward Field, *State of Rhode Island and Providence Plantations at the End of the Century: A History,* 3 vols. (Boston: Mason, 1902), 2:554. Joslin, "Street Railway Lines," 2518. All of the above assigned the month of May 1864. Samuel Rosenberg, "A History of Street Railways in Rhode Island" (M.A. thesis, University of Rhode Island), 6; and Albert W. Claflin, "The Providence Cable Tramway," *Rhode Island History* 5 (Apr. 1946): 41, both claimed March 1864. Greene, *Providence Plantations,* generalized it to the winter of 1863–64, while the informative article "The Union Railroad" intimated the beginning of 1864.

20. *Pawtucket Gazette,* 27 May, 3 June 1864.

21. *Providence Morning Star,* 11 Feb. 1883.

22. *Providence Journal,* 3 Oct. 1863. The ballot also included a constitutional amendment to broaden the suffrage by allowing honorably discharged Civil War veterans, regardless of national origin, the right to vote. It lost handily, partly because the *Journal*'s editors opposed the enfranchisement of mainly Irish veterans. *Providence Daily Post,* 9 Nov. 1864.

23. Bradley H. Clarke, *The Boston Transit Album* (Boston: Boston Street Railway Association, 1977), 3. By 1880 mergers had reduced the number to six in Boston. *Providence Journal,* 8, 9 Nov. 1864.

24. Joslin, "Street Railway Lines," 2519. "The Union Railroad," *Providence Journal,* 19 Nov. 1877. *Acts and Resolves of the General Assembly of the State of Rhode Island in Relation to the Several Horse Railroad Companies, Consolidated under the Name of the Union Railroad Company* (Providence: Providence Press, 1869), 34–36. Rosenberg, "History of Street Railways," 6–7. Claflin, "Providence Cable Tramway," 41–43.

25. "When the First Horse Car Ran in Providence Fifty Years Ago," undated newspaper article in "Scrapbook." *Trollier,* 13 Oct. 1917; The *Trollier* was a weekly publication of the Rhode Island Company, successor to the Union Railroad, issued for one year in 1918–1919. *Providence Journal,* 23 Feb., 3 May, 12, 28, 29 June 1865. "The Union Railroad," *Providence Journal,* 19 Nov. 1877. "Girdle the City," *Providence Evening Telegram,* 21 Dec. 1895. *Manufacturers and Farmers Journal,* 7, 10, 24 Aug. 1865.

26. *Providence Journal,* 23 Jan. 1867.

27. *Providence Morning Star,* 30 Dec. 1872, 3 Jan. 1873. Molloy, "Motormen," chap. 2.

28. *Providence Journal,* 18 Dec. 1867, 15 Nov. 1869. *Providence Morning Star,* 11 July 1874. *Providence Morning Herald,* 21 May 1873. *Resolutions of the City Council of the City of*

Providence with Reports, 1871–1872 (Providence: Hammond, Angell, 1872), resolution 524.

29. *Providence Morning Herald*, 31 Jan. 1868. *Providence Morning Star*, 30 Dec. 1872.

30. *Providence Morning Herald*, 4 Apr., 6 May 1873.

31. Ibid. "The Union Railroad," *Providence Journal*, 19 Nov. 1877; 1, 8, 27 June 1865. *Manufacturers and Farmers Journal*, 24, 31 July, 7 Aug. 1865.

32. *Charters of the Rhode Island Company and Its Subsidiary Companies together with General and Special Acts, and Franchise Agreements with Cities and Towns* (Providence: Snow & Farnham, 1912), 91. The Rhode Island Company was the successor to the Union Railroad in 1902.

33. *Acts and Resolves of the General Assembly* (Providence: Knowles & Anthony, 1855), 117. *Providence Journal*, 23 Mar. 1864. *Acts and Resolves of the General Assembly of the State of Rhode Island in Relation to the Several Horse Railroad Companies, Consolidated under the Name of the Union Railroad Company* (Providence: Providence Press, 1869), 53. *Manufacturers and Farmers Journal*, 11 Aug. 1864. *An Ordinance for the Regulation of Hacks, Omnibuses, Drays, Trucks, &c. Reported by the Standing Committee on Police, August 8, 1864* (Providence: Knowles, Anthony, 1864). *An Ordinance in Relation to Railroads, Reported by the Standing Committee on Railroads, November 28, 1864* (Providence: Knowles, Anthony, 1864).

34. *Providence City Documents*, "Newspaper Reports" (June–Dec. 1863). *Providence Daily Post*, 16 Mar. 1864. *Providence Evening Press*, 14 July 1864. *Manufacturers and Farmers Journal*, 11, 15 Aug. 1864. *Providence Journal*, 15 Mar. 1864.

35. *Manufacturers and Farmers Journal*, 18 Mar., 15 Aug. 1864.

36. *Providence Journal*, 23 Feb. 1869.

37. *Providence Journal*, 7, 15 June 1864.

38. *Providence Journal*, 12, 28 June 1865.

2. AN EXCEPTIONALLY INTELLIGENT CLASS OF MEN

1. *All Aboard*, 1 Jan. 1924, 1 Feb. 1927. Undated newspaper articles, "Scrapbook."

2. *Trollier*, 30 Mar., 6 Apr. 1918. Undated newspaper articles, "Scrapbook."

3. Undated newspaper article, "Scrapbook."

4. Herbert Gutman, *Work, Culture and Society in Industrializing America* (New York: Vintage Books, 1966), 108. Herbert Gutman, "The Worker's Search for Power: Labor in the Gilded Age," in H. Wayne Morgan, ed., *The Gilded Age: A Reappraisal* (Syracuse, N.Y.: Syracuse University Press, 1963), 43. Paul M. Taillon, "Manhood, Whiteness, and the Fraternal Culture of the Railroad Brotherhoods" (paper presented at the Pullman Strike Centennial Conference, Terre Haute, Ind., 24 Sept. 1994), 3, 6, 9.

5. *American Railway Journal*, June 1889, 131. Samuel P. Hays, "The Changing Political Structure of the City in Industrial America," *Journal of Urban History* 1 (Nov.

1974): 8. David N. Smith, "Management Strategies, Working Conditions, and the Origins of Unionism: The Case of the Tramway and Omnibus Industry, 1870–1891," *Journal of Transport History* 8 (Mar. 1987): 33.

6. David Nye, *Electrifying America: Social Meanings of a New Technology, 1880–1940* (Cambridge: MIT Press, 1990), 13–14.

7. "Eighty Years Ago," *Providence Journal*, 29 Jan. 1882. "An Old Time Journey," *Providence Journal*, 10 July 1892. *Providence Journal*, 23 June 1901.

8. "The Union Railroad," *Providence Journal*, 19 Nov. 1877. "When the First Horsecar Ran," undated newspaper article, "Scrapbook." *All Aboard*, 1 May 1927.

9. *Providence Journal*, 17 Jan. 1892. *Providence Morning Star*, 11 Apr. 1886. *All Aboard*, Nov. 1929. His first day on the job in 1903, a holiday, Chris Daniels labored seventeen straight hours without a break (interview with Chris Daniels, Pawtucket, R. I., 17 June 1976).

10. *All Aboard*, 1 Jan. 1924, 1 Mar. 1925. In New York City, being late five minutes earned a two-day suspension (*Street Railway Journal*, Feb. 1886, 114).

11. *Providence Morning Star*, 18 Jan. 1883, 26 May 1884, 21 Nov. 1885. *All Aboard*, 1 Mar. 1927.

12. *All Aboard*, 1 Dec. 1925, 1 Jan. 1926, 1 Mar. 1927. "The Union Railroad," *Providence Journal*, 19 Nov. 1877. *Rules for the Conductors and Drivers of the Union Railroad Co.* (Providence: Gladding & Brother, 1865), 5. *Providence Journal*, 17 Jan. 1892.

13. "The Union Railroad," *Providence Journal*, 19 Nov. 1877. *All Aboard*, 1 Jan. 1926. Henry V. A. Joslin to George L. Vose, railroad commissioner, 18 Apr. 1891 (the letter is in the author's collection, hereafter cited as DSM Collection). *Street Railway Journal*, Apr. 1886, 199; July 1886, 336. The Amalgamated Association of Street Railway Employes of America lauded one of its first contracts in Detroit for including a ten-hour day, but at eighteen cents an hour for horsecar workers and twenty cents for electric streetcar employees. An 1898 survey reflected fewer hours but wages that lagged behind those paid by the Union Railroad in this period (*Motorman and Conductor*, Mar. 1895, Apr. 1898).

14. *Providence Journal*, 3, 13 Dec. 1887. One transit historian remarked that all companies wanted reliable employees but considered transportation work unskilled and undeserving of high wages (Emerson Schmidt, *Industrial Relations in Urban Transportation* [Minneapolis: University of Minnesota Press, 1937], 81). In Chicago, wrote the *Street Railway Journal*, "the Superintendent has a right to discharge a man because he don't look honest or because he don't look sober, or because he wants to reduce the force, or because he wants to put another man in the discharged man's place" (*Street Railway Journal*, Aug. 1885, 220). One railway official suggested boarding the employees in barracks to make them more dependent (*Street Railway Journal*, Apr. 1886, 201).

15. *Rhode Island Industrial Statistics Report, 1888* (Providence: E. L. Freeman & Son, 1889), 80. "When the First Horse Car Ran in Providence Fifty Years Ago," undated newspaper article in "Scrapbook." *All Aboard*, 1 Jan. 1926, Nov. 1929. *Providence Morning Star*, 11, 14 Mar. 1886. Taillon, "Manhood," 12–13.

16. *All Aboard*, 1 Jan. 1926, June 1931. "The Union Railroad Company," *Providence Journal*, 19 Nov. 1877, 9 June 1891, 29 Oct. 1890. The *Street Railway Journal* suggested, "In small cities and towns it is usually best to select the employes from among the residents of the place in which the road is located, and such as are favorably known, and well endorsed, but for lines in large cities it is claimed that the country-bred men make by far the best employes" (May 1891, 256).

17. "The Union Railroad," *Providence Journal*, 19 Nov. 1877, 27 Nov. 1892. *Rules. Providence Morning Star*, 20 Aug. 1885. Rules for crews on New York's Metropolitan [Horse] Railroad appeared in *Street Railway Journal*, July 1886, 335–36. Regulations differed only slightly between properties.

18. "The Union Railroad," *Providence Journal*, 19 Nov. 1877. *All Aboard*, 1 Mar. 1925. Undated newspaper articles in "Scrapbook." In England signs on the trams offered rewards to the public for turning in conductors (Smith, "Management Strategies," 44).

19. Mark Twain, "A Literary Nightmare," *Atlantic Monthly* 37 (Feb. 1876): 167–69. Twain crafted a humorous article describing the mesmerizing effect of the jingle. A slightly different version appeared in "The Union Railroad," *Providence Journal*, 19 Nov. 1877. In 1980 an elderly neighbor of mine, Mrs. Harold Blaine, actually recited the jingle, saying she had learned it from an uncle when she was a child.

20. In Boston fifty conductors employed a small device with a bell to mimic the ring of the bell punch to steal fares (*Providence Morning Star*, 9 May 1882). One transit historian told of employees stealing registers for their own use on the cars (Schmidt, *Industrial Relations*, 77), a legend I heard repeated about several trolley conductors in Rhode Island during the 1930s (*Providence Journal*, 17 Jan., 27 Nov. 1892; 15 July 1944). The Amalgamated implored its members to be honest to preserve the union's reputation (*Motorman and Conductor*, Mar. 1898). Brian J. Cudahy, *Cash, Tokens and Transfers: A History of Urban Mass Transit in North America* (New York: Fordham University Press, 1982), 15, 25.

21. *Providence Journal*, 18 Apr. 1870, 21 Dec. 1872; 13 Aug. 1877; 10 July, 22 Sept. 1879.

22. "The Union Railroad," *Providence Journal*, 19 Nov. 1877. *All Aboard*, 1 Jan. 1926. *Providence Morning Star*, 15 Dec. 1880. Robert Wheeler, "The End of an Era," *Providence Sunday Journal Magazine*, 16 May 1948. *Providence Journal*, 17 Jan. 1892, 15 July 1944. From its inception in 1892, the Amalgamated lobbied for mandatory vestibules, achieving its first success in Ohio. One of its national officers perished at the controls of his trolley in Milwaukee in 1893, actually freezing to death. *Motorman and Conductor*, Mar. 1895. *Motorman, Conductor, and Motor Coach Operator*, Sept. 1942. ATU staff, *A History of the Amalgamated Transit Union* (Washington, D.C.: Amalgamated Transit Union, 1992), 14. The Amalgamated trumpeted its vestibule successes: "The sick and death rate in our organization in the places where the vestibule is used, has decreased 25 per cent, showing the great benefit to the health and happiness of the employe" (*Motorman and Conductor*, Apr. 1897). The general manager of the Albany Railway Company had

a different opinion: "To place such operator in such position that having ears he cannot hear, having eyes he cannot see, and having a tongue and voice he cannot use them" (*Street Railway Journal*, Apr. 1899, 243). In New York City the crews had to provide firewood for stoves on the vehicles (Sarah M. Henry, "The Strikers and Their Sympathizers: Brooklyn in the Trolley Strike of 1895," *Labor History* 32 [summer 1991]: 331).

23. *All Aboard*, 1 Mar. 1925, Nov. 1929. *Providence Morning Star*, 27 Dec. 1872, 3 Feb. 1873, 21 Jan. 1875, 24 Jan. 1878, 2 Mar. 1886. *Providence Evening Bulletin*, 14, 16, 17 Jan. 1874.

24. *Providence Morning Star*, 5 Mar. 1873; 4, 5 Jan. 1878; 12 Dec. 1879; 11 Apr. 1881. *Providence Journal*, 29 Nov. 1880, 26 Jan. 1883, 3 Nov. 1890. *All Aboard*, 1 Jan. 1926. Nye, *Electrifying America*, 105.

25. *Rules*, 5–6. *The People*, 16 Jan. 1886. *Rhode Island Industrial Statistics Report, 1888*, 80. *Providence Morning Star*, 23 Jan. 1875; 3, 24, 25 Jan. 1877; 2 Feb. 1878; 28 Dec. 1880; 8 Feb. 1881; 2 Feb. 1882; 8 Feb. 1886. *Providence Journal*, 18 Jan., 5 Feb., 16, 27 Dec. 1867; 17 Jan. 1892. *Union Railroad Guide* (Providence: Rhode Island Printing, 1879).

26. *Semi-Annual Report of the Railroad Commissioner, Made to the General Assembly at Its January Session, 1876* (Providence: Providence Press, 1876), 23. *Providence Journal*, 20 Aug. 1890, 1 Nov. 1891, 27 Nov. 1892. *Manufacturers and Farmers Journal*, 27 Feb. 1868. *Providence Morning Star*, 24 Mar., 9 June, 14 Oct. 1873; 10 June 1878; 5 Mar. 1880; 23 Nov. 1883; 11 Sept. 1884; 14 Jan., 11 Mar. 1886.

27. *Manufacturers and Farmers Journal*, 22, 29 Aug. 1864. *Providence Journal*, 5 Sept. 1867, 14 Aug. 1889, 29 Aug. 1890. *Providence Morning Star*, 26 May 1879, 21 Apr. 1882. *An Ordinance for the Regulation of Hacks, Omnibuses, Drays, Trucks, &c. Reported by the Standing Committee on Police, August 8, 1864* (Providence: Knowles, Anthony, 1864). *Rules*, 19–22. In New York, reported the *Street Railway Journal*, the "driver is put to a constant strain every moment he is on his car" (Apr. 1886, 199). Long after the disappearance of horsecars, the transit industry would admit just how hard the job used to be. The *Street Railway Journal* wrote, "With all these duties he must stand exposed to the splashing of the mud, the beating of the rain and snow, with his line in one hand and the other hand constantly on the brake" (12 Oct. 1901, 541).

28. *Providence Morning Star*, 26 May 1875, 27 Jan. 1883, 8 July 1886. *All Aboard*, 1 Jan. 1924, 1 Jan. 1926. *Semi-Annual Report of the Railroad Commissioner, 1875* (Providence: Providence Press, 1875), 14; *1880*, 36; *1884*, 40.

29. "The Union Railroad," *Providence Journal*, 19 Nov. 1877. "Streetcar Service: Development and Extension of Union Railroad Lines," *Providence Journal*, 1 Mar. 1891. *All Aboard*, 1 Mar. 1925. *Providence Journal*, 28 Feb. 1871, 20 Mar. 1875. *Street Railway Journal*, Mar., Apr. 1885; June 1889.

30. *Rules*, 11. Amasa Sprague disliked mistreatment of horses. He owned two teams that carried freight from Providence to Cranston before the railway. Once he observed a teamster strike one of his beloved horses with a whip. He immediately fired

the driver and drove the team back himself (undated newspaper article in "Scrapbook"). *Providence Morning Star,* 3 Dec. 1879, 20 June 1884. *Motorman and Conductor,* July 1895. *Motorman, Conductor, and Motor Coach Operator,* Sept. 1942. *The Amalgamated Transit Union: A Brief History* (Washington, D.C.: Amalgamated Transit Union, 1985), 1. *The People* 23 (Jan. 1886). The Amalgamated complained that the Boston Humane Society posted signs reading "Please blanket your horses," while "the drivers were working eighteen hours with insufficient clothes to protect them from the storm" (*Motorman and Conductor,* Mar. 1898).

31. *Providence Morning Star,* 21 Jan. 1874, 16 Sept. 1875, 4 Dec. 1879, 24 Sept. 1882. *Providence Journal,* 18 Jan. 1887, 25 Sept. 1893. *Manufacturers and Farmers Journal,* 27 July 1865.

32. Obituaries and retirement stories are in undated newspaper articles in "Scrapbook." *Rules and Regulations* (Providence: Rhode Island Printing, 1884), 3, 18.

33. "Scrapbook," *Providence Journal,* 22 Apr. 1888, 10 Sept. 1901.

34. *All Aboard,* 1 Jan 1926, 1 May 1927. "Scrapbook," *Trollier,* 30 Mar. 1918. *Providence Sunday Journal Magazine,* 16 Nov. 1930.

35. *Providence Morning Star,* 8 July 1873; 17 Aug. 1874; 4 Aug., 2 Oct. 1883. *Providence Journal,* 22 Apr. 1888, 20 Sept. 1889, 17 Jan. 1892. *All Aboard,* June 1931. "The Union Railroad," *Providence Journal,* 19 Nov. 1877. The *Street Railway Journal* counseled against allowing crews to carry packages or messages (June 1891, 293–301).

36. *Providence Morning Star,* 21 Mar. 1886. *Providence Journal,* 17 Jan. 1892. The close relationship was a national phenomenon: "They take a friendly interest in their passengers, and are on a fraternal footing with those who regularly patronize the line. They know who live in every house along the way, and all the family histories" (Sylvester Baxter, "The Trolley in Rural Parts," *Harper's New Monthly Magazine* 97 [June 1898]: 65). Taillon, "Manhood," 2.

37. *Providence Morning Star,* 9 Aug. 1885. *Manufacturers and Farmers Journal,* 16 Nov. 1865. *Providence Journal,* 17 Jan. 1892. The Amalgamated suggested that all passenger complaints should be in writing: "It would stop the old dyspeptic grumbler, who reports the conductor because he could [not] read his mind or see him around the block, or the one who reports the motorman slipping a crossing or not knowing that he wanted a car when he was in the middle of the block talking to some one" (*Motorman and Conductor,* Apr. 1897).

38. *All Aboard,* 1 Dec. 1926. "Scrapbook." *Providence Morning Star,* 7 July, 28 Dec. 1876; 8 Dec. 1879; 24 Mar. 1881; 27, 28 Sept., 26 Dec. 1883; 6 Feb., 27 Apr., 17, 21 Sept., 11 Oct. 1886. *Providence Journal,* 5 Sept., 26 Dec. 1888. The *Street Railway Journal* warned against the acceptance of gifts and close passenger rapport (June 1891, 295).

39. *Providence Journal,* 21 July 1870. "The Union Railroad," *Providence Journal,* 19 Nov. 1877, 22 Jan. 1888. *Providence Morning Star,* 1 Sept. 1881; 20 Nov. 1882; 24, 26 Mar. 1885; 7, 18 Feb., 6 Oct. 1886. Nye, *Electrifying America,* 105.

40. "Scrapbook." "The Union Railroad," *Providence Journal,* 19 Nov. 1877. Wil-

liam Kirk, ed., *A Modern City: Providence, Rhode Island and Its Activities* (Chicago: University of Chicago Press, 1909), 102–3.

41. "Ye Olden Days," *Contact*, Feb. 1929. The New England Power Company published this monthly employee magazine. NEPCO was the parent company for Narragansett Electric Company, which owned the United Electric Railways, the second successor to the Union Railroad. The magazine irregularly carried stories about streetcar history. *Manufacturers and Farmers Journal*, 15 Dec. 1864. *Providence Morning Star*, 24 Mar., 19 Sept. 1873; 14 June 1877; 13 Mar. 1880; 19, 22 Oct. 1882; 24 June, 1, 17 Oct. 1884; 23 Nov. 1885. *Providence Journal*, 22 Feb. 1888, 11 Feb. 1889, 10 Nov. 1891.

42. *Census of Rhode Island, 1895* (Providence: E. L. Freeman & Sons, 1898), 293–94, 401, 434, 516. Republican Party boss Charles R. Brayton wrote to U.S. senator and future owner of state transit operations Nelson W. Aldrich, recommending Dr. H. S. Flynn to the local Board of Examining Physicians. Brayton assured Aldrich that the doctor "is not Irish as his name would indicate" (Nelson W. Aldrich Papers [hereafter cited as NWA Papers], Library of Congress, Brayton to Aldrich, 12 July 1897, reel 22, containers 31–32). An informal survey by the author of railway employee's names during the horsecar era uncovered only a rare Irish, French, or other "foreign" name. Almost all horsecar workers were of English extraction. For the story of the Irish in the state, see Patrick T. Conley, *The Irish in Rhode Island* (Providence: Rhode Island Publications Society, 1986). *Street Railway Journal*, Nov. 1885, 10. The president of the Sixth Avenue line in New York City complained that the Knights of Labor did not discriminate against the immigrants he hired: "Their condition of membership has no grades; but the most ignorant employe, who may have arrived last week from a foreign country, has the same standing as the faithful employe of years." Frank Curtis, "The Labor Question, in View of Labor Organizations and Recent Strikes," *Street Railway Journal*, Oct. 1888, 247. Daniel Sutherland, *The Expansion of Everyday Life, 1860–1876* (New York: Harper & Row, 1989), 179.

43. John S. Gilkinson, *Middle-Class Providence, 1820–1940* (Princeton: Princeton University Press, 1986), discusses the growth of clubs, fraternal organizations, and mutual benefit associations in chapter 4, "The Club Idea." *Providence Morning Star*, 14 Nov. 1882; 1, 3, 8, 16, 22 May, 19 Sept. 1884.

44. *Census of Rhode Island, 1885*, 460. Paul Buhle, "The Knights of Labor in Rhode Island," *Radical History Review* 17 (spring 1978). Gilkinson, *Middle-Class Providence*, 7. *Quarterly Report of District Assembly 99, K. of L.* (Boston: Cooperative Printing and Publishing, 1886), 14.

45. *Providence Morning Star*, 3 May, 18, 27 Nov., 2 Dec. 1884; 14 Jan., 24 Nov. 1885; 12 Jan. 1886; 31 Mar. 1888; 17 Jan. 1889; 24, 27 Mar. 1890. Buhle, "Knights," 41–44. Jonathan Garlock, *Guide to the Local Assemblies of the Knights of Labor* (Westport, Conn.: Greenwood Press, 1982). The Amalgamated retold the story of the Knights' organizing efforts with mixed opinions (*Motorman and Conductor*, Dec. 1897, Feb. 1898; see also George E. McNeil, *The Labor Movement: The Problem of To-Day* [New York: M. W. Hazen, 1888], 383–86). Taillon, "Manhood," 1.

3. THINGS WERE REDUCED TO A SYSTEM

1. Daniel Longstreet, "Events Which Led Up to the Formation of the American Street Railway Association," *Street Railway Journal*, Nov. 1892, 656; Oct. 1893, 656. In November 1994, Brown University acquired over one hundred of Longstreet's Civil War letters to his sister in Providence. His aptitude for detail and discipline are evident as a teenage soldier.

2. Ibid.

3. Ibid. Omnibus drivers often had an agreement with the vehicle's owner to keep part of the proceeds, a practice which seemed to influence horsecar conductors. After the turn of the century, the Amalgamated endorsed automatic fare registers to eliminate the suspicion of stealing, Longstreet's goal three decades earlier (undated article in "Scrapbook").

4. Longstreet, "Events," Oct. 1893, 656–57. *Street Railway Journal*, May 1888, 128; Oct. 1893, 656; Feb. 1886, 113. Longstreet was also active in the Grand Army of the Republic, as were a number of other traction employees. He was the last surviving member of the GAR Rodman Post in Providence when he died in 1937 (obituary in "Scrapbook").

5. *Providence Morning Star*, 30 June 1873. *Street Railway Journal*, June 1889, 152; Oct. 1893, 656.

6. William McLoughlin, *Rhode Island: A History* (New York: W. W. Norton, 1978), 167. Charles Carroll, *Rhode Island: Three Centuries of Democracy*, 4 vols. (Lewis Historical Publishing, 1932), 2:766. Welcome Arnold Greene, *The Providence Plantations for Two Hundred and Fifty Years* (Providence: J. A. & R. A. Reid, 1886), 96. *Providence Morning Star*, 11 Feb., 9 May 1876; 19 Jan. 1889; 2, 6, 7, 21 May, 7 June 1881. *Statement of Z. Chafee, Trustee, to the Creditors of A. & W. Sprague Mfg. Co., and Others* (Providence: E. A. Johnson, 1886), 28–29.

7. Longstreet, "Events," Oct. 1893, 658.

8. "The Union Railroad," *Providence Journal*, 19 Nov. 1877. *All Aboard*, 1 Jan. 1928. "Girdle the City," *Providence Evening Telegram*, 21 Dec. 1895. *Providence Journal*, 14 May 1867. Manure sales were an important source of income for horsecar companies (William D. Middleton, *The Time of the Trolley* [Milwaukee: Kalmbach Publishing, 1967], 24). Union Railroad, *Annual Report* (Providence: Rhode Island Printing, 1880). The company subcontracted horseshoeing in 1878. *Street Railway Journal*, Feb. 1885, 69. Brian J. Cudahy, *Cash, Tokens and Transfers: A History of Urban Mass Transit in North America* (New York: Fordham University Press, 1982), 45. Longstreet, "Events," Oct. 1893, 658.

9. Sam Bass Warner, *Streetcar Suburbs: The Process of Growth in Boston, 1870–1900* (Cambridge: Harvard University Press, 1962), chap. 3. Greene, *Providence Plantations*, 97. "Ye Olden Days," *Contact*, Feb. 1929.

10. John Stilgoe, *Borderland: Origins of the American Suburb, 1820–1839* (New Haven:

Yale University Press, 1988), 131. Raymond Mohl, *The New City: Urban America in the Industrial Age* (Arlington Heights, Ill.: Harlan Davidson, 1985), 27–28. Providence workers continued to live close to work sites long after the introduction of electric trolleys (William MacDonald, "Population," in William Kirk, ed., *A Modern City: Providence, Rhode Island and Its Activities* [Chicago: University of Chicago Press, 1909], 41–42). Oscar Handlin, on the other hand, reported Irish immigrants in Boston using the horsecar to move out of the city (*Boston's Immigrants, 1790–1865: A Study in Acculturation* [Cambridge: Harvard University Press, 1941], 106). Robert McCulloch, "Street Railways: A Review of the Past and a Forecast of the Future," *Street Railway Journal,* 12 Oct. 1901.

11. *Providence Journal,* 2 Feb. 1867. *Providence Morning Star,* 26 Jan. 1884.

12. *Providence Journal,* 24 Aug. 1865, 22 July 1867. *Providence Morning Star,* 20 Mar. 1872. *Providence Morning Herald,* 31 Jan. 1868.

13. *Providence Journal,* 27 June 1865. *Providence Morning Star,* 20 Feb. 1883. Robert O. Christensen, *Elmwood, Providence* (Providence: Rhode Island Historical Preservation Commission, 1979), 7, 11, 15, 31.

14. *Providence Journal,* 1 June, 5 Oct. 1865; 7 Feb., 27 Apr., 27 May 1867. "The Union Railroad," *Providence Journal,* 19 Nov. 1877. Christensen, *Elmwood,* 11, 15.

15. *Providence Journal,* 30 June 1869, 30 June 1870. "The Union Railroad," *Providence Journal,* 19 Nov. 1877.

16. *The Providence Directory, 1891* (Providence: Sampson, Murdock, 1891). *Street Railway Journal,* Apr. 1886, 201; Sept. 1886, 158; Oct. 1897, 635. Sarah M. Henry, "The Strikers and Their Sympathizers: Brooklyn in the Trolley Strike of 1895," *Labor History* 32 (summer 1991): 339.

17. *Providence City Directory, 1891* (Providence: Sampson, Murdock, 1891).

18. *All Aboard,* 1 Dec. 1925, 1 Jan. 1926. *Providence Journal,* 18 Apr. 1893, 22 Feb. 1895.

19. *Providence Morning Herald,* 5 May 1870. *Providence Morning Star,* 28 June 1873. *Providence Riding School for Ladies and Gentlemen* (Providence: J. A. & R. A. Reid, n.d.), 4.

20. *Providence Morning Star,* 14 May, 1 Aug., 16, 17, 20 Oct. 1877; 16 July 1878. "Ye Olden Days," *Contact,* Feb. 1929. *Stranger's Guide and Time Table of the Union Railroad Co., July 4, 1871* (Providence: Millard, Gray & Simpson, 1871).

21. *Providence Morning Star,* 11, 22 May, 17 July 1878; 9 June 1883; 21 May 1884. "Ye Olden Days," *Contact,* Feb. 1929. Roy Rosenzweig, *Eight Hours for What We Will: Workers and Leisure in an Industrial City, 1870–1920* (New York: Cambridge University Press, 1983). *Union Railroad Guide* (Providence: R.I. Printing, 1879).

22. *Providence Journal,* 7, 8, 13 Oct. 1887; 6 June 1890. Narragansett Real Estate Company, *Cottage Homes* (Providence: J. J. Ryder, n.d.).

23. Christensen, *Elmwood,* 12. *Providence Journal,* 18 May, 18 Oct., 20 Nov. 1889. D. M. Thompson, *Exposition of the Proposed Improvement of Greenwich Street, and a General Review of the Policy, and Public Improvements in Other Cities* (Providence, 1889), 21–23. Thompson also wrote a pamphlet under the auspices of the Advance Club encour-

aging improvements in local neighborhoods (*The Crisis: Shall the Advance of the Material Progress of the City of Providence Be Arrested by Political or Factional Interests* [Providence: E. A. Johnson, 1891]). Hiram Howard, *A Plea for Progress* (Providence: Rhode Island Printing, 1890), 16–17, 48. Middleton noted the enriching effect expanded service had on real estate values as well as wealthy opposition to that expansion (*Time of the Trolley*, 79).

24. *Providence Morning Star*, 2 Apr. 1881; 4, 15 Nov. 1883; 23 June 1885. Middleton chronicled similar opening-day celebrations nationally (*Time of the Trolley*, 75). "Mount Pleasant: Suburban Homes of Salaried Workers," *Providence Journal*, 13 Nov. 1887.

25. *Providence Journal*, 21 May 1864, 26 Feb. 1867, 16 Feb. 1869, 1 Mar. 1891, 3 Apr. 1892. *Providence Morning Star*, 21 Feb. 1880. "Mount Pleasant," *Providence Journal*, 13 Nov. 1887. *Manufacturers and Farmers Journal*, 14 Dec. 1865, 20 Apr. 1870.

26. "Mount Pleasant," *Providence Journal*, 13 Nov., 3 Dec. 1887; 1 Apr. 1892. *Semi-Annual Report of the Railroad Commissioner, 1876* (Providence: Providence Press, 1876), 16. *Railroad Commissioner's Report, 1890* (Providence: E. L. Freeman & Son, 1890), 55. "Ye Olden Days," *Contact*, Feb. 1929. Union Railroad, *Annual Report*, 1876, 16; 1877, 7, 15.

27. Albert W. Claflin, "The Providence Cable Tramway," *Rhode Island History* 5 (Apr. 1946): 41–53. *Providence Morning Star*, 20 Apr. 1884.

28. *Street Railway Journal*, Jan. 1888, 30.

29. *Providence Journal*, 16 Mar. 1869. *Providence Morning Star*, 13 Mar. 1884.

30. *Providence Journal*, 15 Oct. 1887. A special U.S. government report in 1905 declared: "In numerous cases real estate syndicates have built railways for the purpose of rendering their lands accessible to the people and increasing their price." Department of Commerce and Labor, Bureau of the Census, *Special Report: Street and Electric Railways, 1902* (Washington, D.C.: Government Printing Office, 1905), 30.

31. *Providence Journal*, 15 Oct., 3 Dec. 1887. *Street Railway Journal*, Feb. 1888, 48.

32. *Providence Journal*, 9, 12, 14, 23 Dec. 1887; 21 Feb. 1888; 28 Apr., 17 May, 12, 18, 20, 23 June, 10, 14, 24, 26 July, 10 Aug., 20 Sept., 8, 10 Dec. 1889. The minutes of the city's railroad committee were blank during most of these hearings.

33. *Providence Journal*, 12, 25 Dec. 1889; 14, 18, 23, 27, 29 Jan., 24, 25 Oct., 11, 26 Nov. 1890. Providence Board of Trade *Journal*, Feb. 1890, 28.

34. *Providence Morning Star*, 11 Apr. 1876; 27 Feb., 1, 13 Mar., 10 Apr. 1877; 22 Oct. 1880. *Providence Journal*, 19 May 1891. *Report of the Joint Committee* (Providence, 1881), 4.

35. *Providence Morning Star*, 21 June, 15 Nov., 2 Dec. 1881; 24 Feb., 3 Mar. 1882. *Union Railroad Company . . . Petition for an Amendment of Charter* (Providence: E. L. Freeman, 1882), 2–3.

36. *Providence Journal*, 8 Aug. 1870. *Providence Morning Star*, 3 May, 1 Aug. 1881. *Acts and Resolves of the General Assembly . . . in Relation to the Several Horse Railroad Companies* (Providence: Providence Press, 1869).

37. *Union Railroad Company . . . Petition.* More specific analysis is difficult because many routes passed through several distinct socioeconomic areas.

38. *Providence Morning Star,* 27 Aug., 17, 19, 22, 27, 30 Oct., 8, 14 Nov., 17, 18, 29 Dec. 1885; 12 Jan., 20 Apr. 1886.

39. *Providence Morning Star,* 5 Dec. 1882; 5 May, 21 June, 21 Sept., 18 Nov. 1883; 26 Jan., 29 Sept., 17 Oct. 1884; 19 Mar. 1885.

40. *Providence Journal,* 27 May, 25 July 1888.

41. *Street Railway Journal,* May 1890, 233; Nov. 1892, 656; Mar. 1893, 147. Management's plea for solidarity was a partial response to bickering over dues payments (Cudahy, *Cash,* 5).

42. *Street Railway Journal,* Nov. 1893, 719.

4. THE SUGAR RAILROAD

1. David Nye, *Electrifying America: Social Meanings of a New Technology, 1880–1940* (Cambridge: MIT Press, 1990), 85.

2. Cited in Nye, *Electrifying America,* 151. William Dean Howells, *A Hazard of New Fortunes* (1890; New York: Bantam Books, 1960), 60–61. Terence V. Powderly, *The Path I Trod: The Autobiography of Terence V. Powderly* (New York: Columbia University Press, 1940), 229. "The department store could never have attained its present importance except through the aid of the street railway" (Department of Commerce and Labor, Bureau of the Census, *Special Report: Street and Electric Railways, 1902* [Washington, D.C.: Government Printing Office, 1905], 29).

3. *Electrical World,* 2 Feb. 1895, 125.

4. *Evening Telegram,* 20 June 1894. Edward E. Higgins, "Studies of the Comparative Economy of Horse and Electric Traction," *Street Railway Journal,* Mar. 1896, 209. Brian J. Cudahy, *Cash, Tokens and Transfers: A History of Urban Mass Transit in North America* (New York: Fordham University Press, 1982), 51. Harold C. Passer, *The Electrical Manufacturers, 1875–1900* (Cambridge: Harvard University Press, 1953), 226, 264. Nye, *Electrifying America,* 90, 233. Burton J. Hendrick, "Great American Fortunes and Their Making: Street Railway Financiers," *McClure's Magazine* 30 (Nov. 1907): 33. A. J. Scopino, Jr., "Community, Class, and Conflict: The Waterbury Trolley Strike of 1903," *Connecticut History* 24 (1983): 30. *Special Report,* 10.

5. *Street Railway Journal,* Nov. 1892, 657. *Charters Granted by the General Assembly of the State of Rhode Island to the Railroad Companies Having Tracks in the City of Providence* (Providence: Providence Press, 1887), 191. For a description of the Providence experiments, see *Providence Magazine,* Nov. 1923, 35. The law firm of Miner and Roelker drew up the agreements for "Brayton's Motor Engines." William Roelker would later become a key player on the Rhode Island transit scene as a close associate of Nelson Aldrich (Roelker Papers, Rhode Island Historical Society Library, "Ledger," 10 Jan. 1873, box

1). John Anderson Miller, *Fares, Please!: From Horse-Cars to Streamliners* (New York: D. Appleton-Century, 1941), 56–57. "Anniversary of the First Trolley Trip in New England," undated newspaper article in "Scrapbook." *Rhode Island State Census, 1885* (Providence: E. L. Freeman & Son, 1887), 89. *Providence Journal*, 30 July, 2, 3, 4, 6, 14, 26 Aug., 15, 18, 29 Sept., 6, 11, 12, 13, 20, 23 Oct., 5, 12, 17, 22 Nov. 1887. *Charters of the Rhode Island Company and Its Subsidiary Companies together with General and Special Acts, and Franchise Agreements with Cities and Towns* (Providence: Snow & Farnham, 1912), 267–70. *Railroad Commissioner's Report, 1890* (Providence: E. L. Freeman & Son, 1890), 45–46, 53–56. Marcel Fortin, ed., *Woonsocket, Rhode Island: A Centennial History, 1888–1988* (Woonsocket: Woonsocket Centennial Committee, 1988), 22–23. *Providence Morning Star*, 13 Oct. 1886; *Providence Evening Bulletin*, 29 Nov. 1886.

6. *Providence Journal*, 25 Feb., 19 Apr., 2, 11, 20, 23, 26, 30 June, 14, 27 July, 8, 11 Aug. 1889; 4 June 1890. Donald M. O'Hanley, *Newport by Trolley!* (Cambridge, Mass.: Boston Street Railway Association, 1976), 7. William Astor to Nelson Aldrich, 5 July 1889, NWA Papers, reel 20, containers 27–28. *Taggart v. Newport Street Railway*, 16 RI 668 (1890). Nye, *Electrifying America*, 91. *Street Railway Journal*, Dec. 1889, 386. Barbara Schreier and Michele Majer, "The Resort of Pure Fashion: Newport, Rhode Island, 1890–1914," *Rhode Island History* 47 (Feb. 1989): 34.

7. *Street Railway Journal*, Aug. 1890, 401. *Providence Morning Star*, 13 Oct., 29 Nov. 1886. *Providence Journal*, 18, 21, 23 Apr., 10 May, 3 Oct. 1889; 7 Mar. 1890.

8. *Providence Journal*, 13 Mar., 12 Apr., 25, 27 May 1890; 14 June 1892; 2 Mar. 1902. The hiring of politicos was common practice among street railway companies (Melvin G. Holli, *Reform in Detroit: Hazen S. Pingree and Urban Politics* [New York: Oxford University Press, 1969], 45–46). When he was city solicitor, Van Slyck spoke before a legislative committee that was considering charter amendments for the Union Railroad. He asked members "to recollect that in 1864, when weak, the company was polite, and asked for privileges; now grown strong by success, it demands a re-arrangement of its contract" (*Providence Morning Star*, 24 Mar., 31 May 1882).

9. *Providence Journal*, 21 June, 1, 2, 24, 25 July 1890.

10. *Providence Journal*, 2, 5 Sept., 24, 28 Oct., 2, 11 Nov., 9 Dec. 1890. *Railroad Commissioner's Report, 1890*, 40–41. Beginning with this report, the railroad commissioner issued a separate bound volume of yearly reports rather than a smaller appendage to general assembly proceedings. Letter from Henry V. A. Joslin, secretary, Union Railroad, to George L. Vose, chairman, Joint Committee on Railroads, 18 Apr. 1891, DSM Collection. Emerson Schmidt, *Industrial Relations in Urban Transportation* (Minneapolis: University of Minnesota Press, 1937), 17.

11. *Providence Journal*, 20 Jan., 6, 11, 25 Feb., 31 Mar., 1, 2 Apr., 19 May, 1891. *Board of Trade Journal* 2 (Feb. 1891): 1. Fear of electric power was common in the United States: "Public opposition to electric traction was widespread at the beginning . . . and stories of electrocution figured large in the conversation of village philosophers everywhere" (Schmidt, *Industrial Relations*, 17). Letter from D. F. Hayden, Providence city clerk, to Jesse Metcalf, president, Union Railroad, 3 Apr. 1891, DSM Col-

lection. Robert C. Power, "Rhode Island Republican Politics in the Gilded Age: The G.O.P. Machine of Anthony, Aldrich, and Brayton" (honors thesis, Brown University, 1972), 148.

12. *Providence Journal*, 21, 25 Jan. 1892. *Railroad Commissioner's Report, 1892* (Providence: E. L. Freeman & Son, 1893), 50–53. *Street Railway Journal*, July 1891, 371.

13.Scott Molloy, "Motormen, Moguls, and the Machine: Urban Mass Transit in Rhode Island" (Ph.D. diss., Providence College, 1991), chap. 7.

14. *Providence Journal*, 23, 24, 29 June 1891. *Report of the Joint Special Committee Appointed by the City Council to Examine into and Report upon the Matter of a Cross Town Street Railway and Transfer Tickets* (Providence: Snow & Farnham, 1895), 16–19. *Railroad Commissioner's Report, 1892* (Providence: E. L. Freeman & Son, 1893), 52–53. As late as 1920 a Brown University professor claimed that the general assembly had "emasculated" Providence by usurping the role of the city council (James Quayle Dealey, *Political Situation in Rhode Island* [Providence, 1928], 38). The piece was originally a series of articles in the *Providence Journal* in 1920. Elsewhere, in 1909, the same author declared: "There is little doubt that the existing rates of franchise taxes could be increased considerably with a liberal return on the actual investment in these quasi-public corporations" (quoted in William Kirk, ed., *A Modern City: Providence, Rhode Island and Its Activities* [Chicago: University of Chicago Press, 1909], 202).

15. *Providence Journal*, 1, 3, 9, 10, 25, 29 July, 15, 16 Dec. 1891.

16. Short biographies of the two are in the *Rhode Island Manual, 1889–1890* (Providence: E. L. Freeman & Son, 1889), 317, 321; see also John S. Gilkinson, *Middle-Class Providence, 1820–1940* (Princeton: Princeton University Press, 1986), 186–87. Howard to Capron, 27 Nov. 1891, Rider Collection, box 149, no. 31.

17. *Providence Journal*, 5 Jan., 19 Apr. 1892. Mary Cobb Nelson, "The Influence of Immigration on Rhode Island Politics, 1865–1910" (Ph.D. diss., Harvard University, 1954), 213. *Street Railway Journal*, May 1892, 318.

18. *Providence Journal*, 22, 23, 28, 30 Apr., 10 May 1892.

19. *Providence Journal*, 3, 5 Feb. 1893. The syndicate offered $250 a share to Union Railroad president Jesse Metcalf as long as he did not insist on that price for other stockholders. Early, unintended publicity led to a bidding war, which inflated the stock to $250 a share anyway ("Memorandum of Understanding," 7 Jan. 1893, NWA Papers, reel 21, containers 29–30).

20. *Providence Journal*, 4, 5, 7, 9, 12, 17 Feb. 1892. Charles Hall, superintendent of People's Edison Illuminating and Power Company in Riverpoint, Rhode Island, warned that an unnamed woman was purchasing more stock in the electric company in anticipation of a future trade for United Traction and Electric Company shares, perhaps as part of a previous deal involving Union Railroad securities (Hall to Aldrich, 22 Nov. 1893, NWA Papers, reel 21, containers 29–30).

21. *Providence Journal*, 21 July 1892; 18, 22, 23, 28 Feb. 1893. William Roelker, then a lawyer for the Union Railroad, falsely denied the charge: "In regard to Mr. Brennan's statement about a Philadelphia syndicate, there was not a shadow of truth

in the statement." Roelker, acting in Aldrich's behalf, wrote a series of identical letters to Pawtucket Street Railway stockholders tendering and withdrawing various offers for shares (Roelker to Lyman Goff, 29 May, 17 June, 8 July 1893, Roelker Papers, box 3). Goff, in a letter to Nelson Aldrich in 1901 on another subject, still complained about the shortchanging deal for his pivotal stock: "I regret however that I obtained about thirty five dollars per share less than all the rest of the stockholders" (Goff to Aldrich, 30 Dec. 1901, NWA Papers, reel 23, containers 33–34).

22. *Providence Journal*, 28 Feb., 1, 23 Mar., 29 Sept. 1893. *New York Times*, 20 June 1894. There was some difficulty providing detailed financial information about the Union Railroad to New York financiers. William Roelker wrote, "I find that the system of accounting is . . . antiquated, it being the same that was in use upon the horse railroad system a number of years ago." He had Aldrich supply the required data (Roelker to Clark, Dodge & Company, 10, 14 Mar. 1894, Roelker Papers, box 3). One of the discussion topics at a Squantum Club meeting in East Providence was a proposed takeover of the Interstate Railway in nearby Massachusetts (John E. Searles to Aldrich, 26 Oct. 1893; Searles to Adrian Joline, 26 Oct. 1893, NWA Papers, reel 21, containers 29–30). Aldrich also corresponded with other senators seeking control of railways in Denver, Colorado, and Dubuque, Iowa (Edward Wolcott to Aldrich, 16 Nov. 1898; W. B. Allison to Aldrich, 24 Dec. 1898, NWA Papers, reel 22, containers 31–32). Jerome Sternstein, "Corruption in the Gilded Age Senate: Nelson W. Aldrich and the Sugar Trust," *Capitol Studies* 6 (spring 1978): 14–37.

23. *New York Times*, 20, 21 June 1894. "Memorandum of Agreement," 7 Jan. 1893, NWA Papers, reel 21, containers 29–30.

24. *New York Times*, 20, 21 June 1894. *Providence Journal*, 29 Mar., 11 Apr. 1892. *Providence Evening Telegram*, 20 June 1894. Lincoln Steffens, "Rhode Island: A State for Sale," *McClure's Magazine* 34 (Feb. 1905): 347. John E. Searles, treasurer of the American Sugar Refining Company and a close confidant of the senator, was soon after named a director of the traction company. He asked Aldrich to arrange a large personal loan for him from a Providence bank (Searles to Aldrich, 26 July 1893, NWA Papers, reel 21, containers 29–30).

25. *Providence Journal*, 22, 23, 24, 25 Mar. 1893. *Pawtucket Evening Post*, 12 May 1894.

26. *Providence Journal*, 25 Mar. 1893. *Street Railway Journal*, Mar. 1897, 160–61.

27. *Providence Journal*, 25, 28, 31 Mar. 1893.

28. *Providence Journal*, 3, 5, 14 Apr., 11 May 1894. *Providence News*, 11 May 1894.

29. *Providence Journal*, 11 May 1894. *The Amalgamated Transit Union: A Brief History* (Washington, D.C.: Amalgamated Transit Union, 1985), 2–3. Emerson Schmidt, *Industrial Relations in Urban Transportation* (Minneapolis: University of Minnesota Press, 1937), 106–7. Later in his life, Gompers wrote, "No organization received more of my thought and personal attention than the street carmen. Conditions among them were deplorable—long hours, little pay, practically no home life, irregular work" (Gompers, *Seventy Years of Life and Labor: An Autobiography*, 2 vols. [New York: E. P. Dutton, 1925],

1:350). See Stuart B. Kaufman, ed., *The Samuel Gompers Papers* (Urbana, Ill: University of Illinois Press, 1991) for various letters to and from Gompers about transit workers. *Motorman and Conductor,* Feb. 1898.

30. *The Amalgamated Transit Union: A Brief History,* 4–5. *Proceedings of the First Annual Convention of the Amalgamated Association of Street Railway Employes of America* (Detroit: Amalgamated Association, 1892). Kaufman, *Samuel Gompers Papers* 1:351. Schmidt, *Industrial Relations,* 123. *Motorman and Conductor,* Feb. 1898.

31. *Providence Journal,* 11 May 1894. *Justice* (weekly publication of the Rhode Island Central Labor Union, A. F. of L.), 19 May 1894. A similar scenario occurred in Connecticut when another New Jersey concern took over a local horsecar enterprise, and transit crews feared an influx of "Jerseymen" (Marc Stern, "Traction and Tradition: A Preliminary Look at Bridgeport's Labor History" [paper presented to the Association for the Study of Connecticut History, Hartford, Conn., 11 Nov. 1978].

32. *Providence Journal,* 11 May 1894.

33. *Providence Journal,* 17, 18, 29 May, 1 June 1894. "Report of the President," Third Annual Convention, Amalgamated Association of Street Railway Employes of America, Oct. 8–12, 1894. Minutes are at the headquarters of the Amalgamated Transit Union, Washington, D.C.

34. *Providence Journal,* 18 June, 14 July, 2 Aug. 1894. *Constitution and By-Laws of Conductors and Motormen's Union, No. 39 of Providence, R. I.* (Providence: M. J. Cummings, 1894), 8 (DSM Collection). Voting figures were tabulated by checking the names of Union Railroad employees with a listing of those who paid poll taxes in 1892. Poll-tax books are at Providence city hall. Local union members displayed a continuing animus to centralized authority when they complained about the high cost of the twenty-five-cents monthly dues. The national president was forced to remit a portion to the local ("Report of the President," 1894).

35. *Providence Journal,* 3 Apr., 16 Aug., 22 Sept., 6, 17 Oct. 1894. W. F. Kelly, "The Selection and Management of Employes," *Street Railway Journal,* Nov. 1896, 716.

36. *Motorman and Conductor,* Mar. 1900, Sept. 1901. *Street Railway Journal,* Sept. 1897, 545; July 1889, 198; 18 May 1901, 593–94. Cudahy, *Cash,* 145. Schmidt saw them as precursors to welfare capitalism (*Industrial Relations,* 96).

37. *Official Souvenir History of the Street Car Mutual Benefit Association* (Providence: Journal of Commerce, n.d.). *Providence Journal,* 27 Mar. 1890, 25 Nov. 1893. Schmidt wrote that railways often turned to mutual benefit associations at the first sign of a union (*Industrial Relations,* 95–96). In Detroit a former Knights of Labor carmen's assembly reorganized under the auspices of such a group (Richard J. Oestreicher, *Solidarity and Fragmentation: Working People and Class Consciousness in Detroit, 1875–1900* [Chicago: University of Illinois Press, 1986], 223–25). English owners used mutual benefit associations to impede union growth (David N. Smith, "Management Strategies, Working Conditions, and the Origins of Unionism: The Case of the Tramway and Omnibus Industry, 1870–1891," *Journal of Transport History* 8 [Mar. 1987]: 48). The Amalgamated emphasized the union's health insurance, a death-and-disability benefit of fifty dollars.

The union had to draw on this fund for general expenses in 1897. *Motorman and Conductor,* Dec. 1895, Apr. 1897. *Street Railway Journal,* Nov. 1889, 332; Oct. 1890, 498; Feb. 1896, 112.

38. *Providence Journal,* 2 Aug. 1894, 22 Feb. 1895. *The Street Car Mutual Benefit Association* (Providence: P. F. Ludwig, 1901). *20th Century Illustrated History of Rhode Island Central Trades and Labor Union* (Providence, 1901), 396. *Program,* First Grand Concert, Street Car Mutual Benefit Association, Rider Collection, box 439, no. 39. The Amalgamated encouraged socials and dances (*Motorman and Conductor,* Jan. 1900). *Street Railway Journal,* Nov. 1896, 684.

39. *Providence Journal,* 18 Apr., 8, 9 May 1895. Sidney Rider, in *Book Notes* 12 (4 May 1895).

40. *Providence Journal,* 22 May, 23 Dec. 1893; 23, 24, 31 Jan. 1895. Scott Molloy, "100th Anniversary of the Labor Movement in Rhode Island," *Old Rhode Island* (Sept. 1993): 10–15. *Rhode Island Industrial Statistics Report, 1893* (Providence: E. L. Freeman & Son, 1894).

41. *Providence Journal,* 7 Feb. 1893; 12, 25 Jan., 25 Sept. 1894. *Official Souvenir History of the Motormen and Conductors Social Club, Division No. 3* (Providence, 1904), 23–24. Although Union Railroad directors snuffed out the union drive, a group of carmen formed a social club. There is no direct evidence that this club, or several similar organizations, nurtured the union concept. However, the leader of one eventually became union president (*Motorman and Conductor,* June 1897).

5. THE TROLLEY HABIT

1. *Providence Journal,* 17 Jan. 1897.

2. *Providence Journal,* 17 Jan. 1897. "The introduction of electrically propelled cars has raised the standard of intelligence required of street railway employes, and has raised their daily wages from ten to twenty percent" (Edward E. Higgins, "Studies of the Comparative Economy of Horse and Electric Traction," *Street Railway Journal,* Mar. 1896, 207).

3. *Board of Trade Journal* (Feb. 1891), 531. For accounts of what happened to horses and horsecars, see *Providence Journal,* 2 Apr., 6, 20 Sept., 13 Nov., 11, 12 Dec. 1893; 8, 27 Jan., 21 Feb., 23 Aug. 1894; 10, 22 Jan., 29 Mar., 26 June 1895; 7 Aug. 1898; 20 Jan., 28 Mar., 12 Aug. 1900. Henry V. A. Joslin, "Street Railway Lines of Rhode Island," in William T. Davis, ed., *The New England States: Their Constitutional, Judicial, Educational, Commercial, Professional and Industrial History,* 4 vols. (Boston: D. H. Hurd, 1897), 4:2521–23. The Branford Trolley Museum in Connecticut owns the pieces of a Rhode Island horsecar. The last horsecar in Rhode Island ran on the seasonal resort of Block Island and operated into the early years of the twentieth century (Samuel Rosenberg, "A History of Street Railways in Rhode Island" [M.A. thesis, University of Rhode Island], 34).

4. *Providence Journal*, 11 Aug. 1895, 18 Dec. 1898, 14 Jan. 1900. Carmela E. Santoro, *The Italians in Rhode Island* (Providence: Rhode Island Publications Society, 1990).

5. *Providence Journal*, 26 June 1894, 30 Nov. 1896, 20 Apr. 1902. Amusement parks and resorts were revenue boosters for street railways and a lucrative investment opportunity for traction companies. The *Street Railway Journal* carried four articles on this subject in 1897 (Feb., Mar., May, and June). An earlier article warned, "Care should also be exercised in providing attractions that will draw only a desireable class of patrons" (Sept. 1892, 544). David Nye attributed a secularizing influence to the trolley, which changed Sunday from a day of religious observance to one of entertainment (*Electrifying America: Social Meanings of a New Technology, 1880–1940* [Cambridge: MIT Press, 1990], 92). The industry tried to deflect religious criticism and blame labor: "It has outraged religion and profaned the Sabbath, by holding most of its business meetings on that day, and devoting its sacred hours to excursions and amusements" (*Street Railway Journal*, Oct. 1890, 498).

6. *Providence Journal*, 2 Nov. 1896, 9 Aug. 1898, 21 June 1899. Nye, *Electrifying America*, 111.

7. The U.S. Department of Commerce and Labor reported, "It is complained that the presence of laborers in a crowded car is often distasteful to many of the passengers and that, in some cases, their working clothes soil those of the other passengers" (Department of Commerce and Labor, Bureau of the Census, *Special Report: Street and Electric Railways, 1902* [Washington, D.C.: Government Printing Office, 1905], 41). *Providence Journal*, 1 Dec. 1892, 7 Aug 1893, 15 Apr. 1900.

8. *Providence Journal*, 26 June 1898, 25 June 1899. *Trolley Trips from Providence Out* (Providence: Providence Journal Co., 1901). Robert O. Jones, *Narragansett Pier, Narragansett, Rhode Island* (Providence: Rhode Island Historic Preservation Commission, 1978). David Nye wrote, "Riding the trolley became a new kind of tourism, and it became a subject of painting and poetry" (*Electrifying America*, ix, 120).

9. *Providence Journal*, 30 June, 24 Nov. 1901. *Special Report*, 295.

10. *Providence Journal*, 10 Dec. 1898; 2 July, 11 Aug. 1899; 24 Nov. 1901. Nye, *Electrifying America*, 114, 119.

11. *Providence Journal*, 11, 26 July, 11 Aug. 1895; 22 May, 9 July, 5 Aug. 1896; 5, 6, 17 Aug. 1898; 13, 22 July, 5 Aug. 1899; 26 July 1900. Kenneth T. Jackson, *Crabgrass Frontier: The Suburbanization of the United States* (New York: Oxford University Press, 1985), 112. At the Amalgamated's 1899 convention, the "question of drawing the color line in Ritual and Constitution was discussed at some length, and it was stated by delegates from the South that they had never seen a colored man on a street car." However, William Mahon addressed groups of black trade unionists when in the South. *Motorman and Conductor*, May 1899, Sept. 1901. Nye, *Electrifying America*, 120.

12. David Thelan, *The New Citizenship: Origins of Progressivism in Wisconsin, 1883–1906* (Columbia, Mo.: University of Missouri Press, 1972), 277. Henry C. Binford wrote, "The revolt against transportation drew upon a sense of betrayal and a fear of corporate power that went back to the [eighteen] forties" (*The First Suburbs: Residential*

Commuters on the Boston Periphery, 1815–1860 [Chicago: University of Chicago Press, 1985], 210). Henry Demarest Lloyd, who helped initiate the Progressive era with his landmark work *Wealth against Commonwealth*, took on the street railway owners in another book, *The Chicago Traction Question* (1903). He criticized transit shortcomings and excoriated the industry's proprietors: "More dangerous than foreign invaders who come giving notice, and more destructive, these foes of our own household have surreptitiously, treasonably, corruptly, possessed themselves of our property, our government, our rights, and now claim a private estate in these in practical perpetuity" (17). Such sentiment spread nationally during this period.

13. *Providence Journal*, 7 June, 6 Oct. 1892; 8 Dec. 1893; 4, 14 Feb. 1894; 1 Feb. 1898; 15 Feb. 1899.

14. *Providence Journal*, 7 Aug., 3 Sept., 6 Oct., 16, 24 Nov. 1892; 8, 23 Mar., 15, 23, 29 Apr., 14 May, 16 July, 1, 2 Aug., 7 Nov. 1893; 13, 14 Aug., 2 Sept. 1894; 12 Feb. 1899; 1 Apr. 1900. Richard Longstreth, *East Providence, Rhode Island* (Providence: Rhode Island Historic Preservation Commission, 1976), 32. Joseph Conforti, *Our Heritage: A History of East Providence* (White Plains, N.Y.: Monarch Publishing, 1976), chap. 6. William Byron Forbush to Nelson W. Aldrich, 21 Dec. 1893, NWA Papers, reel 21, containers 29–30. "Franchise Agreement between the Town of East Providence and the Union Railroad," 15 Oct. 1892, in *Charters of the Rhode Island Company and Its Subsidiary Companies together with General and Special Acts, and Franchise Agreements with Cities and Towns* (Providence: Snow & Farnham, 1912), 152–55.

15. *Providence Journal*, 10 June 1892, 15 Mar., 21, 23, 30 Nov. 1893. Robert O. Jones, *Warwick, Rhode Island* (Providence: Rhode Island Historic Preservation Commission, 1981), 35.

16. *Providence Journal*, 19, 21 July 1894; 22 May 1895; 10 July, 13 Nov., 18 Dec. 1898; 29 Jan., 21 Mar., 24 May, 3 June, 20 Sept. 1899. *Railroad Commissioner's Report, 1894* (Providence: E. L. Freeman & Son, 1895), 35–36. Robert Elliot Freeman, *Cranston, Rhode Island* (Providence: Rhode Island Historic Preservation Commission, 1980). Ancelin V. Lynch, *Foster, Rhode Island* (Providence: Rhode Island Historic Preservation Commission, 1982), 38–40. Congressman Capron invited Nelson Aldrich to visit Greenville to meet William Winsor, "our wealthiest and most prominent citizen," who had land to sell for the trolley route into northern Rhode Island (Capron to Aldrich, 26 Sept. 1898, NWA Papers, reel 22, containers 31–32). William Roelker to Aldrich, 8 Nov. 1893, Roelker Papers, box 3.

17. *Providence Journal*, 23, 28, Dec. 1893; 16 July 1894; 4 July 1895; 24 May 1899. Joslin, "Street Railway Lines," 4:2526–2527. Rosenberg, *History of Street Railways*, 23–25. John Searles to Nelson Aldrich, 1 Nov. 1893, NWA Papers, reel 21, containers 29–30. Bicycles proved to be an unanticipated competitor in the 1890s (Scott Molloy, "Motormen, Moguls, and the Machine: Urban Mass Transit in Rhode Island" [Ph.D. diss., Providence College, 1991], chap. 8).

18. *Providence Journal*, 7, 29 June 1892; 1 Jan., 14 Feb. 1893; 5 Mar. 1902.

19. *Providence Journal*, 20 Nov. 1892; 21 May, 16 July 1893; 6, 25 Oct., 5, 17, 24 Nov. 1895. Freeman, *Cranston*, 26–28.

20. *Providence Journal*, 6 Oct. 1892; 2, 20 Sept. 1894; 24 July 1895. *What It Was and As It Is* (Providence: Isaac L. Goff, ca. 1900). Jackson, *Crabgrass Frontier*, 115.

21. *Providence Journal*, 25 Dec. 1898; 5 Feb. 1899; 23 June, 7 July 1901.

22. *Providence Journal*, 2 Dec. 1900; 15 Mar., 12 July 1901. Nye, *Electrifying America*, 10, 119.

23. *Providence Journal*, 14, 15 Apr., 5, 9 May 1895. William Roelker to Nelson Aldrich, 9 May 1893, Roelker Papers, box 3. The American Street Railway Association lambasted concessions made by railways to cities to secure franchises and particularly singled out Mayor Pingree of Detroit (*Street Railway Journal*, Feb. 1896, 112; Feb. 1897, 104). The organization went so far as to assert, "The service rendered by an operating company is in all cases sufficient compensation for the use of streets" (*Street Railway Journal*, Aug. 1894, 503). Richard Hofstader reported that the era's businesses "looked for the sure thing, for privileges, above all for profitable franchises and for opportunities to evade as much as possible of the burden of taxation" (*The Age of Reform: From Bryan to F.D.R.* [New York: Alfred A. Knopf, 1955], 173). Sylvester Baxter, "The Trolley in Rural Parts," *Harper's New Monthly Magazine* 97 (June 1898): 69.

24. *Providence Journal*, 2, 28 Apr., 1, 9, 10, 11, 17, 18 May 1895; 25 Jan. 1896. David Hayden, Providence city clerk, to Nelson Aldrich, 9 Apr. 1896, NWA Papers, reel 21, containers 29–30. John S. Gilkinson impressively described the reform ferment and class arrangements of that impulse in *Middle-Class Providence, 1820–1940* (Princeton: Princeton University Press, 1986), chap. 5, "Corporate Greed and Partisan Exigency." Although a handful of council Democrats continually antagonized the Union Railroad, Rhode Island's restricted suffrage prevented reformers from augmenting their ranks with enfranchised working-class voters to clean out the elite aldermanic chambers. The carrier and the GOP machine usually muzzled dissenting voices by running well-financed opposition campaigns. One transit historian wrote, "Even more than railroad men, transit operators depended on political connections and influence" (Charles W. Cheape, *Moving the Masses: Urban Public Transit in New York, Boston, and Philadelphia, 1880–1912* [Cambridge: Harvard University Press, 1980], 209). In partisan Democratic primaries, Brayton financed candidates to sap the reformers' zeal and treasury. In the general assembly, where Democrats were as scarce as in the city's aldermen's quarters, Brayton at times provided a favor or bribe to corral bipartisan support for a controversial bill, such as a franchise act. When assembly critics— usually Democrats, infrequently Republicans—crossed the power establishment at the statehouse, the machine mobilized a scorched-earth political policy.

25. *Providence Journal*, 3, 4, 5, 6 May, 1, 2, 9 June, 3 Sept. 1895. Progressives wisely targeted several Union Railroad supporters on the council who held traction stock and voted on matters favorable to the company despite a blatant conflict of interest. Energies were funneled into races to defeat these candidates rather than mounting a grapeshot attack. Several reform candidates ran on an independent ticket, and a number of Democrats ran under both party designations. Labor unions mobilized their members to defeat Union Railroad partisans. Neighborhood associations held numerous rallies to support "men who will perform their duties in a better, purer,

cleaner, more honest and more business-like manner than is done at present" (*Providence Journal*, 9 Oct. 1895). The watchword was "business-like," emphasizing efficiency and implying support for those with wealth who worked for a living. Advocates of honest government temporarily eschewed party politics, particularly at the local and state levels. "Nonpartisan" joined "business-like" as tandem slogans (Robert C. Power, "Rhode Island Republican Politics in the Gilded Age: The G.O.P. Machine of Anthony, Aldrich, and Brayton" [honors thesis, Brown University, 1972], cited the UPP pamphlet as part of the Rider Collection, but no one at the John Hay Library at Brown University could locate it). In Chicago, thousands of trade unionists marched on city hall with ropes threatening to hang any politicians who voted for a franchise extension (Georg Leidenberger, "From Machine to Reform Politics: Chicago Trade Unions and the Movement for the Municipal Ownership of Streetcars at the Turn of the Century" [paper presented at the Pullman Strike Centennial Conference, Terre Haute, Ind., Sept. 23–24, 1994], 9).

26. Cheape, *Moving the Masses*, 209. *Providence Journal*, 11, 27, Nov. 1892. Mary Cobb Nelson, "The Influence of Immigration on Rhode Island Politics, 1865–1910" (Ph.D. diss., Harvard University, 1954), 167, 223. Jerome Sternstein, "Corruption in the Gilded Age Senate: Nelson W. Aldrich and the Sugar Trust," *Capitol Studies* 6 (spring 1978): 321. Paul Buhle, "The Knights of Labor in Rhode Island," *Radical History Review* 17 (spring 1978): 60–65. Carl Gersuny, "Uphill Battle: Lucius F. C. Garvin's Crusade for Political Reform," *Rhode Island History* 39 (May 1980): 57–61. William MacDonald, "Population," in William Kirk, ed., *A Modern City: Providence, Rhode Island and Its Activities* (Chicago: University of Chicago Press, 1909), 51. Nancy Apgar, "The Life and Times of General Charles R. Brayton: A Study in Boss Rule" (honors thesis, Brown University, 1961), 42. Brayton complained to Aldrich that a Republican senator, who owed his position to the machine, went on vacation during a key campaign (Brayton to Aldrich, 24 Apr. 1904, NWA Papers, reel 24, containers 35–36).

27. *Providence Journal*, 20, 22, 25, 26, 29, 30 Oct., 6, 7, 10, 11, 17, 21, 23, 24, 25 Nov. 1895. Gilkinson, *Middle-Class Providence*, 191. Patrick T. Conley, *Democracy in Decline: Rhode Island's Constitutional Development, 1776–1841* (Providence: Rhode Island Historical Society, 1977), 132.

28. *Providence Journal*, 27, 28 Nov. 1895; 5, 7 Jan., 21 Feb., 3, 10 Mar., 4, 10 Oct., 4 Nov. 1896; 5 Jan., 2, 4, 6, 8 Apr. 1897. Nelson, "Influence," 247. Power, "Rhode Island Republican Politics," 7. Elmer Cornwell, Jr., "A Note on Providence Politics in the Age of Bryan," *Rhode Island History* 19 (Apr. 1960): 37–38. Gilkinson, *Middle-Class Providence*, 192–93.

29. *Providence Journal*, 26 Jan. 1896. Steve Babson, *Working Detroit* (New York: Adama Books, 1984), 14–15. Emerson Schmidt, *Industrial Relations in Urban Transportation* (Minneapolis: University of Minnesota Press, 1937), 115. Melvin G. Holli, *Reform in Detroit: Hazen S. Pingree and Urban Politics* (New York: Oxford University Press, 1969).

30. "Minutes," Joint Special Committee . . . Transfer Tickets, 209–13. *Providence*

Journal, 30 Mar. 1895; 14, 15, 17 Mar. 1896. David Hayden to Nelson Aldrich, 2, 23 Mar. 1896, NWA Papers, reel 21, containers 29–30.

31. Nelson W. Aldrich, *Arguments of Nelson W. Aldrich, President of the Union Railroad Company before the Judiciary Committee, House of Representatives, April 27, 1896, on Petition of Providence to Amend charter of the Union Railroad Company and Compel It to Grant Transfers* (Providence: E. L. Freeman, 1896).

32. Forty-seven of fifty major American systems used transfers rather than stations. Aldrich never mentioned a judgment he sought from the Twin City Rapid Transit Company of Minneapolis about the impact of transfers there. Just four months before the senator's speech, the company's auditor replied: "Under proper restrictions, we are of the opinion that the use of transfers will increase rather than decrease the gross revenue." The American Street Railway Association seconded this view: "A liberal system of transfers is coming to be generally recognized as one of the best means for promoting traffic that managers can employ" (Aldrich, *Arguments*, 3, 5, 13; J. F. Calderwood to Nelson Aldrich, 24 Dec. 1895, NWA Papers, reel 21, containers 29–30; *Special Report*, 42, 304; *Street Railway Journal*, Aug. 1893, 523). The editors endorsed transfers more fervently with each passing year (*Street Railway Journal*, Nov. 1894, 680–81; 5 Oct. 1901, 435). The Amalgamated reported that the Union Railroad had the third largest track capitalization in the country, behind only New York and Pennsylvania. The state was second in funded debt per mile of track (*Motorman and Conductor*, Sept. 1895). Ernest S. Griffith, *A History of American City Government: The Conspicuous Failure, 1870–1900* (New York: Praeger, 1974), 188.

33. Aldrich, *Arguments*, 27.

34. *Providence Journal*, 7 Apr., 7 May, 18, 19, 22 June, 23 Aug., 15 Sept. 1896. Mary Josephine Bannon, ed., *Autobiographical Memoirs of Hon. Patrick J. McCarthy* (Providence: Providence Visitor Press, 1927). *Board of Trade Journal* 3 (Sept. 1895). Power, "Rhode Island Republican Politics," 179. Sidney Rider, in *Book Notes* 12 (4 May 1895). Samuel Chipman Smart, *The Outlet Story, 1894–1984* (Providence: Outlet Communications, 1984), 14–21. "Minutes," Joint Special Committee . . . Transfer Tickets, 229. *Outlet Bulletin*, 9 Nov. 1901. "Minutes," Blackstone Improvement Society, 12 May 1896. The pin is in the DSM Collection.

35. *Providence Journal*, 10 Oct. 1895, 15 Mar. 1896, 31 Dec. 1897. Nelson, "Influence," 227, 273. "Minutes," Blackstone Improvement Society, 7 June 1893. Hiram Howard, *A Plea for Progress* (Providence: Rhode Island Printing, 1890), 44. D. M. Thompson, *The Crisis: Shall the Advance of the Material Progress of the City of Providence Be Arrested by Political or Factional Interests* (Providence: E. A. Johnson, 1891), 5. Brayton to Aldrich, 19 Jan. 1901, NWA Papers, reel 23, containers, 33–34. Raymond Mohl pointed out the limited impact reform groups exerted in this era: "Their successes often resulted from short-lived bursts of reform zeal or depended on the energy of a few committed leaders" (*The New City: Urban America in the Industrial Age* [Arlington Heights, Ill.: Harlan Davidson, 1985], 114).

36. *Providence Journal*, 10 Apr. 1897, 3 Jan. 1899. Sidney S. Rider, in *Book Notes* 25

(25 Jan. 1908); 27 (10 Dec. 1910). Lincoln Steffens, "Rhode Island: A State for Sale," *McClure's Magazine* 34 (Feb. 1905): 349. Robert E. Falb, "Marsden J. Perry: 'The Man Who Owned Rhode Island'" (honors thesis, Brown University, 1964), 27. Nelson, "Influence," 222–23. *Special Report*, 147. Robert Grieve, "Political Debasement of Rhode Island," *State*, 4 Nov. 1905. *Springfield Republican*, 13 Feb. 1903, in Rider Collection, "Historical Newspaper Cuttings relating to Men and Things in Rhode Island, following the Year 1875" 9:23.

   37. *Providence Journal*, 2, 28 Apr., 1, 9, 10, 11, 17, 18 May 1895; 25 Jan. 1896; 23 Apr., 20 May 1898. David Hayden, Providence city clerk, to Nelson Aldrich, 9 Apr. 1896, NWA Papers, reel 21, containers 29–30. Nelson Aldrich to Providence mayor William C. Baker, 22 Apr. 1898, in *Charters of the Rhode Island Company*, 167. "Minutes," Joint Special Committee to Confer with the Union Railroad on Transfer Tickets, 27 Feb. 1896, 1.

6. WE NEVER USED TO BE IN SUCH A HURRY

   1. David Nye, *Electrifying America: Social Meanings of a New Technology, 1880–1940* (Cambridge: MIT Press, 1990), 90. Alfred D. Chandler, Jr., *The Visible Hand: Managerial Revolution in American Business* (Cambridge: Harvard University Press, 1977), 193–94.

   2. *Providence Journal*, 16, 17 Sept. 1893; 8, 13, 14, 16, 19, 27 Mar., 8 Nov. 1894; 13 Jan. 1901; 21 Mar. 1902. C. Ernest Saunders and Earl Brown, *The Street Railway Strike in Providence and Pawtucket* (Providence: Franklin Press, 1902), 5–6. Mark Ciabattari, "Urban Liberals, Politics and the Fight for Public Transit, San Francisco, 1897–1915," 2 vols. (Ph.D. diss., New York University, 1988), 1:182. The *Street Railway Journal* proclaimed that trolleys were "no more dangerous to occupants of the streets than cars drawn by animal power" (Oct. 1892, 597).

   3. *Providence Journal*, 17 Apr., 9, 10 July 1894; 2 June 1895; 19 Aug. 1896. Saunders and Brown, *Street Railway Strike*, 42. *Providence Evening Telegram*, 20 June 1894. The Amalgamated counseled its members to study the new motive power to make themselves more skilled (*Motorman and Conductor*, July, Aug. 1895). The rationalization of the Dubuque, Iowa, system brought quick service improvements and even wage increases. After a short time, however, management introduced a demerit process for employees, and crews complained about "the terror of the schedule" (Ralph Scharnau, "The Dubuque Streetcar Strike, 1903," ms., 6–7).

   4. *Providence Journal*, 4 Feb., 8 Mar., 5, 23 June, 10 Nov. 1894; 8 Jan. 1896; 1 Oct. 1899; 2 Dec. 1900. Passengers apparently had some measure of revenge in the winter when wind-driven snow occasionally covered all poles, forcing motormen to stop at virtually every corner. The Union Railroad came up with an innovative way to paint these poles using a double ladder, receiving national attention (*Street Railway Journal*,

Sept. 1896, 547). The journal also noted, "There is no doubt that not a few street railway companies have given the people a service too frequent to be profitable to stockholders" (*Street Railway Journal*, July 1899, 455). Nye, *Electrifying America*, 99. Chandler,
Visible Hand, 193–94.

5. Henry V. A. Joslin, "Street Railway Lines of Rhode Island," in William T.
Davis, ed., *The New England States: Their Constitutional, Judicial, Educational, Commercial, Professional and Industrial History*, 4 vols. (Boston: D. H. Hurd, 1897), 4:2524. *Providence Journal*, 9 Nov. 1899; 23 Aug., 21 Nov., 17, 18 Dec. 1900; 6 Apr., 2 June 1901. The honor
of driving the first vestibuled car went to the oldest employee. The *Street Railway Journal*
had endorsed vestibules a decade earlier (May 1890, 230).

6. *Providence Journal*, 28 Oct., 22, 25 Nov., 12 Dec. 1894; 15 Apr. 1895; 5, 7, 12
Dec. 1897; 1 Aug., 18 Dec. 1898. "The Problem of Rapid Transit in Cities," *International Socialist Review* 4 (July 1903): 42.

7. *Providence Journal*, 7 Aug. 1898; 18 Feb. 1900; 9, 23 June, 7 July 1901.

8. *Providence Journal*, 10 Feb. 1895. George M. Hall wrote the poem.

9. See the annual reports of the railroad commissioner for individual descriptions and summaries of steam and electric railway accidents. Department of Commerce and Labor, Bureau of the Census, *Special Report: Street and Electric Railways, 1902*
(Washington, D.C.: Government Printing Office, 1905), 15. *Motorman and Conductor*
cited inattentive pedestrians as the cause of accidents (Apr. 1897). In New York, street
railway accidents and tampered franchises mobilized passengers to support crews
(Sarah M. Henry, "The Strikers and Their Sympathizers: Brooklyn in the Trolley
Strike of 1895," *Labor History* 32 [summer 1991]: 347–48).

10. *Providence Journal*, 8 Apr., 31 July, 9 Aug., 25 Sept. 1894; 30 Jan., 19 Aug.
1895; 11 June 1900. *Railroad Commissioner's Report, 1900* (Providence: E. L. Freeman &
Son, 1901), 63–66. The *Street Railway Journal* estimated the compensation costs for children killed in accidents between $120 and $5,000 ("The Value of a Child's Life," Dec.
1898, 799). David Nye pointed out, "For children, the trolley was not transportation,
but a dangerous, forbidden, and therefore exciting toy" (*Electrifying America*, 104).

11. *Providence Journal*, 3, 11, 13, 15, 17, 18, 19, 20, 21, 22 June 1900. The Amalgamated claimed that there were fewer problems on organized properties (*Motorman and Conductor*, June 1895). The most prominent and active lawyers were future
Providence mayor P. J. McCarthy; Joseph Osfield, future father-in-law of Pawtucket
mayor John Fitzgerald; and P. J. Quinn, former Knights of Labor official and future
judge.

12. *Providence Journal*, 21, 25, June, 12 Aug., 28 Nov. 1900. A. K. Baylor, "Power
Brakes upon Electric Cars" (*Street Railway Journal*, Mar. 1896, 185). "New and inexperienced men are inducted into the service in large numbers and after being schooled for
a few days are given exclusive, absolute and independent control of a car running
through crowded city thoroughfares and populous suburbs" (*Street Railway Journal*, Oct.
1897, 635). The Amalgamated made the installation of air brakes a legislative priority

(Sidney L. Harring, "Car Wars: Strikes, Arbitration, and Class Struggle in the Making of Labor Law," *Review of Law and Social Changes* 14 [1986]: 868).

13. *Providence Journal*, 20 Mar., 7, 27 Sept. 1895; 26 May 1897; 2 Sept. 1898; 24 Feb. 1899; 17 June 1900. Saunders and Brown, *Street Railway Strike*, 4. *Special Report*, 75. The Amalgamated cautioned its members to "carry out the rules and report every accident, no difference how trifling, for your own protection and for the protection of the company for whom you work" (*Motorman and Conductor*, Dec. 1899).

14. *Providence Journal*, 3 Jan., 20 Sept. 1895; 1 Sept. 1896; 17 Jan., 26 May 1897; 18 Dec. 1898; 11 Feb., 31 July 1901; 5 Jan. 1902. *State*, 23 Dec. 1905. An East Providence resident asked Nelson Aldrich for leniency for the offending employee (David Ray to Nelson Aldrich, 23 Sept. 1895, NWA Papers, reel 21, containers 29–30).

15. *Providence Journal*, 1 May 1894; 5 Jan., 25 Apr., 6 Nov. 1895; 1 Nov. 1896; 27 June 1897. *Railroad Commissioner's Report, 1895* (Providence: E. L. Freeman & Son, 1897), 34–35. David Hayden to Nelson Aldrich, 18 Nov. 1893, NWA Papers, reel 21, containers 29–30. The fender choice was not an easy one: "During the last three years probably more patents have been granted in this country for street car fenders than any other invention" (*Street Railway Journal*, July 1896, 419). Nye, *Electrifying America*, 99.

16. *Providence Journal*, 25, 29, 30 July, 1, 20, 22 Aug., 5, 6 Sept. 1897. Robert Babcock wrote, "Traction companies' balance sheets, management policies, and operating procedures often became political issues" ("Will You Walk? Yes, We'll Walk!: Popular Support for a Street Railway Strike in Portland, Maine," *Labor History* 35 [summer 1994]: 374).

17. *Providence Journal*, 13 Sept., 17 Oct. 1894; 18 Nov., 15, 30 Dec. 1900; 17 Feb. 1901.

18. *Providence Journal*, 11 July, 3, 8 Aug., 8 Nov. 1894; 7 Mar. 1895; 27 Jan. 1901; 6 May 1902. Nye, *Electrifying America*, 105.

19. *Providence Journal*, 6 July, 8, 21 Sept., 2, 19 Nov., 12 Dec. 1894; 21 Mar. 1896; 17 Jan. 1897.

20. John T. Winterich, *Another Day, Another Dollar* (Philadelphia: J. B. Lippincott, 1942), 156, 165. "No doubt it is a surprise to many to learn that street railway men are discharged for obeying the laws of nature" (*Motorman and Conductor*, Aug. 1896).

21. *Providence Journal*, 27, 29 July, 1 Sept. 1915. Emerson Schmidt, *Industrial Relations in Urban Transportation* (Minneapolis: University of Minnesota Press, 1937), 81–85. *Motorman and Conductor*, Feb. 1907. Daniel T. Pierce, "The Strike Problem upon Electric Railways," *Annals* (American Academy of Political and Social Science) 37 (Jan.–June 1911): 93.

22. *Providence Journal*, 14 July 1901; 27, 29 July, 30 Sept. 1915.

23. *Providence Journal*, 2, 9 July 1899; 28 Apr. 1901.

24. Approximately 359 of the 489 crew members who lived in Providence in 1901 owned their own homes (*The Providence Directory* [Providence: Murdock, 1901]). The DSM Collection contains a *Providence Journal* file entitled "United Electric Rail-

ways Co., Retirements," with articles as late as 1940. The "Scrapbook" contains dozens of testimonials from an earlier generation.

25. *Providence Journal*, 31 July, 9 Aug. 1894; 15 July 1900. Saunders and Brown, *Street Railway Strike*, 6. Residents of Portland, Maine, supported a nine-hour railway day for reasons of safety (Babcock, "Will You Walk?" 385).

26. *Providence Journal*, 21, 23, 28 Mar. 1900; 8 Mar., 17, 29 May, 18 June, 10 July 1901. *Rhode Island Industrial Statistics Report, 1900* (Providence: E. L. Freeman & Son, 1901), 65. *Motorman and Conductor*, Aug., Sept. 1901.

27. *Providence Journal*, 11 Oct., 1, 24 Nov., 5 Dec. 1901.

28. *Providence Journal*, 24 Nov. 1901. *Street Railway Journal*, 26 Oct. 1901, 638. The organization also admitted it was "a novelty to not a few of our readers" (ibid.). A few months later, after member criticism, the magazine wrote: "The plan as announced may be considered by some as quixotic philanthropy at the expense of the stockholders" (*Street Railway Journal*, 15 Mar. 1902, 329).

29. *Motorman and Conductor*, Nov., Dec. 1901; 15 Feb. 1902. Saunders and Brown, *Street Railway Strike*, 8.

30. *Providence Journal*, 22 Nov. 1901; 3, 10 Jan., 5 Feb. 1902. *Evening Telegram*, 30 Nov. 1901.

31. *Providence Journal*, 12, 15 Mar. 1902. Saunders and Brown, *Street Railway Strike*, 22. Other states had already reduced the hours for railway workers (Harring, "Car Wars," 869).

32. *Street Railway Journal*, 3 May 1902, 544. *Motorman and Conductor*, Feb. 1898. In 1912 some Boston carmen complained about plans to reduce hours to nine with a loss of pay (Harring, "Car Wars," 869).

33. *Providence Journal*, 23 Mar. 1902. *Providence News*, 5 July 1902.

34. *Providence Journal*, 26 Mar., 6 Apr. 1902. *Evening Telegram*, 24, 25 Mar. 1902.

35. *Providence Journal*, 5 Apr. 1902. *Evening Telegram*, 14 Mar., 4, 5, 7, Apr. 1902. Mary Cobb Nelson, "The Influence of Immigration on Rhode Island Politics, 1865–1910" (Ph.D. diss., Harvard University, 1954), 260. Robert E. Falb, "Marsden J. Perry: 'The Man Who Owned Rhode Island'" (honors thesis, Brown University, 1964), 29–31. Samuel Rosenberg, "A History of Street Railways in Rhode Island" (M.A. thesis, University of Rhode Island), 35–37. *Motorman and Conductor*, Apr. 1902. David Hayden to Nelson Aldrich, 18 Nov. 1893; Charles Brayton to Nelson Aldrich, 29 Sept. 1902; Adin Capron to Nelson Aldrich, 6 Oct. 1902, NWA Papers, reel 23, containers 33–34.

36. *Providence Journal*, 19 Mar., 2, 3, Apr. 1902. *Springfield Republican*, n.d., in "Historical Newspaper Cuttings," Rider Collection 10:39.

37. *Providence Journal*, 4 Apr. 1902. Garrett D. Byrnes and Charles H. Spilman, *The Providence Journal: 150 Years* (Providence: Providence Journal Co., 1980), 234–35.

38. *Providence Journal*, 22 Apr., 13, 17, 25, 29 May 1902. Rosenberg, "History," 35–39. Falb, "Marsden J. Perry," 30–31. Some merger material can be found among the papers of Samuel Colt, president of the Industrial National Bank in Providence.

Colt was a Bristol resident and financial confidant of Aldrich and Perry (Colt Family Papers, Special Collections, University of Rhode Island, box 103, folder 53). Chandler, *Visible Hand*, 193. The United Traction and Electric Company, for example, proffered a 5-percent rate of return and one share of Rhode Island Company stock for every four shares owned by Union Railroad stockholders. Marsden Perry pushed hard to get the most for his Narragansett Electric Company shares, holding out as long as possible for a better deal, as substantiated in an internal memorandum: "This latter [agreement] more nearly conforms with the bonus of Securities stock given by the Traction Company than the offer of one share of Securities Company to eight shares of Narragansett Company." At the time, United Traction and Electric stock spiraled handsomely to 121.

39. *Providence Journal*, 15, 16, 17 Apr. 1902. Saunders and Brown, *Street Railway Strike*, 9, 25.

40. *Providence Journal*, 22 Apr., 28 May 1902. *Motorman and Conductor*, Apr. 1902. *Evening Telegram*, 9, 14 Apr. 1902.

41. *Railroad Commissioner's Report, 1892* (Providence: E. L. Freeman & Son, 1893), appendix, 48–49. *Railroad Commissioner's Report, 1903* (Providence: E. L. Freeman & Son, 1904), 74–75. *Special Report*, 6, 10, 12.

7. I BELIEVE IN USING HEROIC METHODS

1. David Graham Philips, "The Treason of the Senate," *Cosmopolitan* 40, no. 5 (Mar. 1906): 618.

2. Patrick T. Conley, *An Album of Rhode Island History* (Norfolk, Va.: Donning, 1986), 161–65. John Buenker, "Urban Liberalism in Rhode Island, 1909–1919," *Rhode Island History* 30 (1971): 36.

3. Patrick T. Conley and Paul Campbell, *Providence: A Pictorial History* (Norfolk, Va.: Donning, 1982), 98. Conley, *Album*, 161–65. Charles Carroll, *Rhode Island: Three Centuries of Democracy*, 4 vols. (Lewis Historical Publishing, 1932), 2:653–56. The machine was particularly solicitous to the populous French Canadians. Rep. Adin Capron wrote to Aldrich seeking help in 1897 because "our friend Lt. Gov. Pothier and the French Canadians seem not a little stirred up over the fact that Mr. Authier—the L'Esperance editor—has failed to secure a plum." A year later Brayton secured funds to keep the friendly French newspaper in business (Capron to Aldrich, 27 Aug. 1897; Brayton to Aldrich, 11 Feb. 1898, NWA Papers, reel 22, containers 31–32). John Buenker charted the hypocrisy of Rhode Island Irish in not championing the political rights of Catholic newcomers from Italy or the already established French Canadian community: "Irish leaders proved as reluctant to grant them power and recognition as did the Yankees, a condition which allowed the Republicans to cull a sizeable portion of the new stock vote" ("Union Liberalism," 38). James Quayle Dealey labeled the

economic suffrage restrictions as "the only survival in the United States of the old-fashioned, colonial property qualifications" ("Government," in William Kirk, ed., *A Modern City: Providence, Rhode Island and Its Activities* [Chicago: University of Chicago Press, 1909], 160). Ellen Hartwell, "Political Extremism and the Quest for Absolutes in Rhode Island, 1900–1935" (honors thesis, Brown University, 1980), 5. William J. Jennings, Jr., "The Prince of Pawtucket: A Study of the Politics of Thomas P. McCoy" (Ph.D. diss., Providence College, 1985), 11–12.

4. *Providence Journal*, 22 Mar. 1896. Conley, *Album*, 161–65. Mary Cobb Nelson, "The Influence of Immigration on Rhode Island Politics, 1865–1910" (Ph.D. diss., Harvard University, 1954), 212.

5. The interview was reprinted by local reformers and distributed in pamphlet form (*To the People of Rhode Island: A Disclosure of Political Conditions and an Appeal for Their Reform, Articles Reprinted from the New York Evening Post*, with a forward by local bishop William McVickar, n.p., n.d.; in DSM Collection, 26).

6. Nelson, "Influence of Immigration," 229. The *Springfield Republican* article was reprinted in the *Providence Evening Times*, 14 Mar. 1900. William Roelker, when not working with Brayton and Aldrich to assist the Consolidated or Union Railroads, free-lanced his services to other lines. He wrote a series of letters to Jeremiah P. Robinson of New York City, who sought to incorporate the Point Judith Railroad Company in southern Rhode Island: "I have handed your charters in to the General Assembly today," Roelker wrote in March 1892, "and it will be continued to the May session of the General Assembly at Newport, when I will endeavor to have it passed." Roelker charged a "moderate" fee of only $100, apparently in response to a bargain offer of stock in the new project (Roelker to Robinson, 15, 22 Mar., 2 Aug. 1892, Roelker Papers, box 2).

7. *Providence Journal*, 1, 6 Mar. 1896; 6 Apr. 1897; 4 May 1902. Lincoln Steffens, "Rhode Island: A State for Sale," *McClure's Magazine* 34 (Feb. 1905): 339. *To the People of Rhode Island*, 33. Lincoln Steffens wrote an article in the first issue of a reform newspaper, the *State*, entitled, "What Can Rhode Islanders Do?" (17 June 1905).

8. *Providence Journal*, 20 Sept., 5 Nov. 1899. Carroll, *Rhode Island* 2:676.

9. *Pawtucket, Rhode Island* (Pawtucket: Rhode Island Historical Preservation Commission, 1978).

10. *Providence Journal*, 11, 22, 25 Oct. 1899.

11. *Providence Journal*, 5, 25, Nov. 1899; 2 Jan., 20, 28, 31 Mar., 29 Apr., 13 May 1900.

12. *Providence Journal*, 27 May 1891; 25, 26, 27, 28 May 1900. Nelson, "Influence of Immigration," 268. Herbert Gutman, "The Worker's Search for Power: Labor in the Gilded Age," in H. Wayne Morgan, ed., *The Gilded Age: A Reappraisal* (Syracuse, N.Y.: Syracuse University Press, 1963), 50–51. William Harrison Taylor, ed., *Legislative History and Souvenir of Rhode Island, 1899 and 1900* (Providence: E. L. Freeman & Sons, 1900), 162. This work contains very comprehensive biographical sketches of state dignitaries and legislators.

13. *Providence Journal*, 28, 29, 30 May 1900. Nelson, "Influence of Immigration," 267–68. John S. Gilkinson, *Middle-Class Providence, 1820–1940* (Princeton: Princeton University Press, 1986), 195, 197.

14. *Providence Journal*, 4, 5, 7, 28 June, 6 July 1900.

15. *Providence Journal*, 6, 10, 18, 19, 23 Aug., 2 Oct. 1900; 10 Feb. 1901. Originally the Union Railroad planned to ignore the narrow-gauge problem despite franchise language "that said Company shall within two years from the date of this contract change the gauge of its tracks . . . to the standard gauge." Roelker wrote to Aldrich, declaring, "As far as [Marsden Perry] and I are concerned we do not see that it is either wise or practicable to widen gauges in Pawtucket or Lincoln, or to do anything more than equip our present lines there electrically." Mayor Henry Tiepke and city aldermen agreed to waive the gauge provision in a franchise amendment in June 1894, a few months after Roelker contacted Aldrich (14 Mar. 1894, Roelker Papers, box 3). James Jenks to Aldrich, 26 Apr. 1898, NWA Papers, reel 27, containers 31–32. *Charters of the Rhode Island Company and Its Subsidiary Companies together with General and Special Acts, and Franchise Agreements with Cities and Towns* (Providence: Snow & Farnham, 1912), 182, 184. Frank M. Bates, Pawtucket city treasurer, provided tax figures to Albert A. Taber, Providence's assistant city solicitor (Bates to Taber, 26 Aug. 1897, DSM Collection).

16. *Providence Journal*, 8 Aug., 21, 25 Oct. 1900; 3 Apr. 1902. Interview with Catherine Hagan, Fitzgerald's daughter, 25 June 1976, Cumberland, R. I. Mayor Hazen Pingree of Detroit used a similar ethnic coalition (Melvin G. Holli, *Reform in Detroit: Hazen S. Pingree and Urban Politics* [New York: Oxford University Press, 1969], 146).

17. *Providence Journal*, 7, 31 Aug., 5, 7, 8, 11, 18 Nov. 1900.

18. *Providence Journal*, 20, 21, 22 Oct., 2 Dec. 1900. *Charters of the Rhode Island Company*, 183. In Detroit, Mayor Pingree tested a transfer case and was personally ejected from a trolley (Holli, *Reform*, 108).

19. *Providence Journal*, 22 Nov., 20 Dec. 1900; 6, 8 Jan. 1901.

20. Lyman B. Goff to Aldrich, 30 Dec. 1901, NWA Papers, reel 23, containers 33–34.

21. *Providence Journal*, 30, 31 Mar., 3, 7 Apr. 1901. Dealey, "Government," 164–66. The general assembly empowered the mayor of Providence to choose the three police commissioners in 1906 but subject to the approval of the aldermen: a city version of the Brayton Act.

22. *Providence Journal*, 28 Mar., 2 May, 2, 13 June 1900. *Providence Evening Telegram*, 25 June 1901.

23. *Providence Journal*, 18, 25 June, 2 July, 13 Aug. 1901. *Motorman and Conductor*, Aug., Sept. 1901.

24. *Rhode Island Industrial Statistics Report, 1902* (Providence: E. L. Freeman & Son, 1903), 129.

25. *Providence Journal*, 19, 22 Apr., 5, 12, 23 May 1902.

26. *Providence Journal*, 8 Apr., 5, 12, 23, 25, 27, 30 May 1902. *Evening Telegram*, 6, 9, 23 May 1902.

27. *Providence Journal*, 5, 12, 23, 26 May 1902. Garvin outlined his theory in a letter to the *Providence Journal*, 20 Apr. 1902.

28. *Providence Journal*, 12, 23, 24, 25, 26 May 1902.

29. *Providence Journal*, 13 Apr., 4 May 1902.

30. *Providence Journal*, 20, 22 Mar., 15, 17 May 1902. Although the media called the change in work schedules an eight-hour day, it was really a forty-eight-hour week. Construction workers labored nine hours daily and three additional hours on Saturday morning. Fitzgerald notably pushed the change for manual workers rather than white-collar employees or fire and police personnel. He outlined his philosophy of fewer hours as a way to increase wages and economic prosperity in a Labor Day article (*Labor Day Journal and Program* [Providence: Wm. R. Brown, 1901]).

31. *Providence Journal*, 24 Feb., 5, 20, 21, 22 Mar., 8, 11, 13, 16, 25, 30 Apr., 1, 2, 4, 6, 9, 11, 14, 15, 17, 18 May 1902. The Rhode Island Central Trades and Labor Union, headquartered in Providence and made up of representatives of unions throughout the state, handled both city and state problems. When Pawtucket joined Newport with city-oriented labor bodies, the state organization dropped Rhode Island from its title and replaced it with Providence. A new state labor body soon developed apart from the decentralized labor councils (*Providence Journal*, 11, 24, 26 May 1902).

32. *Providence Journal*, 5 Mar., 8, 30 Apr., 25 May 1902.

33. *Providence Journal*, 23, 28, 30 May 1902.

34. *Providence Journal*, 19 Mar. 1902.

35. *Providence Journal*, 23, 24, 25, 26 Mar. 1902.

36. *Providence Journal*, 28 Mar., 4 Apr. 1902.

37. *Providence Journal*, 6 Apr., 18, 23 May 1902.

38. *Providence Journal*, 6 Apr., 18, 23, 25 May 1902.

8. FITZGERALD'S REBELLION

1. *Providence Journal*, 17 May 1902. *Pawtucket Evening Times*, 2 June 1902. The *Evening Telegram* reported that Potter agreed to abide by the law, if it passed, as early as March 24 (25 Mar. 1902). C. Ernest Saunders and Earl Brown, *The Street Railway Strike in Providence and Pawtucket* (Providence: Franklin Press, 1902), 27. The authors worked for the Union Railroad in Providence as blue-uniform men. The history was more of a souvenir advertisement book to raise funds than a comprehensive report, but the limited narrative did provide valuable detail and a union perspective. The 108-page pamphlet contained hundreds of local business solicitations. It sold for twenty-five cents a copy and included several strike photographs. Sidney L. Harring, "Car Wars: Strikes,

Arbitration, and Class Struggle in the Making of Labor Law," *Review of Law and Social Changes* 14 (1986): 870.

2. *Providence Journal*, 1 June 1902. *Pawtucket Evening Times*, 18 June 1902. Saunders and Brown, *Street Railway Strike*, 25. *Lochner v. New York*, 198 U.S. 45; 25 S. Ct. 539; 49 L. Ed. 937 (1905).

3. *Providence Journal*, 1 June 1902. Saunders and Brown, *Street Railway Strike*, 27.

4. *Providence Journal*, 2 June 1902.

5. "Reports of the International President and General Executive Board, 1901–1903," 8 Oct. 1902, 107. The records are at the headquarters, Amalgamated Transit Union, Washington, D. C. Rezin Orr was one of the union's founders. He had attended the first convention and was a former member of the Knights of Labor (Emerson Schmidt, *Industrial Relations in Urban Transportation* [Minneapolis: University of Minnesota Press, 1937], 122).

6. *Motorman and Conductor*, Oct. 1902. Strikers in Providence and Pawtucket haggled over which city should get the $200 ("Reports of the International President," 8 Oct. 1902, 107–8). Superintendent Potter as well as an anonymous letter writer attacked the national union for being shabby to strikers over this issue (*Providence Journal*, 24, 29 June, 4, 6 July 1902). Striking Providence teamsters, whose own walkout overlapped the streetcar strike by a few days, had experienced similar problems obtaining strike benefits from the parent union in May. The *Providence Journal* publicized these difficulties, although the situation was quickly corrected by the national Teamsters Union (19 May 1902).

The first president of the Amalgamated, William J. Law, excoriated wildcat strikes as injurious to the union at the second annual convention in Cleveland in October 1893: "Such rules and conditions should be laid down as would make it impossible for any division of this Association to engage in a strike save as a matter of the very last resource and over a grave question of principle only" ("Proceedings of the Second Annual Convention"). William D. Mahon, the union's president for the next fifty-three years (1894–1946), spoke just as harshly at the following convention in Milwaukee in the depression year of 1894: "And I recommend that the constitution be amended in such a way that no local can go on strike until the National officers have been called in and arbitration offered, and in this way many disastrous strikes can be avoided" ("Proceedings of the Third Annual Convention").

A national conclave just prior to the 1902 Rhode Island strike had rejected a dues increase to finance a separate defense account for such situations. John Arno blamed the lack of strike funds as one of the walkout's two major weaknesses but admitted he had overestimated the amount of money available from the national union treasury (*Providence Journal*, 7 July 1902; also see Saunders and Brown, *Street Railway Strike*, 52). For a broader framework, see Harring, "Car Wars," 851–52. William Mahon commented later in his career, "I would sooner face the world with an organization of 10,000 men with $1,000,000 in their treasury than I would with an organization of 10,000,000 men and $10,000 in their treasury." Emerson Schmidt, who interviewed Mahon, added, "One of the reasons for the success of the International, it appears, was the authority over impulsive, inexperienced, and at times ignorant local officers" (Schmidt, *Industrial Relations*, 125, 221). Gompers took credit for influencing Mahon to enforce discipline among the railway locals in such situations (Samuel Gompers, *Seventy Years of Life and Labor: An Autobiography*, 2 vols. [New York: E. P. Dutton, 1925], 1:354).

Rezin Orr, in a subsequent Rhode Island organizing drive in 1908, defensively explained that Vetter had not shared orders with the local union to postpone the strike until Orr arrived in Providence. The national officer alleged that Vetter told the membership "he had the fullest endorsement of the international body" for the walkout (*Evening Tribune*, 6 June 1908). The Amalgamated provided only $250 in the Dubuque walkout (Ralph Scharnau, "The Dubuque Streetcar Strike, 1903," ms., 32).

7. *Providence Journal*, 2, 4 June 1902. Tiepke wrote to Arno immediately after the walkout: "I beg to remind you of my suggestion made prior to the strike to the effect that the constitutionality of the law could be tested without resorting to a strike" (*Providence Journal*, 6 July 1902). In his capacity as commissioner of industrial statistics, he officially added, "Nothing was gained by the strike, which was doomed to be a failure from the second day after it began" (*Rhode Island Industrial Statistics Report, 1902* [Providence: E. L. Freeman & Son, 1903], 133). Approximately 60 percent of all street railway employees working in cities the size of Providence earned between $2.00 and $2.25 per day the year of the walkout. Old-timers were definitely paid above the national average (Department of Commerce and Labor, Bureau of the Census, *Special Report: Street and Electric Railways, 1902* [Washington, D.C.: Government Printing Office, 1905], 99).

8. *Providence Journal*, 15, 24 May, 4, 11 June 1902. *Evening Telegram*, 2, 3, 4, 11, 16 June 1902. *Rhode Island Industrial Statistics Report, 1902*, 155. The union history claimed eight hundred joined the organization. A petition for a ten-hour day submitted to the state legislature by railway employees in May was signed by seven hundred (Saunders and Brown, *Street Railway Strike*, 31). Approximately 109 conductors and 116 motormen received premium wages, although conductors earned twenty-five cents more a day than their colleagues at the controls ("Scrapbook"). Electrical linemen at the railway struck on their own in 1907 and won a partial victory. Orr admitted in 1908 that too much emphasis had been placed on blue-uniform men in 1902 to the exclusion of workers in other crafts ("Scrapbook").

9. *Providence Journal*, 4, 5 June 1902. *Evening Telegram*, 4 June 1902. *Pawtucket Evening Times*, 7 June 1902.

10. *Providence Journal*, 5 June 1902. *Evening Telegram*, 5 June 1902.

11. *Providence Journal*, 6 June 1902. *Evening Telegram*, 6 June 1902.

12. Ibid.

13. Ibid.

14. Ibid.

15. *Providence Journal*, 6, 7 June 1902. *Evening Telegram*, 6, 7 June 1902.

16. *Providence Journal,* 4, 5, 6, 7, 8, 9, 14, 18 June 1902. Saunders and Brown, *Street Railway Strike,* 39. Providence police had recently gained valuable strike experience during the May walkout of teamsters. Reserves had been assigned overnight duty to stem violence and accompany scab drivers on their rounds. Teamster officials went out of their way to disassociate the union from violent acts, meeting with the police commissioners on several occasions to reduce tension and condemn a medical colleague of Dr. Lucius Garvin who called the public safety board a scab operation (*Providence Journal,* 3, 18, 20 May 1902). The Providence Police Commission had recently been organized into a tight, disciplined unit by a controversial act in the Republican legislature (*Providence Journal,* 3 June 1900). John S. Gilkinson, *Middle-Class Providence, 1820–1940* (Princeton: Princeton University Press, 1986), 197. Mary Cobb Nelson, "The Influence of Immigration on Rhode Island Politics, 1865–1910" (Ph.D. diss., Harvard University, 1954), 268. Charles Carroll, *Rhode Island: Three Centuries of Democracy,* 4 vols. (Lewis Historical Publishing, 1932), 2:673. Carroll wrote that police "ruthlessly" enforced the law and claimed a naval battalion was secretly ensconced in Providence in case of further violence (Carroll, *Rhode Island* 2:670).

The company refused to provide free tickets to uniformed fire fighters despite a request from the Providence board of fire commissioners in 1896. It was standard practice in the industry to give police free tickets (*Street Railway Journal,* June 1891, 295). All complimentary tickets, except for employee passes, were discontinued after the establishment of transfer tickets soon after the strike in July 1902 (Providence Board of Fire Commissioners to Nelson Aldrich, 27 Aug. 1896, NWA Papers, reel 21, containers 29–30).

17. *Providence Journal,* 4, 5, 6, 7, 8 June 1902. *Pawtucket Evening Times,* 7 June 1902. *Evening Telegram,* 4, 7 June 1902. *Providence Sunday Journal Magazine,* 16 Nov. 1930. Saunders and Brown, *Street Railway Strike,* 39. Daniel T. Pierce, the former Philadelphia railway official, remarked about the power of "the odium that falls to the lot of the 'scab'" ("The Strike Problem upon Electric Railways," *Annals* [American Academy of Political and Social Science] 37 [Jan.–June 1911]: 94).

18. "Scrapbook." *Providence Journal,* 6 June 1902, 4 Jan. 1914. Saunders and Brown, *Street Railway Strike,* 4. When the Union Railroad moved to spacious quarters in 1902, Albert Potter was sheltered in an inaccessible suite. The *Providence Journal* mentioned, "The General Manager cannot be buttonholed with the old-time freedom" (6 Apr. 1902).

19. *Providence Journal,* 6 Oct. 1893, 29 Jan. 1900, 24 Nov. 1901, 11 June 1902. *All Aboard,* 1 Jan. 1926. *Pawtucket Evening Times,* 11 June 1902. The Amalgamated's Pittsburgh division reported, "There is an element among the early men who cannot be induced to become members" (*Motorman and Conductor,* Apr. 1900). Paul M. Taillon, "Manhood, Whiteness, and the Fraternal Culture of the Railroad Brotherhoods" (paper presented at the Pullman Strike Centennial Conference, Terre Haute, Ind., 24 Sept. 1994), 1.

20. *Providence Journal,* 22 June 1902. *Evening Telegram,* 17 June 1902. *Pawtucket Evening Times,* 10, 11 June 1902.

21. *Providence Journal*, 6 June 1902. *Evening Telegram*, 6 June 1902. *Pawtucket Evening Times*, 6 June 1902.

22. *Railroad Commissioner's Report, 1902* (Providence: E. L. Freeman & Son, 1903), 56. *Providence Journal*, 6 July 1902. *Evening Telegram*, 27 Mar. 1902.

23. *Providence Journal*, 7 June 1902. *Evening Telegram*, 7 June 1902. *Pawtucket Evening Times*, 7 June 1902.

24. *Providence Journal*, 6 June 1902. Robert E. Falb, "Marsden J. Perry: 'The Man Who Owned Rhode Island'" (honors thesis, Brown University, 1964), 41. One source suggested that deputized sheriffs "kicked back" half their salaries to Brayton's machine, which the Boss ran from White's office in the statehouse (William J. Jennings, Jr., "The Prince of Pawtucket: A Study of the Politics of Thomas P. McCoy" [Ph.D. diss., Providence College, 1985], 11). McCoy, a future mayor of Pawtucket and important architect of the Democrats rise to power in the state, began his career on a Pawtucket trolley in 1905 and helped organize the successful union drive of 1912–13 (Jennings, "Prince," 30). Another student commentator summarized the importance of the GOP-sheriff nexus: "Power over the law enforcement agency warmed the confidence of statewide industrialists for whom labor trouble constituted a real and perpetual threat" (Ellen Hartwell, "Political Extremism and the Quest for Absolutes in Rhode Island, 1900–1935" [honors thesis, Brown University, 1980], 6).

25. *Providence Journal*, 7, 8, 9 June 1902. *Evening Telegram*, 7, 9 June 1902. "Minutes," Common Council, Pawtucket, 7 June 1902. Fitzgerald's refusal to provide police protection to corporations was not that unusual in smaller American towns. During a streetcar strike in Houston, Texas, in 1902 the chief of police said, "This department does not propose to man the company's conveyance with policemen until it demonstrates that protection is absolutely necessary" (cited in Robert E. Zeigler, "The Limits of Power: The Amalgamated Association of Street Railway Employees in Houston, Texas, 1897–1905," *Labor History* 18 [winter 1971]: 75).

26. *Providence Journal*, 5 June 1900; 6, 9, 11, 13, 14, 19, 20, 21, 26, 28 June, 3 July 1902. Judge Isaac Shove dropped charges against five strikebreakers with concealed weapons, saying they had a right to protect themselves and passengers. The same judge turned stone throwers over to a grand jury. Fitzgerald claimed that many sheriffs, who boasted political connections rather than police experience, were unsavory characters who required surveillance themselves. Democrats accused White of employing fees and fines collected by deputies for Republican campaigns (Nelson, "Influence," 274; Carroll, *Rhode Island*, 675). The Central Falls police chief blamed strikebreakers for inciting trouble by taunting crowds, while his counterpart in Cumberland accused the Pawtucket Street Railway of inviting problems by running ill-advised and unannounced trips. Sidney Harring wrote that law enforcement attitudes "never turned on police rank and file sympathies for the workers side but were always related to citywide political questions" ("Car Wars," 136).

27. *Providence Journal*, 9 June 1902.

28. *Providence Journal*, 12 June 1902.

29. *Providence Journal*, 6, 9, 11, 12 June 1902. *Evening Telegram*, 12, 13, 14 June

1902. *Westerly Daily Sun*, 12 June 1902. Utter later served as lieutenant governor (1904), governor (1905–7), and U.S. representative in 1911 until his death a year later. He sent Nelson Aldrich a complimentary article from the *Sun* about the senator's handling of the peace treaty with Spain in 1899 (7 Feb. 1899, NWA Papers, reel 22, containers 31–32).

30. *Providence Journal*, 11, 12, 13 June 1902. Falb, "Marsden J. Perry," 42. Fitzgerald married Clara Osfield, daughter of prominent Pawtucket attorney and former state representative Joseph Osfield, who often litigated injury cases against the Union Railroad. His best man was James Higgins, who in 1907 would become the first Irish Catholic Democrat to be governor of Rhode Island. The Fitzgeralds left on a publicized honeymoon a day before troops were mobilized (*Annual Reports of the Adjutant-General, Quartermaster-General, and Surgeon-General, of the State of Rhode Island, for the Year 1902* [Providence: E. L. Freeman & Sons, 1903]), 4, 11.

31. *Providence Journal*, 13 June 1902. *Westerly Daily Sun*, 12 June 1902. The annual adjutant-general's report made absolutely no mention of this behavior. Brooklyn militia were employed during the nation's first electric streetcar walkout in 1895 and often made their first domestic appearances in similar strikes (Sarah M. Henry, "The Strikers and Their Sympathizers: Brooklyn in the Trolley Strike of 1895," *Labor History* 32 [summer 1991]: 344; A. J. Scopino, Jr., "Community, Class, and Conflict: The Waterbury Trolley Strike of 1903," *Connecticut History* 24 [1983]: 37).

32. *Providence Journal*, 6, 12, 13, 14, 15, 22 June, 8 Aug. 1902. *Pawtucket Evening Times*, 5 June 1902. The militia arrested two union carmen from Brooklyn, New York, who apparently traveled to Pawtucket to assault a scab to settle a score from an earlier strike elsewhere, indicating the use of professional strikebreakers by the company (*Evening Telegram*, 20 June 1902). *Annual Reports of the Adjutant-General*, 14.

In a number of instances, apparently unique to railway strikes, police and militia refused to cooperate (*Motorman and Conductor*, June 1900). Dina M. Young, "The St. Louis Streetcar Strike of 1900: Pivotal Politics at the Century's Dawn," *Gateway Heritage* 12 (summer 1991): 111. Harold E. Cox, "The Wilkes-Barre Street Railway Strike of 1915," *Pennsylvania Magazine of History and Biography* 75 (1970): 86. Sidney L. Harring, *Policing a Class Society: The Experience of American Cities, 1865–1915* (New Brunswick, N.J.: Rutgers University Press, 1983), 37. *Street Railway Journal*, 16 June 1900, 50. The Amalgamated cited one example of a New York militiaman who refused to serve because his brother was a striker. He wrote a poem: "Out there among the strikers, Is the son of my mother; though all the kings of gold command, I will not kill my brother!" (*Motorman and Conductor*, June 1901).

In Pawtucket one military officer, during slack periods while on duty, decorated clay pipes with the inscription "Fitz's War" as souvenirs for other officers. Soldiers used the sobriquet Fitzgerald's Rebellion, and one regiment had a cat named Fitz for a mascot. A hostile letter writer signed a missive "Anti-Rebellion." The *Providence Journal* called Pawtucket "Fitzgeralized" (16, 17, 21, 22, June, 2, 6 July 1902).

33. *Providence Journal*, 13 June 1902.

34. *Providence Journal*, 13, 14, 16 June 1902. *Railroad Commissioner's Report, 1902*, 65.

35. *Providence Journal*, 14, 15, 16 1902. *Annual Reports of the Adjutant-General*, 13–25.

36. *Providence Journal*, 13, 14, 15, 16, 17, 20, 21 June 1902. The railroad commissioner claimed the militia ended disturbances while the commissioner of industrial statistics reported just the opposite. *Railroad Commissioner's Report, 1902*, 65–66. *Rhode Island Industrial Statistics Report, 1902*, 132–33. The eventual cost to the state came to $25,213.06, exceeding the militia's budget for the year and requiring a supplemental appropriation of over $7,000 from the general assembly. Commanders admitted, however, that expenditures were well worth it: "The experience of officers and men acquired in the active duty far exceeded what could be gained from any number of encampments such as we have been accustomed to." The annual Quonset Point retreat, scheduled for later that summer, was canceled due to a lack of funds. The militia also made a case for more modern statewide armories to quell domestic disturbances. At the dedication of the new Westerly Armory in December 1902, Governor Charles Kimball predicted an increase in labor-management conflict and advocated "a well equipped and disciplined militia." The only noncivilian casualty occurred when a soldier accidentally shot himself in the foot. The militia had 1,339 members in 1902; 48 were musicians. *Annual Reports of the Adjutant-General*, 5, 20, 28, 29, 36, 112. *Providence Journal*, 20 Dec. 1902.

One of the riots in Lonsdale in 1902 started when protestors threw rocks from the Moshassuck Cemetery, where another strike incident occurred during the fateful 1934 nationwide general textile strike. That year the National Guard fired on protestors hiding in the graveyard, killing one and wounding several others. The incident was known as the Saylesville Massacre (*Providence Journal*, 16 June 1902; James Findlay, "The Great Textile Strike of 1934: Illuminating Rhode Island History in the Thirties," *Rhode Island History* 42 [Feb. 1983]).

37. *Evening Telegram*, 16 June 1902. *Providence Journal*, 16, 17 June 1902.

38. *Evening Telegram*, 16, 25 June 1902. Within a week of the militia's withdrawal from Pawtucket, management at the American Woolen Company's Saranac Mills in North Smithfield requested troops to protect Italian strikebreakers in a labor disturbance there. Angry crowds gathered daily, the town council protested the company's actions, and local boardinghouse owners refused to rent to scabs. The state militia was mobilized in nearby Woonsocket, but the textile firm withdrew strikebreakers before further confrontations. *Providence Journal*, 16, 17 June, 3, 4, 7 July 1902.

9. WE WALK

1. *Providence Journal*, 20, 25 June 1902. *Railroad Commissioner's Report, 1902* (Providence: E. L. Freeman & Son, 1903), 55, 66. Badges that read "I'll Walk" were used

during the Milwaukee strike of 1896 (David Thelan, *The New Citizenship: Origins of Progressivism in Wisconsin, 1883–1906* [Columbia, Mo.: University of Missouri Press, 1972], 263).

2. *Providence Journal*, 20, 23, 25, June, 9 July 1902. *Evening Telegram*, 17, 19, 25 June 1902. *Annual Reports of the Adjutant-General, Quartermaster-General, and Surgeon-General, of the State of Rhode Island, for the Year 1902* (Providence: E. L. Freeman & Son, 1903), 28. *Railroad Commissioner's Report, 1902* (Providence: E. L. Freeman & Son, 1903), 55, 66.

3. *Providence Journal*, 13, 15, 19, 20, 23, 24, 25, 29 June, 2 July 1902. *Evening Telegram*, 30 June 1902.

4. *Providence Journal*, 7, 10, 11, 12, 13, 17, 20 June 1902. *Evening Telegram*, 11, 12, 13, 16, 17, 19, 25, 27, 30 June, 2 July 1902. Republicans took over the *Telegram* a few years later and changed the name to the *Evening Tribune* (Mary Cobb Nelson, "The Influence of Immigration on Rhode Island Politics, 1865–1910" [Ph.D. diss., Harvard University, 1954], 287). *Pawtucket Evening Times*, 7, 12, 14 June 1902. "Minutes," Board of Aldermen, Pawtucket, 25 June 1902. The *Street Railway Journal* complained that in Milwaukee, "nearly every organized society in the city even the singing societies and some of the churches sided with the strikers and helped to enforce the boycott" (July 1896, 443). In Waterbury, Connecticut, strike supporters wore "We Walk" buttons (A. J. Scopino, Jr., "Community, Class, and Conflict: The Waterbury Trolley Strike of 1903," *Connecticut History* 24 [1983]: 32–33).

5. *Providence Journal*, 7, 22 June 1902.

6. *Providence Journal*, 6, 13, 15, 21, 29 June 1902. *Evening Telegram*, 4, 6 June 1902. In Detroit's riots, "the mob was composed of some of Detroit's most respectable citizens" (Melvin G. Holli, *Reform in Detroit: Hazen S. Pingree and Urban Politics* [New York: Oxford University Press, 1969], 39–40).

7. *Providence Journal*, 4, 17 June, 19 July 1902. *Evening Telegram*, 9, 10, 13, 14, 25, 28 June 1902. Interview with Chris Daniels. *Providence Evening Bulletin*, "Director's Minutes," July 14, 1902. Henry R. Davis, *Half a Century with the Journal* (Providence: Journal Company, 1904), 48. Davis rose through the ranks from paperboy to secretary and corporation cashier. He compiled a valuable index of early *Journal* articles (Garrett D. Byrnes and Charles H. Spilman, *The Providence Journal: 150 Years* [Providence: Providence Journal Company, 1980], 255–59).

The *Journal* did not relent on Outlet advertising until a few months before the strike. Unfortunately, only a few copies of the *Outlet Bulletin* survive at the Rhode Island Historical Society Library. The strike issues are not available.

In attempting to consult the minute books of the *Journal's* directors, I was denied access and instead had to depend on several notations sent by the current secretary. How ironic that a newspaper that often touts its crusading spirit in printing sensitive and private contemporary documents refuses to allow direct examination of its own historical material!

The trial of John Carroll for assaulting the *Journal* reporter became a minor drama. After his arrest, Carroll was brought to the Pawtucket offices of the *Providence*

Journal by Detective John Haberlin. There, newspaper officials interrogated Carroll for three hours in front of the aggrieved correspondent, Albert Rider. Carroll later preferred charges against the nineteen-year police veteran for taking him to the *Journal* office first rather than the station house. Joseph Osfield, Fitzgerald's father-in-law, represented the policeman, who publicly thanked the mayor for not suspending him prior to his hearing before the board of aldermen. A large crowd, allegedly made up of strike agitators, attended Haberlin's examination. The aldermen fired the detective for unprofessional conduct just before Carroll's trial began. The jury split eleven to one for conviction in that case, and Carroll was exonerated. *Providence Journal*, 19 July, 3, 5, 22, 23 Oct., 1, 20 Dec. 1902.

In the San Francisco walkout, all the city's major papers backed the carmen (Mark Ciabattari, "Urban Liberals, Politics and the Fight for Public Transit, San Francisco, 1897–1915," 2 vols. [Ph.D. diss., New York University, 1988], 1:182).

8. C. Ernest Saunders and Earl Brown, *The Street Railway Strike in Providence and Pawtucket* (Providence: Franklin Press, 1902), 32. *Providence Evening Bulletin*, "Directors' Minutes," July 14, 1902. *Outlet Bulletin*, May 1903. Samuel Chipman Smart, *The Outlet Story, 1894–1984* (Providence: Outlet Communications, 1984), 14–22. Eleanor F. Horvitz, "The Outlet Company Story," *Rhode Island Jewish Historical Notes*, Nov. 1974. The Outlet appeared to advertise regularly in labor publications (see *Labor Day Journal and Programme* [Providence: Bannan, 1897]; *Labor Day Journal and Program* [Providence: Wm. R. Brown, 1901]). The latter contained the message "Success to the Unions" on the inside cover. Management at the Outlet practiced progressive labor relations by providing two weeks paid vacation to their own store clerks.

9. *Providence Journal*, 6, 13, 14, 17, 22 June, 6 July 1902. *Evening Telegram*, 9, 17 June 1902. *Providence Visitor*, 7, 21 June 1902. Small businesses in Milwaukee stood with strikers, according to the *Street Railway Journal*: "The association of merchants and trade people took a hand, and so powerful was the surveillance, inquisition and spotting that even the friends of the company are paralyzed with fear and threatened social ostracism, so that they remained at home or patronized the busses" (July 1896, 442).

10. *Providence Journal*, 8, 12, 13, 14, 15, 18, 1902. Volunteer fire fighters expelled a member for returning to the railway during the strike, a father bodily pulled his scab son off a trolley, and supporters crowded the Apponaug courthouse to support a striking conductor charged with reveling. The exonerated carman then preferred charges of false arrest against the railway superintendent who made the original complaint. Clyde, a village in Warwick in 1902, became part of West Warwick when that town was created in 1913. *Evening Telegram*, 4, 5, 9, June 1902. *Providence Journal*, 21 June 1902.

11. *Evening Telegram*, 4, 5, 6, 13 June 1902. Marc Stern compares trolley strikes in Bridgeport and Waterbury, Connecticut ("Traction and Tradition: A Preliminary Look at Bridgeport's Labor History" [paper presented to the Association for the Study of Connecticut History, Hartford, Conn., 11 Nov. 1978], 19).

12. *Providence Journal,* 12, 13, 15, 24 June 1902. Cumberland actually sent a resolution to the railroad commissioner requiring all motormen and conductors to have
two weeks' experience. The commissioner wrote it was not within his purview to approve or disapprove such an ordinance (*Railroad Commissioner's Report, 1902,* 67–69). A
city ordinance in Albany, New York, prohibited the use of "incompetent labor" on railways during a strike in 1901 (Emerson Schmidt, *Industrial Relations in Urban Transportation* [Minneapolis: University of Minnesota Press, 1937], 146).

William D. Mahon, longtime president of the Amalgamated, had visited Providence during the formation of Division 200 in 1901. At the union's national convention, held in Providence in 1917, he ruefully recalled his earlier visit and his lack of respect for Mayor Granger: "It has been a good many years," Mahon told the delegates,
"since I first came to Providence, and I wasn't received by the mayor at that time. I
was rather looked after by his spotters and the secret service men of the railroad
company. We were not received then with brass bands and open arms. We have had
to struggle to build this organization as we have had to struggle to build all of our
unions" (*Motorman and Conductor,* Oct. 1917). The *Outlet Bulletin* also attacked Granger
for his lackadaisical approach to solving the transfer question (24–26 Oct. 1901).

13. *Providence Journal,* 2, 4, 13, 19 June 1902. The Amalgamated did not publicize
the strike but did follow ten-hour litigation in Rhode Island. *Motorman and Conductor*
(July 1902).

14. *Providence Journal,* 8, 10, 12, 15 June 1902. Saunders and Brown, *Street Railway
Strike,* 47. *Railroad Commissioner's Report, 1902,* 66.

15. *Providence Journal,* 27, 28 June 1902.

16. *Providence Journal,* 23, 26, 27, 28, 29 June, 3, 4, 6, 16, 19 July 1902. *Springfield
Republican,* n.d., "Historical Newspaper Cuttings," Rider Collection 10:40. The company apparently had no formal contracts with individual employees (Saunders and
Brown, *Street Railway Strike,* 28). *Rhode Island Industrial Statistics Report, 1902* (Providence:
E. L. Freeman & Son, 1903), 178–79. A circuit court in Saginaw, Michigan, upheld a
ten-hour law for street railway workers in 1898 (*Motorman and Conductor,* Apr. 1898). Agitation for a shorter workday in Rhode Island harked back to the 1830s. A ten-hour
law had passed the state legislature in 1885 but was emasculated by the usual loop-
hole that individual workers could contract separately for longer hours (William S.
Grovesnor, *A Few Questions and Answers on the Proposed Ten Hour Law in Rhode Island,* 1885).
Interestingly, Sidney Rider, the unrelenting critic of the Union Railroad, opposed the
1885 ten-hour law (Robert C. Power, "Rhode Island Republican Politics in the Gilded
Age: The G. O. P. Machine of Anthony, Aldrich, and Brayton" [honors thesis, Brown
University, 1972], 111).

The constitutionality of maximum-hours legislation passed by the states is a major issue in American labor history. The opening years of the Progressive era saw this
question in the forefront of labor agitation. For helpful summaries, see Alfred H. Kelly,
Winfred A. Harbinson, and Herman Belz, *The American Constitution: Its Origins and Development* (New York: W. W. Norton, 1983); and Joseph G. Rayback, *A History of American
Labor* (New York: Free Press, 1966).

17. *Providence Journal*, 22, 24, 27 June, 6, 7 July 1902. Potter graciously allowed strikers who had taken other jobs extra time to return. *Rhode Island Industrial Statistics Report, 1902*, 174.

18. *Providence Journal*, 26, 30 June, 6 July 1902.

19. *Providence Journal*, 7, 8, 9, 10 July 1902. The *Evening Telegram* wrote, "The most notable feature of the difficulty was the loyalty of the people to the men" (8 July 1902). Accounts of bombings, shootings, and derailments appear in the *Providence Journal*, 9, 10, 13, 17, 19, 24, 27, 29, 30 June, 2, 4, 5, 6 July 1902.

20. *Evening Telegram*, 6 July 1902. Saunders and Brown, *Street Railway Strike*, 58. Interview with Fred Armstrong, Sr., Providence, R. I., 18 Jan. 1977.

21. Saunders and Brown, *Street Railway Strike*, 6.

22. The *State*, a reformist Progressive-era newspaper, commented in 1905, "Under all the conditions the strike was a mistake. Legal and political remedies pursued would have proved effectual" (23 Dec. 1905). Samuel Gompers, mentioning an earlier railway conflict in 1900, sympathized: "The first feeling which had come to the men was one of resentment and desire to exercise their new-found power." However, the A. F. of L. leader wired the Amalgamated to rescind the local's charter if the carmen struck (Samuel Gompers, *Seventy Years of Life and Labor: An Autobiography*, 2 vols. [New York: E. P. Dutton, 1925], 1:352–54). The Amalgamated promised alternative transportation: "There will be buses and horses enough in the hands of our organization to equip the small cities, if necessary, and automobiles to operate in the large ones." The national organization did employ wagons in Milwaukee in 1896, but such assistance was sporadic at best. *Motorman and Conductor*, May 1896; Aug., Sept., Dec. 1899; Sept. 1900.

23. *Providence Journal*, 8 June 1902. John S. Gilkinson, *Middle-Class Providence, 1820–1940* (Princeton: Princeton University Press, 1986), chap. 8.

24. *Railroad Commissioners Report, 1902*, 66. *Rhode Island Industrial Statistics Report, 1902*, 130. *Providence Journal*, 29 June 1902. Richard P. Clark, "The Struggle, Victory and Defeat of James P. Reid: A Socialist in Rhode Island, 1893–1912" (M.A. thesis, Rhode Island College, 1972). Paul Buhle, "Italian-American Radicals and the Labor Movement, 1905–1930," *Radical History Review* 17 (spring 1978). John Buenker, "Urban Liberalism in Rhode Island, 1909–1919," *Rhode Island History* 30 (1971): 47.

A brilliant novel about turn-of-the-century Irish American life in Providence used Reid as the model for a character (Jim Trevin): "They tell me this young Trevin is as smart as a whip and don't care a damn about what they say about him. Sure he could let well enough alone if he wanted to and just run that dentist office of his, but he has the bug in his head, do you see. He's a Socialist, all right." Trying to hit a scab motorman, a character in the novel throws a lunch pail through a front window of a trolley "right after the car strike in Pawtucket" (Edward McSorley, *Our Own Kind* [New York: Harper & Brothers, 1946], 207, 281).

25. *Providence Journal*, 26 May 1902. *Evening Telegram*, 13 Mar., 5 Apr. 1902. Nelson, "Influence," 260. Nathaniel Stephenson wrote that Aldrich feared "city workmen" and "those haunting strains of the 'Marseillaise' that now and then blow along

the air from some tempestuous labor meeting" (*Nelson W. Aldrich: A Leader in American Politics* [Port Washington, N.Y.: Kennikat Press, 1930], 101). This autobiography unabashedly defended the senator from all criticism. Stephenson employed an unusual Marxist terminology, albeit from the conservative right, to warn of the Red Decade. Despite his elitist bias, anyone tired of consensus history will find Stephenson's work a welcome relief from the usual prepackaged bromides that pass as historical biographies.

26. *Springfield Republican*, 13 Feb. 1903, in "Historical Newspaper Clippings," Rider Collection 9:23. Brayton to Aldrich, 5 Apr. 1902, NWA Papers, reel 23, containers 33–34. *Providence Journal*, 5 Apr. 1902. *Evening Telegram*, 13 Mar. 1902. *Railroad Commissioner's Report, 1902*, 58.

27. Lincoln Steffens, "Rhode Island: A State for Sale," *McClure's Magazine* 34 (Feb. 1905): 349. *Providence Journal*, 5 June 1902. *Evening Telegram*, 4 June 1902. A student biographer of Marsden Perry agreed with Steffens's appraisal and wrote that the railway authorized passage of the ten-hour law but reneged when the United Gas Improvement Company balked at the higher wages that would accompany it (Robert E. Falb, "Marsden J. Perry: 'The Man Who Owned Rhode Island'" [honors thesis, Brown University, 1964], 39). John Buenker generalized about GOP reaction to public opinion: "The Republicans occasionally had to yield to urban working class pressures by endorsing measures inimical to the interests they generally served. This was always done under duress and usually took the form of a less drastic version of a measure first urged upon them by the Democrats" ("Urban Liberalism," 38).

28. *Outlet Bulletin*, May 1903. Aldrich was still elected by the legislature, not by popular referendum. Stephenson, in hypocritical fashion, asserted on many occasions that Aldrich had a great distaste for Brayton's methods but authorized their use anyway (*Nelson W. Aldrich*, chaps. 2–4).

29. *Providence Journal*, 6 Apr., 3 June 1902. Falb, "Marsden J. Perry," 26, 43, 46. Charles Carroll, *Rhode Island: Three Centuries of Democracy*, 4 vols. (Lewis Historical Publishing, 1932), 2:842. Patrick T. Conley, *An Album of Rhode Island History* (Norfolk, Va.: Donning, 1986), 118. Steffens, "Rhode Island," 350. Power, "Rhode Island Republican Politics," 98.

30. *Evening Telegram*, 4 June 1902. *Providence Journal*, 8 Apr., 8 June 1902.

31. *Providence Journal*, 8 Apr., 8, 17, 27 June, 3 July 1902. *Evening Telegram*, 4, 30 June 1902. Carroll, *Rhode Island*, 674. The Irish led the naturalized registry voters in urban areas, especially in Providence, where they outnumbered their nearest ethnic rivals—the English—two to one (*Providence Journal*, 3 Nov. 1902).

32. *Providence Journal*, 27, 28, 29 June, 2, 3, 4, 6 July 1902. *Evening Telegram*, 1 July 1902. Many organized workers voted Republican at the time. Elmer Cornwall pointed out that Providence Democrats went for McKinley over Bryan in 1896 despite the latter's courting of blue-collar support. Economic prosperity, employer coercion, and ethnic animosities all played a key role in Republican presidential success

("A Note on Providence Politics in the Age of Bryan," *Rhode Island History* 19 [Apr. 1960]: 33–40).
33. *Evening Telegram*, 13, 24, 25 June 1902.

10. THE UNION RAILROAD IS OUR SUPREME COURT

1. *Providence Journal*, 24 Aug. 1902. Carl Gersuny, "Uphill Battle: Lucius F. C. Garvin's Crusade for Political Reform," *Rhode Island History* 39 (May 1980): 62.

2. A protester accused of obstruction during the strike wore a Fitzgerald pin when he went to court. One letter writer, who had signed an earlier diatribe to the *Journal* as "A Sufferer," sent a second missive a week later claiming, "It is rumored that an ambitious young man is working this strike business to boom his candidacy for a higher office than the one he now holds." He signed this letter, "Still A Sufferer" (*Providence Journal*, 10, 29 June, 2, 6 July 1902).

3. *Providence Journal*, 24 Aug., 1, 3 Sept. 1902. The Pawtucket rally attracted thousands of area residents. Trolley service was so patronized that scores actually rode on streetcar roofs, prompting the *Journal* to admit ironically: "No argument was ever advanced to show how lamentably deficient this city is in the matter of street railway facilities" (1, 7 Sept. 1902).

The *Journal* editors complained that workers did too much standing around at Labor Day demonstrations: "The workingman arises the next morning unrefreshed by his brief absence from the bench or forge." The publishers advocated that operatives abandon working-class solidarity for individual pursuits and follow the example of clerks, bankers, businessmen, and lawyers, who spent "a day of relaxation at the beach or countryside" (1 Sept. 1902).

4. *Providence Journal*, 1 Sept. 1902. The chairman of the Amalgamated's general executive board in Washington viewed the 1909 Philadelphia strike as a continuation of the American Revolution and the Civil War (C. O. Pratt, "The Sympathetic Strike," *Annals* [American Academy of Political and Social Science] 36 [July–Dec. 1910]: 140).

5. Charles Carroll, *Rhode Island: Three Centuries of Democracy*, 4 vols. (Lewis Historical Publishing, 1932), 2:674, 684. Joseph P. Manton to Aldrich, 16 Dec. 1902, NWA Papers, reel 23, containers 33–34. Garvin himself was born in Tennessee. John Buenker (*Urban Liberalism and Progressive Reform* [New York: Scribners, 1973]) parted the Progressives into two contending national camps, not unlike the Rhode Island scene: new-stock, urban liberals; and old-stock, patrician reformers. Future governor Theodore Francis Green, though young at this time, was a patrician with a bright future.

6. Garvin, meanwhile, still expected the nomination with solid backing from small-town caucuses. He was worried, however, and wrote to his close ally and Democratic Party chief, Patrick H. Quinn of Warwick, suggesting that Republican Charles

Boss Brayton might try to bribe Democratic delegates into voting for Fitzgerald. Garvin apparently felt that Republicans viewed him as a more formidable opponent than the mayor. Out of character, he went so far as to suggest to Quinn that a secret ballot might harm his chances, and he therefore sought a recorded public vote at the convention. *Providence Journal*, 20, 24, 26, 29 Sept. 1902. Gersuny, "Uphill Battle," 63. Gersuny suggested that Fitzgerald may have been in league with Brayton, but there is no evidence to substantiate that claim. It was the kind of rumor the *Journal* would have been sure to advance to embarrass the mayor. Just before the general election, the newspaper ran a story claiming that Fitzgerald's uncle, a government engraver in Washington, was promoted with help from Brayton (*Providence Journal*, 26 Oct. 1902). The mayor's subsequent assistance to Garvin belied any collusion.

The *Journal* and the Republicans may have feared Fitzgerald more than Garvin. He was an unpredictable personality who had humiliated the machine on several occasions by mobilizing militant popular support. David Patten, a *Journal* reporter from a later era, characterized Fitzgerald "as a leader who fired the spirits of men. . . . Party leaders hated the sight of the little man who was as bristly as a porcupine. He loved to upset their plans; loved to fight for the underdog; enjoyed rumpling the hair of the big shots" (David Patten, *Rhode Island Story* [Providence: Providence Journal Co., 1954], 42).

There was only one formal labor endorsement during the caucuses. The influential and erudite Providence Typographical Union endorsed Garvin for the second year in a row. The printers' stand underscored labor's initial unease in the realm of politics. In 1901, for example, a motion to endorse Garvin was ruled out of order by the union president on the grounds that "it introduced partisan politics into the Union." Rank-and-file members successfully appealed the ruling of the chair, and "democracy triumphed." Providence Typographical Union no. 33, *Printers and Printing in Providence, 1762–1907* (Providence: Providence Printing, 1907), 149. *Providence Journal*, 9 Sept. 1902.

7. *Providence Journal*, 2 Oct. 1902. Davis served split terms as governor in 1887–88 and 1890–91.

8. *Providence Journal*, 25, 30 Sept., 2 Oct. 1902.

9. *Providence Journal*, 8, 9, 23, 24, 26, 27, 28 Sept., 2 Oct. 1902. Brayton, who was constantly upbraided by critics for exploiting disproportionate representation in country towns, charged that Garvin's victory was fashioned by an equally unrepresentative rotten-borough system in the Democratic caucuses that gave these same rural areas more weight than those in the cities. Providence, for example, elected only 26 delegates of the 220 at the convention. Much of Garvin's support came from old-line Yankee Democrats in the countryside. Garvin, however, did enjoy significant support among Irish leaders such as Democratic Party chieftain Patrick Quinn (Mary Cobb Nelson, "The Influence of Immigration on Rhode Island Politics, 1865–1910" [Ph.D. diss., Harvard University, 1954], 272).

10. *Providence Journal*, 7, 8, 12 Aug. 1902. Marsden J. Perry to F. E. Mason, 14 Aug. 1902, DSM Collection. One letter to the editor praised management for rewarding employees with a higher stipend while the union welshed on strike benefits (*Providence Journal*, 17 Aug. 1902).

11. *Providence Journal*, 19 Apr. 1903. "Scrapbook."

12. *Providence Journal*, 9 Aug., 16 Nov. 1902. For a description and history of Aldrich's magnificent home, see E. L. D. Seymour, "The Aldrich Estate at Warwick Neck," *Country Life*, Feb. 1919.

13. *Providence Journal*, 8, 12, 17, 24 Aug., 4, 15, 16 Sept. 1902. The Providence County grand jury returned "true bills" on only half the twenty-two obstruction and rioting charges during the strike but upheld ten-hour violations against the railway company (*Providence Journal*, 8, 22 Oct. 1902).

14. *Providence Journal*, 11, 12, 14, 31 July, 7, 10, 14 Sept., 3, 7 Oct., 7 Nov. 1902. The Rhode Island Company earned a positive story when it cut suburban fares in two towns (*Providence Journal*, 30 Oct. 1902).

15. *Providence Journal*, 8 Sept., 9, 10 Dec. 1902. Department of Commerce and Labor, Bureau of the Census, *Special Report: Street and Electric Railways, 1902* (Washington, D.C.: Government Printing Office, 1905), 121–23. Robert E. Falb, "Marsden J. Perry: 'The Man Who Owned Rhode Island'" (honors thesis, Brown University, 1964), 30–31. Burton J. Hendrick, *The Age of Big Business: A Chronicle of the Captains of Industry* (New Haven: Yale University Press, 1919), 135. Samuel Rosenberg, "A History of Street Railways in Rhode Island" (M.A. thesis, University of Rhode Island), chap. 4. Benjamin A. Jackson, president, United Traction and Electric Company, to United Gas and Improvement Company, 26 May 1902, Roelker Papers, box 3.

In 1915, two years after the Rhode Island Company signed an initial contract with the carmen's union, both parties went to arbitration to settle terms of the second agreement. The union attorney called the railway "the wonder of the financial world." He ridiculed the company for introducing twenty-one pages of explanations and charts just to explain its complex setup: "The labyrinthian ways through which we have been led to find out just what the Rhode Island Company is, and what its present financial condition is, are the most mystifying, bewildering, extraordinary places in which I have ever been. There are small roads and large roads, leased roads and owned roads, consolidated roads, holding companies, improvement companies, security companies, navigation companies, and all sorts of companies." *Providence Journal*, 30 Sept., 20, 27 Oct. 1915.

Burton Hendrick noted the existence of a loosely drawn syndicate that controlled most of the nation's urban railways. The United Gas and Improvement Company was in the forefront of that alliance ("Great American Fortunes and Their Making: Street-Railway Financiers," *McClure's Magazine* 30 [Nov. 1907, 33–48; Dec. 1907, 236–50; Jan. 1908, 323–38]).

16. *Providence Journal*, 10 Oct. 1902. Joseph P. Manton to Aldrich, 16 Dec.

1902, NWA Papers, reel 23, containers 33–34. A chronological listing of their correspondence is in *Nelson W. Aldrich: A Register and Index of His Papers in the Library of Congress* (Washington, D. C.: Library of Congress, 1973), 92. Republicans even renounced traditional campaign rallies in areas where they expected a popular majority. Cranston, for example, abandoned any demonstration as "an unnecessary expense and bother." The *Journal* seemed more concerned than Republican operatives about a low-key effort when it decried the lack of party spending and warned: "Democratic control of the two branches would insure a redistricting scheme of some kind, radical enough in character to cause decade after decade to roll by without again witnessing a Republican majority in either branch" (*Providence Journal*, 1, 2 Nov. 1902).

17. Joseph P. Manton to Aldrich, 16 Dec. 1902, NWA Papers, reel 23, containers 33–34.

18. *Providence Journal*, 6, 10, 11, 12, 15, 16 Oct., 3 Nov. 1902. The Democratic Party's ward committee on Smith Hill in Providence emphasized the labor connections of several candidates. Dennis McCarthy, standing for alderman, was touted as a forty-year member of the Brotherhood of Locomotive Engineers. Dennis Donovan, running for a city council seat, was a member of the jewelry workers union. John Devlin, another council candidate, was an attorney who represented teamsters in their 1902 strike ("Democratic Ward Committee, Letter of Endorsement," 13 Oct. 1902, Rider Collection Broadsides).

19. *Providence Journal*, 25, 26 Oct., 1 Nov. 1902.

20. *Providence Journal*, 28, 29, 30, 31 Oct., 2 Oct., 2 Nov. 1902. *Springfield Republican*, 13 Feb. 1903. "Historical Newspaper Cuttings," Rider Collection 9:23.

21. *Providence Journal*, 26 Oct., 2, 3 Nov. 1902. Fitzgerald also stumped for Garvin on other occasions, joining former Providence city councilman and Knights of Labor activist Luke Kavanaugh on a foray into East Greenwich (*Providence Journal*, 29 Oct. 1902).

Although Fitzgerald and Garvin apparently made peace quickly, James Higgins attacked the seventy-nine-year-old Garvin as late as 1920, at the height of the Red Scares. In a speech before the Veterans of Foreign Wars in Providence, Higgins assailed Garvin; James Reid, the Olneyville dentist who became the only socialist elected to the Rhode Island legislature; and other local radicals for sponsoring the ten-year-old People's Forum, a leftist lyceum. Although Garvin had not been active in the organization for a couple of years, Higgins stung the former governor by unfairly implicating him in events he had no connection to: "Now, I don't consider every single tax advocate or Socialist a traitor," Higgins declared. "What I do say that is when, in order to carry out their ideas, they preach and practice murder, treason, and burglary, they're going too far." Garvin died on October 2, 1922, and the *Journal* editors gave him an ambiguous editorial eulogy: "He sought office or honors only as they offered opportunity for promoting the causes to which he dedicated himself." *Providence Journal*, 5, 14 Jan. 1920; 3 Oct. 1922.

22. *Providence Journal*, 1, 3 Nov. 1902.

23. *Providence Journal*, 5, 6, 7, 27 Nov. 1902.

24. *Providence Journal*, 5 Nov. 1902.

25. *Providence Journal*, 5, 6, 9, 16, 20 Nov. 1902.

26. *Springfield Republican*, 13 Feb. 1903, "Historical Newspaper Cuttings," Rider Collection 9:23. *Providence Journal*, 4, 5, 6 Dec. 1902. Rathbun was proud of his youthful labor on the family farm in West Greenwich and the twelve-hour days he served as a trolley conductor acquiring "considerable practical experience in controlling crowds of men bent on mischief" (William Harrison Taylor, ed., *Legislative History and Souvenir of Rhode Island, 1899 and 1900* [Providence: E. L. Freeman & Sons, 1900], 142). The *State* commented that legal proceedings against the railway's flouting of the ten-hour statute died "a lingering and unnatural death" (23 Dec. 1905).

27. Brayton's pithy quotation appeared in the *Providence Evening Bulletin*, 27 Mar. 1903 (cited in Nelson, "Influence," 273). Brayton to Aldrich, 20 Feb. 1903, NWA Papers, reel 23, containers 33–34.

28. Nelson, "Influence," 271–83. Gersuny, "Uphill Battle," 63–70. William McLoughlin, *Rhode Island: A History* (New York: W. W. Norton, 1978), 162. "Mr. Utter's Record in the Street Railway Strike" (1904) and "Senator Aldrich Responsible" (1904), Rider Broadside Collection. Muckraker David Graham Phillips sarcastically labeled the $200,000 expenditure "a small sum to be got back by a few minutes of industrious pocket-picking in Wall Street" (David Graham Phillips, "The Treason of the Senate," *Cosmopolitan* 40, no. 5 [Mar. 1906]: 629–30). The poem is in "Scrapbook."

29. Falb, "Marsden J. Perry," 49–56. Manton to Aldrich, 16 Dec. 1902, NWA Papers, reel 23, containers 33–34. Manton, who served as chief commissioner to construct a monument to a local Civil War hero in 1910, dedicated the commemorative program to Charles Brayton, a distinguished war veteran (*Col. Henry H. Young in the Civil War* [Providence: E. A. Johnson, 1910], front cover). Nancy Apgar, "The Life and Times of General Charles R. Brayton: A Study in Boss Rule" (honors thesis, Brown University, 1961), 42. Edwin Lefevre, "Aldrich: General Manager of the United States," *American Magazine* 6 (Mar. 1903): 623.

30. Lincoln Steffens, "Rhode Island: A State for Sale," *McClure's Magazine* 34 (Feb. 1905): 353. Lincoln Steffens, *The Autobiography of Lincoln Steffens* (New York: Harcourt, Brace, 1931), chap. 15, 464–69.

Nathaniel Stephenson, Aldrich's obsequious biographer, disparaged Steffens's ability as an author: "It is not certain that his writings have found a permanent place in English literature and perhaps an ungrateful country no longer remembers him" (*Nelson W. Aldrich: A Leader in American Politics* [Port Washington, N.Y.: Kennikat Press, 1930], 267). Ironically, Nelson W. Aldrich, Jr., the senator's great-grandson, branded Stephenson's biography as "dreadfully dull, a hagiography commissioned by the family"; called his namesake "the old crook"; and endorsed Lucius Garvin's attack on corruption in Rhode Island (*Old Money: The Mythology of America's Upper Class* [New York: Alfred A. Knopf, 1988], 5, 9, 17).

CONCLUSION: ANOTHER DORR WAR

1. Melvin G. Holli, *Reform in Detroit: Hazen S. Pingree and Urban Politics* (New York: Oxford University Press, 1969), ix. Scott Molloy, *Division 618: Streetcar Employees Fight for a Union in Rhode Island* (Providence: Division 618, 1977).

2. Patrick T. Conley, *Democracy in Decline: Rhode Island's Constitutional Development, 1776–1841* (Providence: Rhode Island Historical Society, 1977).

3. Cited in Carl Gersuny, "Uphill Battle: Lucius F. C. Garvin's Crusade for Political Reform," *Rhode Island History* 39 (May 1980): 66.

4. Trolley strikers in San Francisco passed out leaflets to patrons: "The carmen appeal to you to vote for public ownership. . . . To you it means better service and a seat for everyone, for us, it means shorter hours and fair wages" (Mark Ciabattari, "Urban Liberals, Politics and the Fight for Public Transit, San Francisco, 1897–1915," 2 vols. [Ph.D. diss., New York University, 1988], 1:220). In Portland, Maine, streetcar crews were "considered by many of their neighbors to be minor celebrities" (Robert Babcock, "Will You Walk? Yes, We'll Walk!: Popular Support for a Street Railway Strike in Portland, Maine," *Labor History* 35 [summer 1994]: 381).

5. Mary Cobb Nelson, "The Influence of Immigration on Rhode Island Politics, 1865–1910" (Ph.D. diss., Harvard University, 1954), 212. Sidney L. Harring, "Car Wars: Strikes, Arbitration, and Class Struggle in the Making of Labor Law," *Review of Law and Social Changes* 14 (1986): 35. David Nye, *Electrifying America: Social Meanings of a New Technology, 1880–1940* (Cambridge: MIT Press, 1990), 98. William J. Jennings, Jr., "The Prince of Pawtucket: A Study of the Politics of Thomas P. McCoy" (Ph.D. diss., Providence College, 1985). Garvin actually joined Roosevelt's Bullmoose Party for several years before returning to the Democratic fold (Gersuny, "Uphill Battle," 71; Richard Hofstader, *The Age of Reform: From Bryan to F.D.R.* [New York: Alfred A. Knopf, 1955], 131). An unusual alliance of patrician and plebeian reformers struggled on in the state until the New Deal. Sidney Harring wrote, "The workers of the period organized themselves for a wide range of ends, some of them contradictory. But on a broad front they had clear legal objectives that were encouraged by democratic values" ("Car Wars," 850, 870).

6. *Providence Journal*, 18, 29 Nov., 28 Dec. 1902. John Buenker, "Urban Liberalism in Rhode Island, 1909–1919," *Rhode Island History* 30 (1971): 38. Daniel T. Rodgers, "In Search of Progressivism," *Reviews in American History* (Dec. 1982): 115–16. Sarah Feldman, "Overworked and Underpaid: The Regulation of Child Labor in Rhode Island, 1880–1920" (honors thesis, Brown University, 1989), chap. 4.

7. Shelton Stromquist, *A Generation of Boomers: The Pattern of Railroad Labor Conflict in Nineteenth Century America* (Chicago: University of Illinois Press, 1987). Harring, "Car Wars," 852. Despite the large number of railway strikes, which often exposed class and political relations in a city, labor historians have given scant attention to these fascinating events. The new labor history, which emphasizes community and worker cul-

ture rather than the old institutional outlook, also pioneered a new interest in local history; yet the street railway situation is often overlooked by both and old new labor historians except for an obligatory mention of a metropolitan strike here or there, as in Philadelphia in 1909. Actually, an examination of the Amalgamated's car wars requires a blending of new and old labor history to fully understand the situation (Ralph Scharnau, "The Dubuque Streetcar Strike, 1903," ms.). Warren Van Tyne, "The Transformation of Labor Relations in Two Industries in the 1890s" (paper presented at the Pullman Strike Centennial Conference, Terre Haute, Ind., 23–24 Sept. 1994), 3. Babcock, "Will You Walk?" 372. For a look at local railroad workers at the time consult William C. Vieira, "I've Been Working on the Railroad: A History of Providence Lodge 66 of the Brotherhood of Railroad Trainmen, 1890–1898," ms., DSM Collection.

Sidney L. Harring estimated that the Amalgamated lost most of its strikes before 1900 and won most of them after. The success rate during the Progressive era seems suspect and may have been influenced by the union's unwillingness to admit total defeat in the pages of its monthly journal ("Car Wars," 849–72). Babcock offers a more realistic victory rate of 60 percent between 1881 and 1905 ("Will You Walk?" 374).

8. Nye, *Electrifying America*, 101. Babcock, "Will You Walk?" 392. The use of jitneys after 1910 helped provide the boycotting public with inexpensive, alternate transportation at no cost to the union (Babcock, "Will You Walk?" 393).

9. Nick Salvatore, *Eugene V. Debs: Citizen and Socialist* (Chicago: University of Illinois Press, 1982), 181–82. Emerson Schmidt, *Industrial Relations in Urban Transportation* (Minneapolis: University of Minnesota Press, 1937), 146–48. Robert E. Zeigler, "The Limits of Power: The Amalgamated Association of Street Railway Employees in Houston, Texas, 1897–1905," *Labor History* 18 (winter 1971): 89. C. O. Pratt, "The Sympathetic Strike," *Annals* (American Academy of Political and Social Science) 36 (July–Dec. 1910): 139.

10. Pratt, "Sympathetic Strike," 139. Philip Foner, *The AFL in the Progressive Era* (New York: International Publishers, 1980), 143–63.

11. Rhodri Jeffreys-Jones, *Violence and Reform in American History* (New York: New Viewpoints, 1978), 80. Holli, *Reform*, ix. Nye, *Electrifying America*, 110. *Motorman and Conductor*, May 1899. Horsecar proprietors complained of muckraking a generation before its heyday (*Street Railway Journal*, Feb. 1886, 113). The Amalgamated inherited its emphasis on arbitration from the Knights of Labor and Hazen Pingree's actions in Detroit (Harring, "Car Wars," 858). Philip Taft and Philip Ross, "American Labor Violence: Its Causes, Character, and Outcome," in Hugh D. Graham and Ted R. Gwor, eds., *Violence in America: Historical and Comparative Perspectives*, 2 vols. (Washington, D.C.: U.S. Government Printing Office, 1969), 1:290. *Harper's Weekly*, 29 July 1899. Dina M. Young, "The St. Louis Streetcar Strike of 1900: Pivotal Politics at the Century's Dawn," *Gateway Heritage* 12 (summer 1991): 6. The Amalgamated continually encouraged its local divisions to enroll and participate in central labor councils. *Motorman and Conductor*, Oct. 1895; Apr. 1897; Jan. 1899; Jan., Feb. 1900; Mar., May 1901. Young,

"St. Louis Streetcar Strike," 5, 9. A. J. Scopino, Jr., "Community, Class, and Conflict: The Waterbury Trolley Strike of 1903," *Connecticut History* 24 (1983): 42.

12. Van Tyne, "Transformation," 5.

13. *Street Railway Journal*, Feb. 1900, 130; 4 May 1901, 531; 1 Mar. 1902, 544. "You cannot watch men too close. It is a great temptation to men to take all they can get from a street car company, thinking they are working long hours and are not getting enough pay for their services, and again the public feel considerably the same way" (*Street Railway Journal*, July 1898, 375). The journal praises the new personnel system, which emphasized retraining rather than suspensions when problems occurred (*Street Railway Journal*, 3 May 1902, 544).

14. Hofstader, *Age of Reform*, 172, 239. Harring discussed the philosophical underpinnings of the Amalgamated's belief in municipal control ("Car Wars," 865). David Thelan, *The New Citizenship: Origins of Progressivism in Wisconsin, 1883–1906* (Columbia, Mo.: University of Missouri Press, 1972), 288–89. Schmidt, *Industrial Relations*, 138–39. Daniel T. Rodgers, "In Search of Progressivism," *Reviews in American History* (Dec. 1982): 115–16. Georg Leidenberger, "From Machine to Reform Politics: Chicago Trade Unions and the Movement for the Municipal Ownership of Streetcars at the Turn of the Century" (paper presented at the Pullman Strike Centennial Conference, Terre Haute, Ind., 23–24 Sept. 1994), 1. Babcock, "Will You Walk?" 397. *State*, cited in John S. Gilkinson, *Middle-Class Providence, 1820–1940* (Princeton: Princeton University Press, 1986), 201.

15. Quoted in Gilkinson, *Middle-Class Providence*, 130. Thelan, *New Citizenship*, 270.

16. *Trollier*, 6 Apr. 1918. Various newspaper accounts of the trip in "Scrapbook."

17. Ibid.

18. Ibid.

INDEX